Saving **PLAY**

MORE REDLEAF BOOKS BY GAYE GRONLUND

Individualized Child-Focused Curriculum: A Differentiated Approach

Planning for Play, Observation, and Learning in Preschool and Kindergarten

Developmentally Appropriate Play: Guiding Young Children to a Higher Level

Why Children Play: A Family Companion to Developmentally Appropriate Play

Focused Observations: How to Observe Young Children for Assessment and Curriculum Planning, Second Edition, with Marlyn James

Focused Portfolios: A Complete Assessment for the Young Child, with Bev Engel

Make Early Learning Standards Come Alive: Connecting Your Practice and Curriculum to State Guidelines, Second Edition

Early Learning Standards and Staff Development: Best Practices in the Face of Change, with Marlyn James

Saving
PLAY

Addressing Standards through Play-Based Learning in Preschool and Kindergarten

Thomas Rendon | Gaye Gronlund

Redleaf Press®
www.redleafpress.org
800-423-8309

Published by Redleaf Press
10 Yorkton Court
St. Paul, MN 55117
www.redleafpress.org

First edition 2017
Cover design by Jim Handrigan
Cover photograph by iStock photo/Frizzantine
Interior design by Wendy Holdman
Typeset in Karmina
Interior photos by Peter Kaser
Printed in the United States of America
24 23 22 21 20 19 18 17   1 2 3 4 5 6 7 8

Library of Congress Cataloging-in-Publication Data
Names: Rendon, Thomas. | Gronlund, Gaye, 1952— author.
Title: Saving play : addressing standards through play-based learning in preschool and
    kindergarten / Thomas Rendon and Gaye Gronlund.
Description: St. Paul, MN : Redleaf Press, 2017. | Includes bibliographical references and index.
Identifiers: LCCN 2016040815 (print) | LCCN 2017004315 (ebook) | ISBN 9781605545301
    (paperback) | ISBN 9781605545318 (ebook)
Subjects: LCSH: Play | Early childhood education—Standards—United States. | BISAC:
    EDUCATION / Teaching Methods & Materials / General. | EDUCATION / Preschool &
    Kindergarten. | EDUCATION / Evaluation.
Classification: LCC LB1140.35.P55 R46 2017 (print) | LCC LB1140.35.P55 (ebook) |
    DDC 372.21—dc23
LC record available at https://lccn.loc.gov/2016040815

Printed on acid-free paper

To my daughters, Caroline and Beatrice,
with whom I would play and play and play and play.

THOMAS RENDON

In memory of my colleague, collaborator, and dear friend Marlyn James.
The early childhood field has lost a true champion.

GAYE GRONLUND

CONTENTS

ACKNOWLEDGMENTS

From Thomas Rendon:
I owe a debt of gratitude to the Play Committee of the Iowa Association for the Education of Young Children, who made it possible for me to develop a presentation on play and standards that became the inspiration for this book. Special thanks go to Tammy Bormann, who both led the play committee for a time and organized the first major update of Iowa's Early Learning Standards. She made sure play featured prominently. Thanks, too, to so many colleagues past and present, at the Iowa AEYC and the Iowa Department of Education who have been my teachers and mentors in all things early childhood. Finally, I want to acknowledge my prime inspiration for the value and importance of play: the work of Stuart Brown, Scott Eberle, and Walter Drew.

From Gaye Gronlund:
Thank you to the great writers and thinkers who influenced my understanding of play, including Elizabeth Jones, Gretchen Reynolds, Renatta Cooper, Vivian Paley, Walter Drew, Kathy Hirsh-Pasek, Roberta Golinkoff, and Stuart Brown.

And thank you to the leaders in early childhood education who have included me in your efforts to write, revise, and enhance your early learning standards:

Judith Paiz and Dan Haggard, New Mexico

Brian Michalski, Rhonda Clark, Karen McCarthy, and Cindy Zumwalt, Illinois

Eileen Nelson, Minnesota

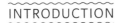

Play and Standards *Can* Go Together

Children's play is under attack. Opportunities for children to engage in child-directed, open-ended play experiences are becoming fewer and fewer. We see it in community settings, in homes, and in many kindergartens and preschools. Drive by playgrounds in many communities and you will rarely see children playing there. The lovely climbing structures and swings stand empty and forlorn-looking. Walk through a busy shopping area, an airport, or other public places and note how many children are mesmerized by electronic devices rather than engaging with their family members in animated conversations and exchanging laughter and smiles. Visit with friends or family and see how children sit passively in front of television or computer screens, their eyes glazed over as they watch. Listen to worried parents describe how they simply cannot allow their children to run and jump and play outdoors unsupervised because of safety concerns. Or hear some say that they are just too busy to find the time for their children to play outside with adult supervision. Watch the commercialization of play as toy companies advertise products that are tied to the latest animated movie or cartoon show. These products do not engage children's creativity, but rather encourage imitation and limited involvement. Other toys are advertised to promote highly focused intellectual gains such as alphabet recognition or letter-sound correspondence with no emphasis on critical thinking, imagination, or problem solving.

In the field of early childhood education, a battle over play is going on. On one side, earnest and sincere educators, grounded in considerable research, make the argument that we must know what children need to learn and have evidence-based instructional practices to teach them, in order to build the strong foundation they need for true academic success. Early learning and Common Core State Standards become the focus of preschool and kindergarten. Play is not seen as a viable strategy for addressing the standards. On the other side are equally earnest and sincere educators who believe that children learn best through their own exploration, driven by their own interests, and nurtured by caring adults. Standards will happen in play naturally, almost accidentally. While both sides have a point to make, we are concerned that play becomes the casualty in this battle. Neither view is helping educators make use of children's play as a curricular strategy, as the richest and most useful context in which real and deep learning can take place.

To emphasize learning more, some educators have replaced play with approaches that we see as shortsighted and that fail the test of developmental appropriateness. They require children to sit and listen for longer periods of time, to produce paper-and-pencil-based work rather than hands-on creations that engage them in a more active way of learning new skills and concepts. We also have concerns that those who advocate for play have not adequately addressed how learning can be enhanced in the early childhood classroom. They have neglected the important tasks of setting clear goals and showing progress in meeting those goals. Both are essential elements in giving teaching purpose and direction. This book is an effort to reconcile these positions so that play can be restored to its proper role as something that is not only fun for kids but also loaded with opportunities for learning.

PLAY IN KINDERGARTENS AND PRESCHOOLS TODAY

Play has been almost completely removed from the kindergarten experiences of most children (Rich 2015). Kindergarten teachers are under tremendous pressure to address standards and improve student achievement. The assumption is that to do so, they must engage in teacher-led lessons where children sit as passive learners, that the development of skills and academic understanding is best addressed through whole-group instruction and paper-and-pencil tasks. The benefits of playtime for children are not seen as academically important. Even recess time has been cut dramatically in recent years with the justification that it takes time away from important learning experiences.

Preschool teachers feel the pressure to limit play as well. They, too, are asked to address standards and prepare children for the rigorous expectations of kindergarten. Family and community members, administrators, and policy makers question whether the time spent in play in preschool classrooms truly helps children meet learning goals. Like kindergarten teachers, preschool teachers often feel conflicted, asking themselves questions such as, "How much time should I allow for child-directed play? What is my role in that play? How can I make sure children are learning what they need to know to be successful in kindergarten?"

OUR PASSION FOR PLAY

We believe passionately that child-directed, open-ended play has a critical role in children's health and well-being in both their social-emotional and cognitive development. We have been in the field of early childhood education for decades, advocating for best practices in programs that serve children from birth through age eight. There is no question in our minds that best practices in early childhood *include play*! Yet we still see play threatened from all sides, relegated to smaller and smaller portions of a child's day in preschool and kindergarten with the goal of enhancing learning of academic skills and concepts. This approach robs children of essential child-directed experiences and devalues the learning that occurs when children play.

This book addresses two critical questions:

1. Can child-directed, open-ended play activities in preschool and kindergarten classrooms address early learning and Common Core standards?
2. Can play be used to reach specific goals and objectives across all developmental domains?

Our resounding answer to both of these questions is *yes*! We strongly believe that teachers *do not* have to sacrifice play for academic achievement. We also recognize that incorporating play in meaningful ways that contribute to learning is not as simple a process as it looks. We think that many teachers are presented with a false dichotomy: play versus academics or play versus standards. We know that play, academics, and standards *can* and *do* work together! It is our sincere hope that this book will inspire others to maintain their passion for play and to advocate for it in their professional settings.

WHO WE ARE

The two of us have different perspectives about play and standards because we serve in different roles as early childhood professionals. Here is more about each of us:

Tom Rendon is a policy maker. As Iowa's Head Start State Collaboration Office coordinator with the Iowa Department of Education, he promotes policies and partnerships that encourage best practices in curriculum and assessment for young children. As a recognized leader in the field, he has served on the governing board of the National Association for the Education of Young Children (NAEYC) and numerous early childhood boards and councils at the state and local level. He is also a member of the Iowa AEYC's Play Committee, which is dedicated to supporting play across early childhood settings in the state. This committee helps early childhood professionals understand and embrace play-based learning through professional development sessions based on the work of play expert Dr. Walter Drew.

Gaye Gronlund is an experienced practitioner. She is an early childhood education consultant and author who formerly taught preschool and kindergarten in both regular and special education programs. Her writing and professional development sessions focus on play-based curriculum, observational assessment, and early learning standards. She is well known for her emphasis on practical suggestions regarding best practices, helping teachers do what is truly best for young children.

Throughout this book, we will engage in conversations from our differing perspectives and invite readers to join us in considering different aspects of fully embracing play in preschool and kindergarten classrooms. Parts 1, 2, and 4 begin with our thoughts about provocative questions, from both a policy-making and teaching perspective. By focusing on these two perspectives, we hope we can offer support and ideas to multiple audiences, including administrators and policy makers as well as classroom teachers.

WHAT YOU WILL FIND IN THIS BOOK

Early in the writing of this book, we read Stuart Brown's important book, *Play: How It Shapes the Brain, Opens the Imagination, and Invigorates the Soul*, in which he explores the topic from the point of view of a physician (2009). In it, Brown shares the groundbreaking work of Scott Eberle, editor of the *American Journal of Play*, and his six steps in the cycle of play (later published in 2014):

- Anticipation—expectation, wonder, curiosity, anxiety, uncertainty, risk
- Surprise—discovery, new sensations or ideas, new perspectives
- Pleasure—it feels good
- Understanding—new knowledge, application of ideas
- Strength—empowerment, confidence, new skills
- Poise—grace, contentment, composure, and sense of balance (ready for anticipation again)

We have organized this book in four parts based on Eberle's model.

Part 1: Anticipation

In chapters 1 and 2, we set the stage, asking questions about play and its proper definition. We show how play actually helps build healthy brains. We show the value of child-directed, open-ended play experiences and the importance of teacher support to enhance such play. In chapter 3, we look at the purposes, design, and implementation of early learning standards for preschoolers and Common Core State Standards for Kindergarten. We address facts and misconceptions regarding both.

Part 2: Surprise and Pleasure

In chapter 4, we show how clearer understanding of play and the purposes of standards leads to new perspectives on teaching and to experiences of gratification, enjoyment, delight, and contentment not only for children but also for teachers and administrators. Linking play and standards, then, becomes a fun and more rewarding way to teach.

In chapter 5, we explore ways to ensure that play is part of the classroom experience for *all* children regardless of abilities, cultural or linguistic backgrounds, or other individual differences.

Part 3: Understanding and Strength

True understanding is taking ideas and applying them in the real world across a variety of settings and situations. Chapters 6 through 12 go deeper with specific suggestions and examples for addressing standards through play experiences in seven domains.

Part 4: Poise

In our final chapters, we hope to leave readers with a sense of confidence by grounding their renewed commitment to play in strong reflection and assessment practices. In chapter 13, we look at how linking play and standards affects assessment. In chapter 14, we offer strategies for advocacy: promoting both play and standards within the context of accountability systems, school reform, and other pressures related to push-down academics.

EMPHASIS ON THE PRACTICAL AND THE DOABLE

Our goal throughout the book is to help early childhood professionals feel supported in their efforts to protect play in their programs. Our target audience is anyone who works on behalf of young children in any kind of early childhood program. We recognize that there are many professional roles in the early childhood field, including family child care providers, educators, teachers, paraprofessionals, directors, administrators, principals, and policy makers. For the sake of consistency, we use the terms "teacher" and "administrator" to describe early childhood professionals.

We strongly believe that embracing play as the most effective strategy to bring about meaningful learning is the right thing to do for young children. When teachers, administrators, and children are in sync, preschool and kindergarten classrooms are more joyful places for all. We sincerely believe that everyone benefits!

ANTICIPATION

CHAPTERS 1 THROUGH 3

The first three chapters of *Saving Play* come under the first step in Scott Eberle's cycle of play: Anticipation. Eberle (2014) describes this stage as including these three elements:

- expectation
- wonder
- curiosity

We have all seen children's delight as new toys, materials, or games are introduced, whether by adults or by other children. They express excitement, interest, and curiosity as they anticipate playing with something or someone new. We hope children's delight inspires wonder in you, the readers, and makes you wonder about what will be offered in the exploration of play and standards in this book. And we hope you will be delighted with the ideas we offer. Our intent is to give you information, support, and strategies for integrating the best ways that young children learn with the expectations that standards define.

In his description of anticipation, Eberle also includes these elements:

- anxiety
- uncertainty
- risk

When trying anything new, most people feel some discomfort. They are outside the familiar and have to accommodate to new thinking or new ways of doing something. We hope the uncertainty we introduce will be at just the right level of challenge so that as early childhood professionals you can consider the questions posed and find solutions that will work in your programs.

In chapter 1, we explore definitions of play and the value of child-directed, open-ended play experiences. In chapter 2, we look more closely at the role of the teacher in this kind of play. And in chapter 3, we delve into early learning standards and the Common Core State Standards for Kindergarten, identifying those standards, considering some of the misconceptions that are circulating about them, and beginning the task of integrating them with child-directed, open-ended play.

CHAPTER 1

The Value of Child-Directed, Open-Ended Play Experiences

PROVOCATIVE QUESTION: What is play?

Tom: The Administrator's Perspective

The difficulty of defining play was brought home to me when I served on the NAEYC governing board. For a number of years, the board and the association had wrestled with developing a position statement on play, and some on the board were impatient with the progress. The reasons for developing the position statement were similar to our purposes here: valuing play as a central asset in the growth and development of young children. One of the staff members showed us a draft version and said part of the holdup was getting a common agreement on a definition of play. They had to define it before they could write about it. That turned out to be a lot harder than anyone anticipated.

Gaye: The Practitioner's Perspective

In my work as a preschool and kindergarten teacher and as a consultant to early childhood educators, I have seen many types of play in action. I am convinced that some play experiences are more beneficial for children than others. In defining play, I think we have to recognize the different types of play. Then we can help teachers set the stage for beneficial play, facilitate it as it occurs, and identify appropriate learning goals and standards that can be linked to beneficial play experiences.

EVERYONE PLAYS

Play is a universal phenomenon. Everyone everywhere—all cultures, all ages—plays. It is not just a human activity. Animals play too. Play is a natural state of being and adds a certain spice to life. In the middle of serious work, an adult may pause to make a joke, act silly, doodle, or throw a crumpled piece of paper into a trash can. Teenagers are known for "goofing off." They hang with friends to relax from the pressures of schooling and organized sports or other activities, to laugh and act childish as they face the daunting task of growing up. Children in the elementary school years spontaneously organize games on playgrounds or in neighborhoods, arguing about rules and relishing the opportunity to use their skills in throwing, catching, or chasing. From seven to eight years of age and on into the teenage years, children strategize at card and board games or challenge each other in video game battles.

Young children delight in play experiences throughout their early years. Babies find their toes fascinating playthings. Toddlers bang wooden spoons in pots, relishing the noise and the imitation of their loved ones cooking. Preschoolers dress up in hats and capes and boots with no purpose other than to pretend to be someone different. Kindergartners organize themselves so that a complex block structure can be completed with a symmetrical design in mind. A preschool or kindergarten child also takes moments of play and turns them toward a serious purpose, such as when a young girl matches picture cards in a memory game. She uses her visual discrimination skills to analyze each picture and her memory skills to find the match. If she is playing with another child or an adult, she may be conversing about the animals or shapes on the cards and increasing her oral vocabulary.

People do not need to be instructed on how to do things like this. Play is a natural way for adults to change the mental tasks in which they are engaged, to take a break from the drudgery of everyday chores, and to make life more pleasant. It is the natural way for children to explore and investigate the world, learning the marvels of nature and how things work, to experience the joy of pretend and the limitless bounds of their imaginations, and to use their muscles, senses, and brains.

SUPPORT FOR PLAY

Many people take play very seriously. In the United Nations Convention of the Rights of the Child, which was ratified by almost every country in the world in 1990 (though, unfortunately, not by the United States), Article 31 reads:

> States Parties recognize the right of the child to rest and leisure, to engage in play and recreational activities appropriate to the age of the child and to participate freely in cultural life and the arts.

This is a powerful statement. No country can write laws or put into practice policies that take away children's right to play.

A key principle in the position statement on "Developmentally Appropriate Practice" from NAEYC reads:

Play is an important vehicle for developing self-regulation as well as for promoting language, cognition, and social competence. (Copple and Bredekamp 2009, 14)

In fact, the word *play* appears thirty-eight times in the thirty-two-page statement. NAEYC and the Division for Early Childhood (Council for Exceptional Children) also include the importance of play in other position statements (which can be accessed at www.naeyc.org /positionstatements and www.dec-sped.org/papers).

Many organizations that focus on young people recognize that play is important because it does so many beneficial things for children. That is why the threat to children's opportunities to play must be taken very seriously. We must save play.

DEFINING PLAY

Defining play is not a simple task. The definition needs to strike the right balance and not be too broad or too narrow. To consider whatever children are doing as playful and important is too broad. To view play as trivial or a mere distraction from the important stuff of life is too narrow. In this book, our definition includes observable characteristics of play that are beneficial to children's development. We consider whether all play is equally valuable, identify different types of play, and determine how they contribute to children's learning. While we show multiple characteristics and types of play, our focus is on child-directed, open-ended play.

When you look up the definition of *play* in *Merriam-Webster's Collegiate Dictionary*, you have to proceed down to the third definition before finding something relevant for this book:

Play: "recreational activity; *esp* the spontaneous activity of children."

Three words are important in this definition: *spontaneous, recreational,* and *activity*.

Spontaneous: Play is not an assigned task. It often begins as an unplanned experience on the part of the player. What occurs is impromptu and unrehearsed.

Recreational: Play is about creating and re-creating. It is also about recreation, amusement, and diversion. It is not only about making and doing things; it is also about relaxation and enjoyment.

Activity: Activity is crucial. When play occurs, things are happening.

Because of its emphasis on fun and experimentation, play promotes a "growth mind-set." Carol Dweck (2006) makes a strong case for the value of the growth mind-set over the fixed mind-set. The growth mind-set views one's personal abilities as something that can always be improved. The fixed mind-set sees personal abilities as limited. Dweck argues that only with the growth mind-set can a person actually do more than he or she, or others (peers and teachers), thought possible. Her extensive research finds that determining one's mind-set, as either "growth" or "fixed," is a strong predictor of future success. When play becomes an avenue for low-risk experimentation, children's abilities inevitably grow. Play allows children to accomplish things outside a high-stakes pass/fail situation. Furthermore, play presents children with a bias toward action, and action teaches just how much each can do.

The Properties of Play

We think giving one all-encompassing definition to play is limiting. Play is complicated and hard to define because so many different kinds of human behavior could be characterized as play. We want to encourage early childhood educators to become observers and investigators of the *phenomenon* of play. When observing play, we encourage adults to ask themselves: what is this experience doing to children's thinking, feeling, and behavior?

In his book *Play: How It Shapes the Brain, Opens the Imagination, and Invigorates the Soul*, Stuart Brown (2009) does not provide a clear definition of play. Instead, he describes seven properties that make play unique from other types of human activities or experiences:

- Play is apparently purposeless (done for its own sake, not for survival or practical value).
- Play is voluntary (not required).
- It has inherent attraction (it's fun; play makes you feel good).
- It provides freedom from time (when fully engaged, we lose sense of the passage of time).
- We experience diminished consciousness of self (we stop thinking about whether we look good or stupid; we are fully in the moment).
- It has improvisational potential (we aren't locked into rigid ways of doing things; we see things in a different way).
- It provides a continuation desire (the pleasure of the experience makes us find ways to keep it going; we want to do it again). (Brown 2009, 17–18)

Here is an example of a play experience that shows many of these properties in action:

Two five-year-old girls decided to play school. They turned over storage containers and called them desks. They brought chairs, papers, and books over to their desks. Each got her backpack from her cubby and pulled out various school supplies. Once they had all of their materials set, they sat quietly, opening their books and turning the pages. They used their pencils to scribble across papers. At one point, one of the girls looked at the other and said, "Time for recess!" They left their desks and went running around the house area together, giggling and laughing. Then they returned to their desks. The other girl said, "Time for lunch!" They pretended to take out their lunchboxes and eat their food together. This pretend play went on for twenty minutes.

Which of the properties of play do you see illustrated in this play scenario?

Defining Play as Child Directed and Open Ended

We are defining play as child directed and open ended. Such play can include all seven properties identified earlier. It is the high-level play in which learning is deeper and more sophisticated.

- The *child-directed* quality is apparently purposeless, fun, self-perpetuating, and, most obviously, voluntary.
- The *open-ended* quality encourages improvisation and creativity, and frees the player to lose himself and not be conscious of time.

We see this as *authentic* play. Child-directedness reminds teachers that play arises from what the child wants to do and not just from what the teacher wants the child to do. If the teacher is involved, it is as inviter, cheerleader, and supporter. Open-endedness encourages teachers to choose materials and play opportunities so that children have many possibilities. Children with a variety of skills and differing understandings can be successful in a variety of ways as they engage in open-ended play experiences. While chaotic and simplistic play can also be child directed and open ended, chances are its abilities to really capture a child's interest for the long term are minimal.

"Apparently Purposeless" on Purpose

Some readers may be troubled by the idea of play being "apparently purposeless." We are aware that teachers are encouraged to be intentional about *all* they do. Outside pressures and expectations deem that classroom time is too short for anything that does not have "purpose." Remember that Brown (2009) says play has *apparent* purposelessness. In other words, a child's reason for engaging in play may be purely for fun, but she cannot stop the learning that occurs while she plays. What we describe in this book is how teachers can observe and understand play so they can see the learning purposes even if the children do not. Play as purposeless should be a reminder to be open to a variety of purposes that may emerge during play or be realized only later in reflection.

Here is an example:

A child may place a toy truck on top of a block tower. The truck rolls off and falls to the ground. That leads the child to figure out what blocks might be added to keep the truck from rolling off the tower. He may create a ramp. He may begin to push the truck around on the floor. Or the child may leave the truck alone and continue to build the tower. The child is following his inclination. All the options are possible. All lead to more play. What determines which option the child selects? Watching, it all seems aimless and accidental. Yet there is a purpose.

THE BENEFITS OF PLAY

Early educators as well as professionals from other fields recognize the many benefits of purposeful, complex play for young children. Research studies and position statements link high-level play to gains in cognitive learning and academic achievement, to physical health, to social-emotional development, and to the development of approaches to learning. In *Individualized Child-Focused Curriculum* (Gronlund 2016), Gaye shares the following benefits of play recognized by various professionals:

- Connections are made to greater academic achievement in the primary grades for children who engage in child-initiated, productive play in the preschool years (Copple and Bredekamp 2009).
- Physical and mental health experts advocate for increased play opportunities for children and warn of dire consequences as children become more sedentary and as kindergartens become less playful (Ginsburg 2007; Miller and Almon 2009).

Here is a list of additional research support for the benefits of play:

- Play positively affects cognitive development, language and literacy, social skills, and the expression of emotions (Rogers and Sawyers 1988).
- A strong association exists between play and self-regulation (Elias and Berk 2002).
- High-functioning play is significantly associated with prosocial behavior, motivation to learn, task persistence, and autonomy (Fantuzzo and McWayne 2002).
- There are connections between play and basic literacy skills and creative problem solving (Zigler, Singer, and Bishop-Josef 2004).
- Elena Bodrova and Deborah Leong (2003) identified five specific characteristics of "mature play" (imaginary situations, multiple roles, clearly defined rules, flexible themes, extensive use of language and long and elaborate play time) they found effective in increasing literacy and enhancing executive function (see also Diamond et al. 2007).

Stuart Brown (2009) summarizes the identified benefits in two categories: effects on the brain and rehearsal for life. Let's consider these two categories in more depth.

Effects on the Brain

When the brain is very young, every experience is an opportunity for the brain to wire together synaptic connections. The science related to brain development over the past fifty years has shown that the quality of those experiences directly determines the nature of the connections. The number and complexity of those connections literally make the brain what it is. When children's brains are engaged in high-level play, they are stimulated to grow and develop in healthy ways (Brown 2009).

When children engage in purposeful, rich play experiences, their neural connections grow stronger and more plentiful. Active play has been found to stimulate neural growth in both the prefrontal cortex and the amygdala. The prefrontal cortex, which lies immediately behind the forehead, is active during planning, personality expression, decision making, and the moderation of social behavior. It is the heart of *executive function* and is what some term as the brain's control tower. As children become deeply engaged in meaningful play, they are developing executive functions, which Ellen Galinsky describes as "the brain functions we use to manage our attention, our emotions, and our behavior in pursuit of our goals. . . . Executive functions predict children's success as well as—if not better than—IQ tests" (Galinsky 2012, 14).

Meanwhile, the amygdala plays the main function in processing memory, emotional reaction, and, like the prefrontal cortex, decision making (Pessoa 2013). Isn't it interesting that these different parts of the brain—memory and emotional reaction—are both necessary for making decisions? In their book *Primal Leadership: Learning to Lead with Emotional Intelligence*, Goleman, Boyatzis, and McKee (2013) write that it is the connections between the prefrontal cortex and the amygdala that build true emotional intelligence. Play is a way to exercise both of these parts of the brain simultaneously.

Play stimulates brain development, even in lower primates, whose brains are much less plastic than those of humans. It is good for all parts of the brain: not just the part that makes one smart, but the parts that make one remember past experiences, control impulses, and feel happy.

Rehearsal for Life

The second category of benefits Brown identifies relates to the function of play as a rehearsal for life. Through play, we can pretend to be or do something before we actually have to do it in real life. This helps us live successful lives. Evolutionary biologists say it helps us survive (Wenner 2009). Some zoologists studying mountain goats noticed that the young goats (kids) played rough-and-tumble games along the edges of very steep cliffs (Brown 2009). These are dangerous games indeed because the kids may misstep and fall to their death. They are having fun, but they are also rehearsing the sure-footedness they will need when they are trying to outrun a coyote or mountain lion. Fun, yes, but also a matter of life and death.

For humans, play becomes a way to fantasize about what might be. Children pretend to be mommies and daddies, taking care of babies, preparing meals, and going off to work. They practice adult roles such as firefighters, cashiers, and teachers. Young children love to engage in superhero play as a way to pretend to be powerful, fearless, and consequential. Such play helps them say, "I matter," and emerges at a time when they sometimes feel weak, scared, and ignored in the adult world. Playing what they are not is a way to become what they want to be.

Through pretend, children can address fears and traumatic situations in their lives. Play provides a safe place to address strong feelings, to relive frightening moments, and to come to some sort of resolution.

Play is also a way to learn how the world works. Observe a child playing intently at a sensory table. You may see him become mesmerized by the pattern the small rake makes as he drags it across the sand or by the effects of a single drop of water squeezed from an eyedropper as it hits the pool. Such exploration helps curiosity bloom into experimentation. Young children are scientific investigators from the earliest ages.

Children are such curious creatures. They explore, question, and wonder, and by doing so, learn. . . . For too many children, curiosity fades. Curiosity dimmed is a future denied. Our potential—emotional, social, and cognitive—is expressed through the quantity and quality of our experiences. And the less-curious child will make fewer new friends, join fewer social groups, read fewer books, and take fewer hikes. The less-curious child is harder to teach because he is harder to inspire, enthuse, and motivate. (Perry 2001, 1)

As a rehearsal for life, play gives children opportunities to put their existing knowledge and skills into practice. Play opens the door to endless possibilities for applying knowledge in new ways and to new situations, or to practice key skills—like balancing on a beam or writing one's name—over and over again.

Children in preschool and kindergarten are "learning to be learners." The better learners they become the more successful they will be in their K–12 careers. They are "rehearsing" for their life as students in elementary, secondary, and higher education settings. Research is showing more connections between the development of effective approaches to learning in the early years and later academic achievement.

CONCLUSION

It's hard to capture the complexity of play in a single phrase or sentence. Identifying the properties of play and considering the many benefits of play help show how important play is in human development. In chapter 2, we explore the importance of teacher involvement in play and the many roles adults can engage in with children in play.

Implementation Ideas for Teachers:
THE VALUE OF OPEN-ENDED PLAY

Reflect about a time you observed children at play. Consider the following questions:

1. How many of the seven properties we have identified were evident?
2. Were the children playing purely for the pleasure of the experience and not for a more defined purpose?
3. Was the play freely chosen?
4. Did they lose themselves in the play?
5. Did it last long?
6. What kinds of things might an adult do to support the child's play?

Practical Considerations for Administrators:
THE VALUE OF OPEN-ENDED PLAY

Take the time to converse about play with the teachers in your program. Ask them the following questions:

1. What memories do you have of playing when you were a child? What kinds of activities did you engage in? What do you think you were learning when you played?
2. How would you define *play*?
3. How much time in your daily schedule is devoted to child-directed, open-ended play indoors?
4. What benefits do you see resulting from children having opportunities to play?

CHAPTER 2

The Importance of Teacher Engagement in Child-Directed Play

PROVOCATIVE QUESTION: **Can play be child directed and open ended *and* include teacher engagement with children as they play?**

Tom: The Administrator's Perspective

I want the answer to this question to be "yes," but I hear concerns from administrators. They want to know whether they can be sure that teachers who implement child-directed and open-ended play experiences are addressing standards, paying attention to learning, and being accountable for student progress. I think it's important that teacher engagement with this type of play is well defined and observable so that an administrator can see the teacher's intentionality and feel confident that children are learning.

Gaye: The Practitioner's Perspective

I think the answer to this question is "yes." But I also recognize that the "how" of that teacher engagement needs more investigation. For children's play to be truly child directed and open ended, teachers must not co-opt children's play or make it completely teacher directed. So, a follow-up question is, what are the best ways for teachers to plan for, support, and facilitate children's play?

FREE PLAY VERSUS PLANNED PLAY

Over time, many preschool and kindergarten teachers have identified a block of time in their daily schedule as "free-play time." During this time, children have the opportunity to choose from a variety of experiences. Commonly, they can choose from the following:

- building with blocks in a designated area
- engaging in dramatic play in a play house or kitchen

- completing puzzles or exploring a variety of manipulatives placed on shelves and in bins that are available for them to pull out and use
- looking at books in a library area
- exploring items from nature with magnifying glasses and other scientific tools
- pretending to write or practicing making the letters they do know with a variety of tools and papers at a writing center
- messing with sand or water at a sensory table; exploring ways to measure, pour, and manipulate it
- creating with a variety of art materials
- exploring musical instruments and listening and dancing to CDs

During this time, teachers allow children to freely choose where they will play, for how long, and with whom. However, in order to offer these choices, teachers must prearrange the environment so that the areas are defined and the appropriate materials are available. In other words, *teachers plan for play*. They have determined the room arrangement and the provision of materials available. This planning provides an inherent structure that helps children engage successfully in a variety of experiences.

In high-quality preschool and kindergarten classrooms, teachers recognize that offering choices to the children brings about more participation and engagement in the activities. Young children do not respond well to constantly being told what to do. As Erik Erikson (1950) identified, they are developing in the age of initiative—trying things out for themselves. Their developing independence and movement toward greater competence propels them to reject constant direction from the adults in their lives. Yet it is not complete freedom from adult guidance that they seek. Children trust adults to provide reasonable choices within the safety of adult guidance (Gronlund 2013, 161).

Because of this teacher planning, calling these blocks of playtime "free play" is really not accurate. In fact, that label can be misleading.

This label does not reflect the amount of thoughtfulness in teacher planning or the amount of learning benefits for the children. In fact, there are often people (children's family members, administrators, community members, policy makers) who think that "free play" really means a "free-for-all." They may think that there is no planning, no teacher intervention, and no purposefulness or learning involved in the play.

Effective early childhood educators know that indeed there is a great deal of planning, teacher involvement, purposefulness, and learning in children's play. Rather than calling playtime "free play," some teachers have re-named this time [Investigation Time, Exploration Time, Discovery Time, Activity Time, Choice Time, Focused Play Time, or Center Time] to reflect its intentionality and importance. (Gronlund 2016, 33–34)

Teachers who are successful in engaging children in high-level play experiences are planful. They are intentional. They think carefully about how to effectively build children's approaches to learning so that they become deeply involved, use their imaginations and critical thinking skills, work cooperatively with others, and benefit from the play experience. Does this intentionality take away from the *authenticity* of play? No. Are the properties of play still observable? Yes. Let's consider some of the properties in light of teacher planning.

Voluntary: Although there is a predetermined set of play experiences, the child chooses where and with what to play.

Inherent attraction and continuation desire: The teacher considers ways to engage children's interests as part of her planning so that the children will perceive that the play is fun and want to keep playing.

Freedom from time and diminished consciousness of self: Teachers make sure ample time is available in the daily schedule for children to get deeply involved in play (forty-five-minute to one-hour blocks are recommended).

Improvisation: Teachers are not necessarily planning what the children have *to do* with the materials available. In fact, they offer more open-ended materials than those with one right use. So, the children have many opportunities to come up with their own ideas and use their creativity.

Effective teaching involves planning. Preschool and kindergarten teachers who recognize play as an important part of their program plan for play in ways that support authentic, high-level engagement for the children.

AMPLE TIME FOR PLAY

Another serious consideration for teachers as they plan for play is the amount of time they allow in their daily schedules for child-directed, open-ended play to develop. Young children do not become deeply engaged immediately. They need time to see what is available, to watch what others are doing, to figure out what they want to do, and then, to get going. Effective teachers recognize that children need a sufficient amount of time for high-level play to develop. Fifteen to twenty minutes is not nearly enough. Instead, recommendations are as follows:

- at least sixty minutes of indoor play at learning centers
- daily outdoor play plus opportunities for physical activities and music and movement indoors (Copple and Bredekamp 2009, 153 and 163)

PLAYFUL LEARNING

Beyond planning for the room arrangement, materials, and time in the daily schedule, teachers also plan for learning goals associated with play. Kathy Hirsh-Pasek and Roberta Michnick Golinkoff (2014) use the term "playful learning." They emphasize the role of the teacher not only in identifying learning goals for play but also in facilitating and guiding the play:

> Playful learning is a whole-child approach to education that includes both free play and guided play. . . . guided play offers a new twist. It refers to play in a structured environment around a general curricular goal that is designed to stimulate children's natural curiosity, exploration, and play with learning-oriented materials. . . . In guided play, learning remains child-directed. This is a key point. Children learn targeted information through exploration of a well-designed and structured environment . . . and through the support of adults who ask open-ended questions to gently guide the child's exploration.

The term "playful learning" provides a wonderful contrast to play that occurs in an unplanned environment. The connection to learning is much more evident, as is the idea that the teacher is intentional in planning and actively facilitating the play experience. But note that the play is still child directed. The teacher is not completely controlling play. Rather, she is gently guiding, facilitating, and asking open-ended questions. She has identified learning goals and uses her skills to integrate them into child-directed play. The emphasis on child direction could not be clearer. Yet the teacher has a significant role as the play experience unfolds.

One caution about these categories—free play versus guided, child directed versus teacher directed, even high level versus low level. They are not fixed and rigid. All play will be more or less free, more or less child directed, more or less high level. What we need to do is develop the skill to observe and evaluate play with these categories in mind.

One of the potentially challenging ideas we are presenting is that some of the learning that takes place while children are engaging in child-directed play is "accidental" or "unanticipated" by the adult. Teachers have to be open to this possibility and ready to recognize when such learning happens. Remember, however, that even with "accidental" learning, teachers still plan—they just make their plans rich enough to create space for the unexpected.

Intentionality, planning, guiding, and facilitating do indeed go together in bringing about playful learning experiences that reflect the properties of meaningful, high-level play. This is the real art of teaching young children and must be recognized, discussed, and developed further. Throughout this book, we plan to do just that.

HOW BEST TO SUPPORT AND FACILITATE PLAY

Just how much guidance should be provided? When is it too little so that the play does not involve deep engagement? And when is it too much so that it takes away the child's enjoyment of the play experience? *Teachers know by observing children engaged in play.* As we said in chapter 1, observation is the way to define play, to identify what properties are evident, to determine whether the child is deeply engaged or not, and to link the play experience to learning. This means teachers cannot assume that they can say to children, "Go play," and then go do something else themselves. They must be *involved* in order to observe. They may not always have to talk with the children or direct the play, but they must be

- nearby,
- watching closely to see what children are doing,
- listening to hear what they are saying, and
- ready to offer assistance.

Teacher involvement in play is recognized as part of best practices in preschool and kindergarten classrooms.

What does the teacher observe during play? A variety of observable behaviors show the child's level of engagement. Let's consider some of them, placing each on a continuum from less developed to more fully developed.

Dependence to Independence

A primary goal of preschool and kindergarten programs is to help children move from dependence to independence. Teachers and family members work with young children on the tasks of dressing and undressing, toileting and feeding, and making one's needs known to others. Making choices and taking the initiative to follow through with them on one's own is another form of independence that develops in the preschool and kindergarten years.

Some children move toward independence more easily than others. The label "terrible twos" is about the move toward independence as two-year-olds declare, "Me do it!" and push their loving caregivers away. Some children, however, hesitate to take risks or try things for themselves. They prefer to be dependent on loved ones into their preschool and kindergarten years. While some of this can be culturally influenced, it is also associated with the child's personality traits and life experiences.

Play can be a way for children to experiment with independence, to take initiative, to try something new on their own. In play experiences, teachers can observe

- the risks children take,
- how often they ask for teacher assistance, and
- if they wait for an adult or another child to do something for them.

Repetitive Actions to Creative Innovation

Toddlers engaged in repetitive actions are right on target developmentally. They try things out again and again to see if the results will be the same. But for three- to six-year-olds, repetitive play is not at the high level of engagement, problem solving, and creativity possible for this age group.

Teachers can watch for the following clues that children are stuck in repetitive engagement:

- Their eyes are glazed and often unfocused.
- Children look bored or say they are bored.
- They are not smiling or laughing.
- They are not coming up with new ideas or ways of using materials.
- They do not stay engaged with the activity for very long.

In contrast, children who are engaged in high-level play are creative innovators. They are coming up with new ideas and ways of using materials or extending play experiences. Teachers can observe these traits:

- bright and focused eyes
- smiling and laughing faces
- combining materials in creative ways
- long engagement in the activity

Poor Self-Control to Self-Regulation

Children in the preschool and kindergarten years are learning self-control and self-regulation. Adults cannot expect them always to be able to inhibit their impulses. Teachers and family members work with children on refraining from hitting and to encourage them to use words to express anger or frustration. They assist them in making choices that are safe and productive rather than dangerous or destructive. Yet some three- to six-year-olds exhibit better impulse control than others. And play is an activity in which they demonstrate their abilities to do so. Teachers can observe for children who are

- being noisy and excessively loud as they play,
- using materials destructively or dangerously,
- laughing hysterically rather than joyfully, and
- excluding particular children in their play groups and being hurtful or mean in doing so.

When teachers observe children in high-level play, they will see them do the following:

- work to solve problems, whether they are physical (like making the puzzle piece fit) or social (like resolving a disagreement)
- need little teacher intervention or assistance but ask for it when needed and then return to their play experience
- change their behavior and inhibit their impulses so that they can keep the play experience going because it is so pleasurable

Frustration to Persistence

Children's level of tolerance for frustration is related to self-control and self-regulation and varies with each child. Again, personality styles as well as life experiences are influential in shaping this capacity. Teachers observing children at play will see them respond to the frustrations that arise in different ways. Each child reacts differently when the block structure won't stand or her playmate takes the toy she wanted. Some children respond to frustration with anger, poor behavior, or total withdrawal from the experience, while other children take frustrations in stride, seem to relish challenges, and move forward with tenacity.

Teachers observe play experiences to determine how each child is doing in relation to independence, creative innovation, self-regulation, and persistence. When a child is showing less-developed behaviors, such as dependence, poor self-control, or low tolerance for frustration, teachers step in quickly to intervene. They may

- need to be directive to keep the play safe,
- give the child suggestions for using materials differently, or
- help the child work out a disagreement with a peer.

Effective preschool and kindergarten teachers have good radar for detecting when children need this kind of intervention and step in as quickly as they can to make the situation more successful.

But what about children who are deeply engaged in play and are showing independence, creative innovation, self-regulation, and persistence? Do they need teacher guidance? Yes! We believe they need it just as much as the children on the other end of the continuum. But the guidance will be different. Rather than intervention, and, yes, even interruption (often for safety's sake), this guidance is "gentler," as Hirsh-Pasek and Golinkoff (2014) say. Teachers

- support and facilitate the play,
- follow the child's lead, and
- join *with* the child in the play experience.

Let's look at ways to support and facilitate high-level play in more depth.

CONSIDER CHANGES TO THE ENVIRONMENT

Preschool and kindergarten teachers know that to engage children in playful learning the classroom environment needs to be carefully organized. Areas are clearly delineated with furniture, shelving, and materials that lead children to engage in different kinds of play. To bring about and support high-level play, then, teachers must continually evaluate how the room arrangement is working and where children are using materials successfully. Sometimes adjustments happen in the moment. A teacher may bring more chairs to a crowded table of playdough users and help them divide the dough so everyone can work with it. Or he may offer a tub of dinosaur figures to a group of block builders to extend the construction they are creating.

Or teachers may think about changes in the environment over time. They may have noticed problems arising in an area or have been concerned that the play in another is not as rich and engaging as it could be. When children misbehave, or when play is not at a high level, the first question teachers ask is, "In what play or interest area of the classroom did this occur?" Then they look closely at that area and evaluate it for particular aspects.

Space

- Is there enough room for the children to move around as they use the materials available so they are not invading each other's personal space?
- Or is the area too large and undefined so that children do not feel a sense of purpose and enclosure?

Quantity of Materials

- Are there enough materials available in the area for the number of children who want to play there?
- Are there some very popular things that are causing disagreements?
- Or are there too many materials so that children are overwhelmed by the choices available?

Engaging and Interesting Materials

- Which materials are children finding most interesting?
- Which are children not using or using inappropriately?
- Are there multiple ways for children to use the materials?
- Are materials open ended or closed ended (that is, having only one right way to be used)?
- Is it time to change some of the materials to add more interest or more challenge?

As teachers ask themselves these questions, they can determine next steps to take regarding each of these aspects of the environment.

Space

- Perhaps a shelf needs to be moved out so that there is more room in the block area and children are not knocking down each other's structures.
- Perhaps the library area is too large and needs to be defined as a smaller, cozier space.
- Perhaps a class meeting needs to be called to discuss the problems that have been arising in the dramatic play area. Children can give their ideas for rearranging the space so that there are fewer disagreements.

Quantity of Materials

- Perhaps too many puzzles are available at the manipulatives area so that children are dumping them all out and having difficulty finding the right pieces for the right puzzle frames. A smaller selection might work more successfully.
- Perhaps the only light blue airplane, which all the boys fight over each day (even though there are many airplanes of different colors), should be put away.
- Perhaps multiple copies of favorite books should be available for children to look at in the class library.

Engaging and Interesting Materials

- Perhaps different writing materials need to be made available to entice children to the writing area, including many different kinds of paper (both lined and unlined, stationery, note cards, index cards) and writing tools (pens, pencils, markers, crayons of differing sizes), so that children can choose what works best for them.
- Perhaps it's time to change the materials in the sensory table from dry to wet sand, or from a full tub of water to individual dishpans of water so that each child has a defined space.
- Perhaps the science area would be better used by the children if they go on a nature walk outdoors and collect leaves, sticks, pebbles, and other items and then decide how to analyze them with tools such as magnifying glasses, and to label and display them in a "nature museum."

Making changes to the environment is a way to facilitate and support high-level play. It is an important teaching strategy and part of the everyday life in a preschool and kindergarten classroom, as well as part of ongoing planning for playful learning.

ENGAGE WITH CHILDREN TO SUPPORT AND ENHANCE PLAY

Teachers can choose from many other strategies to support and facilitate children's play. These strategies involve engaging *with* children in play. In this section, we focus on the following teaching strategies:

- playing alongside children
- modeling
- scaffolding
- providing provocations and challenges
- reflecting with children about their play

Teachers make in-the-moment decisions as they observe children at play to determine which strategy to use. Then, as they interact with the child or group of children, they continue to observe whether the strategy is successful or not. Again, this is at the very heart of effective teaching. Skilled teachers pay close attention to what children are doing and saying and continually adjust their own actions accordingly. Let's look more in depth at these five possible ways to engage with children in play.

Playing alongside Children

When a teacher is nearby as children play, she is communicating that she is interested in what they are doing. She is validating their play experience as she watches and listens. She may smile, give an affirmative comment, or describe what she sees. And she is carefully reading the signals the children are sending her. Throughout, she is asking herself the following questions:

- Are children deeply engaged in what they are doing?
- Do they want to show me what they are doing?
- Do they show interest in including me in the play experience in any way?

She is withholding from stepping further into the children's play until they invite her. If the children do not invite her, she can continue to observe. However, if a child says, "Look what we're doing, Teacher!" she has an opportunity to join with the children:

- She can move closer.
- She can sit alongside them.
- She can continue to make supportive comments.
- She can join in the play herself.

But she does so always with the understanding that the play belongs to the children. *They* further the scenario. She joins *with* them. Rather than taking over the play, the teacher makes sure the children perceive her involvement as an accompaniment to what they want to accomplish rather than an interruption or change. This takes sensitivity. It takes impulse control or self-regulation on the part of the teacher! But it can have great results. Here is an example of a teacher engaging with a child in parallel play. Notice the ways in which he waits for an invitation, joins with the child, refrains from taking over the play, and uses open-ended questions to further the child's engagement.

> Alicia (a four-year-old) was playing independently with a dollhouse. She is a child with identified special needs related to expressive language and, therefore, is not as verbal as some children. Her teacher, Kyle, approached and sat in a chair nearby. Alicia said, "Look, Teacher. It's the mom." Kyle moved closer and picked up a father figure. Alicia said, "It's the dad." "I wonder what the mom and dad are doing?" Kyle asked. Alicia took the father figure from him and placed both figures in chairs at the kitchen table. She then made verbalizations with the dolls

(cont.)

as if they were conversing. She used a higher-pitched voice for the mother and a lower one for the father. Kyle sat and listened, then asked, "Are they talking? What are they talking about?" "The baby," Alicia answered, pulling the baby figure from another room and placing it in the kitchen. Kyle and Alicia continued to engage together at the dollhouse for another ten minutes or so.

Modeling

Modeling is another teaching strategy that can be used to support and enhance children's play. As a teacher joins in play with children, she can model ways to use the materials that may be new or unfamiliar to the children. And as she does so, she can think aloud, describing what she is doing and posing open-ended questions to herself. When teachers first try this, they may feel self-conscious or embarrassed. But as they continue to use this strategy, they will find their discomfort dissipates. Often the children respond with interest in what their teacher is doing and try it out for themselves. Modeling and thinking aloud are valid teaching strategies even in higher grades.

> By verbalizing their inner speech (silent dialogue) as they think their way through a problem, teachers model how expert thinkers solve problems. . . . As students think out loud with teachers and with one another, they gradually internalize this dialogue; it becomes their inner speech, the means by which they direct their own behaviors and problem-solving processes (Tinzmann et al. 1990). Therefore, as students think out loud, they learn how to learn. They learn to think as authors, mathematicians, anthropologists, economists, historians, scientists, and artists. They develop into reflective, metacognitive, independent learners, an invaluable step in helping students understand that learning requires effort and often is difficult (Tinzmann et al. 1990). It lets students know that they are not alone in having to think their way through the problem-solving process.

Modeling and thinking aloud can include introducing something new to children as well as revisiting a familiar play task. Again, open-ended questioning can be included as part of this strategy. Here is an example of a teacher engaged in modeling and thinking aloud:

Patricia, a kindergarten teacher, created a dinosaur play area in response to the interest shown by so many of her students. She placed rocks, magnifying glasses, toy dinosaurs, a balance scale, paper taped to the wall, and stencils in this center. When she introduced the area, she encouraged children to trace and

(cont.)

make rubbings with the stencils, to look at the rocks through the magnifying glasses, to draw dinosaurs, and to weigh the toy dinosaurs. As she observed children exploring the materials, she noticed that they were not engaging with the scale. So she went over and asked if she could join the group there. They agreed, and she sat down next to them and said aloud, "I wonder what we could do with this scale?" When there was no response, she said, "I'm going to see how many dinosaurs can fit on this side of the scale." She began to fill one bucket of the balance scale when Joseph said, "I'll do the other side." Timothy helped him. "How will we know which weighs more?" Patricia asked. " 'Cause it will go down," Joseph replied. Patricia stayed nearby, conversing with the children as they took over using the scale to weigh different groups of dinosaur figures. Other children became involved, predicting what items would be heavier and lighter. Patricia then got some paper and markers and said, "I'm going to make a book that shows what we weighed." She traced the dinosaur figures and created less and more equations as the children engaged with the scale. Some children also joined her in tracing and recording their discoveries.

Scaffolding

The teaching strategies discussed so far facilitate and support children in playful learning experiences with the goal for children to engage in the high-level play that has many benefits for them. One teaching strategy that is particularly effective is scaffolding. What does scaffolding mean in terms of how to interact with children in play?

In the context of classroom interaction, the term *scaffolding* has been taken up to describe the temporary assistance teachers provide for their students to assist them to complete a task or develop new understandings so that they will later be able to complete similar tasks alone (Burns and Joyce 2005).

Scaffolding goes beyond modeling or thinking aloud. It involves an on-the-spot assessment by the teacher of the child's capability to be successful independently in the task at hand. She observes and determines what the child can and cannot do. She assesses the child's potential response when he encounters a problem or is unsuccessful. She asks herself these questions:

- Will he become too frustrated?
- Will he give up altogether?

- Will he become angry?
- Will he relish the challenge?

As the teacher answers these questions in her own mind, she considers how to provide support or scaffolding that is at just the right level. How will she know what that level is? The child will experience success but still perceive that he is the primary accomplisher of the task. Scaffolding, then, will be different for each child in each play situation.

Teachers who use effective scaffolding also know to wait patiently as they figure out how much support to give a child. In the waiting process, they can

- take in the situation and observe closely,
- see if the child will relish the challenge or not,
- ask the child if he wants assistance, or
- consider small amounts of assistance so that the child will stay engaged.

Here is an example of a teacher providing scaffolding to a child in play:

> In her preschool classroom, Lydia saw that Sofia had pulled out the patterning cards and small colored shapes and placed them on the manipulatives table. Lydia pulled a chair nearby and watched as Sofia looked at the cards and successfully matched the manipulatives, creating both AB and ABC patterns. Lydia wondered if she could assist Sofia in creating patterns independent of the cards and asked if Sofia would like to try. She agreed. Lydia asked, "What kind of pattern do you think you'll make?" Sofia said, "I know" and started to lay colored shapes next to each other in no apparent order. "Do you remember what a pattern has to have?" Lydia asked. "Let's look at the card together and see." They analyzed the repeating nature of the patterns on the cards, and then put them away. Lydia guided Sofia as she placed a yellow triangle and a green square. "So if we have these two as our pattern, what has to come next? Is it the yellow triangle or the green square?" Sofia looked at Lydia for a few seconds and then, as if a lightbulb went off, immediately sorted out all of the appropriate shapes from the pile and completed the pattern. "You did it! I wonder if we could try a pattern with three different colors or shapes. What do you think, Sofia? I'll help you if you need it." Together they created an ABC pattern, Lydia adding a shape here and there when Sofia seemed to hesitate.

Providing Provocations and Challenges

When teachers see that children relish challenges and do not need their assistance to be successful, they may consider providing provocations to further complicate what children are doing during play. *Provocations* is a term used in the Reggio Emilia approach to teaching young children, wherein tachers are "listening closely to the children's interests and devising a means for provoking further thought and action" (Gestwicki 2016, 118).

When planning for provocations, teachers need to reflect on what they have observed as children play. They want to determine what level of challenge will be just right to engage the interest of the children and to intrigue them. As Kantor and Whaley write, "The interventions are careful and specific—designed to facilitate children's thinking, to 'provoke' them to go further in their thinking. . . . Rather than constraining children, the teachers are seeking to open up the possibilities for them, just as a maestro helps students learn to play an instrument, but does not make the music for them" (1998, 322).

> The idea is to pay close attention to the child's level of developmental accomplishments and make adjustments in the curriculum not only to match that level but also to challenge the child to move ahead in skills, knowledge, and concepts. Then, the teacher is standing by ready to provide scaffolding and support. (Gronlund 2013, 140–41)

So, scaffolding may be necessary when offering provocations to children as well. The two teaching strategies work hand in hand.

What are some possible provocations for preschool and kindergarten children? Here is a basic list for consideration. However, as we move forward in this book and investigate the role of standards and academics in children's play, we offer many more ideas for possible provocations. Basic provocations may include the following:

- new or different materials
- new or different playmates
- investigative topics, projects, or studies
- incorporation of academic skills (such as reading comprehension, writing, mathematical problem solving, or scientific investigation)
- documenting the play experience and sharing it with others

The following vignette is an example of a provocation planned and implemented by teachers in a kindergarten classroom.

Mrs. Jansen, a kindergarten teacher, had car trouble earlier in the week and shared her frustrating experience with the children in her classroom. They asked her many questions about her car repair and shared stories of their families' experiences with car trouble. She and her coteacher, Mr. Lange, decided to create a car repair area. They covered a table with a blanket and called it the "car." They provided tools, measuring devices, a telephone, a clipboard with paper, writing materials, plastic bottles, and a skateboard (to roll under the car). The students were highly engaged for the entire playtime in this area. They pretended to answer the phone, write down orders, roll under the car with tools, use the measuring items, place fluids in the car, and talk to customers. Mrs. Jansen and Mr. Lange were amazed that the skateboard in the area was used only for its intended purpose of pretending to roll under the car. The children stayed in "character" as they talked to each other about how to fix the car. They used appropriate car and measurement vocabulary to describe what was happening and interacted verbally and cooperatively with one another throughout the activity.

Reflecting with Children about Play

Another way teachers can support and enhance children's play is to encourage them to reflect on their play experiences after the fact. Inviting children to review what they did in play validates it and gives it importance. Asking children their thoughts about their play helps develop communication skills as children remember what they have done and explain it to others. This process can lead to consideration of what they might do differently the next time. Such conversations open the door for the teacher to offer suggestions and ideas as well. Children and teachers can jointly make plans for the next play experience. Teachers can weave in learning goals and challenges so that children take the play further into more complexity and creativity.

Some teachers use technology to engage children in this reflective process. They use handheld devices to either videotape or create an audio recording of what children are doing during play. Then they revisit the recording with the children to engage in reflection. Here is an example of such a discussion:

Early in the day, Jordan, a preschool teacher, asks a group of children, "Before we start playing, do you want to watch the video of what you did yesterday?" "Yes!" chime several children as a few get up and run over to the tablet. Jordan plays the short video and asks, "What's happening here?" "Amelia was sick!" says Sara. Zach agrees. "Yeah, she has diphtheria. Sara saw it on the X-ray. See? There she is looking at the X-ray." "Well, doctors, how will you help our friend today?" asks Jordan. Zach replies, "We need to get her the medicine, but it is far away." Sara suggests having a dogsled relay to get the medicine, connecting yesterday's play to the story of Balto the sled dog, currently popular in the class. The children rush off, gathering props and friends—they need as many dogsled teams as they can get! Soon most of the class is working together on the relay, getting Amelia her medicine in the nick of time. Later in the day, the children watch a video of the dogsled play and revisit their harrowing tale with each other (Foley and Green 2015, 21).

Teachers can ask children to draw and/or write about their play. They can serve as scribes during dramatic play scenarios, writing down the script that children create. Then they can revisit the script with the children and invite them to act it out again. Vivian Paley (1981) has written extensively about her experiences doing this with kindergarten children with wonderful results. The teacher learns more about children's thinking, and children learn how important their play is to their teacher.

CONCLUSION

All of the strategies shared in this chapter work together to support children's play. It's as if teachers and children are involved in a dance together. The teacher is continually determining when the children should take the lead and when she should follow, or when she should be more in the lead role, making changes to the environment, modeling, thinking aloud, scaffolding, or providing provocations.

Observation is a key element. Teachers watch and listen as they decide when to step in and out of children's play. Open-ended questioning is used whether the teacher is playing alongside or scaffolding. The teacher's overarching goal is for children to benefit from the play experience.

We have seen that effective play facilitation is complex. Teachers have many choices to consider and must be constantly evaluating play situations. This is hard work! It is not haphazard or random. It is intentional. And it is essential to the development of play that can be connected to learning, to standards, and to the many benefits for children. The question posed at the beginning of this chapter was, Can play be child directed and open ended *and* include teacher engagement with children as they play?

Yes! We hope we have shown the many ways teachers can engage with children and facilitate and support child-directed and open-ended play.

In the next chapter, we look closely at standards and consider facts and misconceptions about them. More importantly, we show how standards can provide necessary guidance for the learning we desire for children.

Implementation Ideas for Teachers:
TEACHER ENGAGEMENT IN CHILD-DIRECTED PLAY

Think back about the last week in your preschool or kindergarten classroom. Consider the following questions:

1. In what ways did you engage with children in play?
2. Do you feel your engagement supported or enhanced the play? In what ways?
3. Which ideas in this chapter will you try in the future?

Implementation Ideas for Administrators:
TEACHER ENGAGEMENT IN CHILD-DIRECTED PLAY

Schedule some time in the coming week to observe a preschool or kindergarten class when child-directed play will occur. Check with your teachers about the best time during their daily schedules when such an activity is likely to occur. Consider these questions:

1. How was the teacher engaged? Remember to consider how the teacher might have modeled or set up opportunities beforehand.
2. Did you observe parallel play? Modeling? Scaffolding? Providing provocations or challenges? Reflecting with children?
3. From your perspective, what part of the play was the richest in terms of learning?
4. What guidance might you give the teacher about how to be more intentional in the play activity you observed?
5. Share your reflections about all of these questions with teachers and see how your ideas align with their thinking.

CHAPTER 3

Why Standards? Facts and Misconceptions about Early Learning and Kindergarten Standards

PROVOCATIVE QUESTION: Why are standards necessary in early childhood programs?

Tom: The Administrator's Perspective

When the federal initiative Good Start, Grow Smart was launched in 2002, one of my colleagues at the Iowa Department of Education was charged with helping the state develop early learning guidelines. At the time, I was skeptical of such initiatives, thinking guidelines or standards were intended to ratchet up expectations on learning in early childhood settings. I held a traditional view that developmentally appropriate practice rightly placed the emphasis on rich, playful experiences for young children without worrying about what children were learning. In all earnestness, I went up to her and asked, "Are we going to be developing early learning guidelines because we have to? Or do we actually intend to use them in some specific way?" She responded, "Oh, we will be using them for sure." Her response was a turning point for me. Less than four months later, I was asked to give a keynote address at an early childhood conference on the value of standards. I had to be ready. And I was ready, thanks to our brief but definitive conversation. Standards are to be used and should be taken seriously.

Gaye: The Practitioner's Perspective

As I travel the country and talk with early childhood educators, I hear confusion about standards. I think people tend to confuse the standards themselves with the way they are implemented. And often their implementation is not developmentally appropriate. It's essential that we clear up misunderstandings and learn the facts about standards and the best ways to implement them in preschool and kindergarten classrooms.

WHAT CHILDREN DESERVE

In this book, we show again and again that play and standards can fit together. But we never want to compromise the integrity of either play or standards in order to make them "fit" better. We believe that standards and play can be linked so that teachers can do what they are supposed to do: teach young children in ways that are right for them. In this chapter, we clarify what standards are, what they mean for early education, and the best ways to implement them.

Unfortunately, we have seen examples of practices that either do harm to play or fail to address the standards. Teachers or administrators may think they are providing play opportunities for children just by making teacher-led instruction more playful. They may also short-change the standards by not focusing on all of them or by allowing a kind of "good enough" attitude to dilute a required level of rigor or mastery relating to specific skills or knowledge. Neither is acceptable. Neither is optimal learning. Children deserve better.

- Children deserve to be challenged.
- Children deserve instruction that introduces them to new things and pushes them beyond their existing abilities.
- Children deserve an education that prepares them to survive and thrive in the world in which they live.
- Children deserve to learn about things that interest them as well as things that will be important for them to know.
- Children deserve to learn through a wide variety of experiences and approaches.
- Children deserve to be affirmed and supported as learners capable of learning.

Adults are obligated to provide all of this for children. That is what high-quality early childhood education is all about.

WHAT ARE STANDARDS?

Standards can provide the foundation for high-quality preschool and kindergarten education. Sometimes called guidelines, standards guide curriculum, instruction, and assessment. They express what adults want for children. They embody core values to ensure that society progresses and improves. They are a set of goals, perhaps even dreams, for what children will know and achieve. Like blueprints in architecture, standards are the blueprints in education. They are detailed drawings, sketches, or outlines. They describe expectations for children's learning at different ages that will help them survive and thrive into adulthood.

We also must clarify what standards are *not*:

- They are *not* an assessment.
- They are *not* a curriculum.
- They are *not* a set of instructional practices.

Standards should be seen as the aspirations of our society that have been paired with knowledge of child development.

In this book, we focus on early learning standards for preschool children and on standards for kindergartners. We will refer to several different sets of kindergarten standards, including the following:

- Common Core State Standards for Kindergarten
- Next Generation Science Standards
- College, Career, and Civic Life (C3) Framework for Social Studies State Standards
- Grade-Level Outcomes for a Variety of K–12 Standards for Physical Education, Social Studies, and Social-Emotional Development

What Standards Mean for Early Education

Professional recommendations show us the potential benefits of both early learning and Common Core standards. For preschool children:

> The first years of life are critical for later outcomes. Young children have an innate desire to learn. That desire can be supported or undermined by early experiences. High-quality early childhood education can promote intellectual, language, physical, social, and emotional development, creating school readiness and building a foundation for later academic and social competence. By defining the desired content and outcomes of young children's education, early learning standards can lead to greater opportunities for positive development and learning in these early years. (NAEYC and NAECS/SDE 2002, 2)

For kindergarten and beyond:

> High standards that are consistent across states provide teachers, parents, and students with a set of clear expectations to ensure that all students have the skills and knowledge necessary to succeed in college, career, and life upon graduation from high school,

regardless of where they live. These standards are aligned to the expectations of colleges, workforce training programs, and employers. The standards promote equity by ensuring all students are well prepared to collaborate and compete with their peers in the United States and abroad. Unlike previous state standards, which varied widely from state to state, the Common Core enables collaboration among states on a range of tools and policies. (CCSS 2015a)

Sharon Lynn Kagan and colleagues (2013) state that standards provide

- quality,
- equity,
- consistency, and
- transparency.

Let's look at each in turn.

Quality

First, standards shape *quality* by raising a high bar. Standards lay out what is necessary for children to learn in order to survive and thrive in the future. Standards encourage teachers to be more conscious about what children are taking away from experiences in the classroom. They are an important ingredient in providing a *high-quality* early learning program.

Equity

Standards provide a foundation for *equity* because they identify what we want every child to know and be able to do. Standards were designed to identify high expectations for *all* children, thus reducing the disparities from community to community in how much and how well children learn. As John Hattie reminds us, expectations are subtle but powerful influences on teacher behavior and child success:

> Students *know* they are treated differently in the classroom due to expectations held by teachers, and are quite accurate in informing on how teachers differ in the degree to which they favor some children over others with higher expectations. (Hattie 2009, 124)

Consistency

Standards promote *consistency*. When standards are adopted by a preschool program, a school district, a city, a state, or a nation, they help ensure that all domains are considered and will be addressed by each teacher in every classroom. When teachers teach content only from their favorite units or rely only on what children want to learn, there is a danger that some important domains will be ignored. Standards help remind us of our full responsibilities when it comes to teaching children.

Consistency also means horizontal and vertical alignment so that standards are properly sequenced and knowledge and skills build logically and progressively. Similarly, having some assurance that children are learning the same things in preschools or kindergarten provides stability. Consistency gives coherence to the educational system.

Transparency

Being accountable to standards provides *transparency*. When standards are published, displayed in classrooms, included in curricular planning and assessment procedures, and explained to parents and family members, educators are making clear the learning that is going on in preschool and kindergarten classrooms. This transparency signals that early childhood educators are involved in important work far beyond just keeping children safe and healthy. Being transparent allows for collaboration with children's family members and other teachers. Teachers can link what they are doing with the programs of caregivers and teachers who supported children in their infant and toddler years. And they can facilitate a smooth transition with elementary school teachers who will take over when children move forward into the primary grades.

ISSUES ABOUT STANDARDS

Some professionals in the field of early childhood education have not welcomed the development of standards or have been unsure how they should best be implemented. Many see them as a step away from more constructivist approaches whereby children learn from their own interests and initiatives. They see the standards movement as responsible for high-stakes testing, for a doubling down on teacher-directed instructional strategies, and for the elevation of unnecessary and inappropriate higher academic expectations in both preschool and kindergarten.

We agree that careful consideration should be given to standards-based educational practices. We also think, however, that there is confusion between the content of the standards and their implementation. Let's look more closely at each of the issues raised in the preceding paragraph.

Issue 1: Standards Are Not Always Based on Knowledge of How Children Grow and Learn

It is true that the content of standards must be based on knowledge of child development so that the expectations are appropriate for the age. Teachers should pay attention to how young children learn in the implementation process. If there are disagreements concerning specific benchmarks in the standards, educators can continue to dialogue and fine-tune the expectations so that they are indeed developmentally appropriate for preschool or kindergarten children. Doing so is about curricular strategies, not the content of the standards themselves.

Issue 2: Standards Do Not Take into Account Children's Needs, Capacities, Cultures, and Unique Characteristics

As they implement standards in their curriculum, effective teachers take into account the needs and capacities of individual children. Standards identify high expectations for *all* children. This ensures equity. If standards are written so that they address individual needs, they might lower expectations for some and excessively challenge others.

Considering cultural differences is important. The following cautionary statement urges ongoing attention to cultural diversity:

> Our youngest children are our most culturally diverse. Early learning standards must take this diversity into account. In addition, many children transition from culturally familiar child care programs and family environments into settings that do not reflect their culture or language. These discontinuities make it difficult to implement early learning standards in effective ways. (NAEYC and NAECS/SDE 2002, 3)

Some state early learning standards address cultural diversity by incorporating sections on dual-language learners or development of cultural awareness in the social studies domain.

Issue 3: Standards Can Lead to Teaching Skills in Ways That Are Not Effective or Meaningful, to the Narrowing of the Curriculum, and to Less Time for Play and Hands-On Learning

We agree! That's why the focus of this book is on *how* standards are implemented. We know it is possible to teach to standards and still be effective and meaningful. We show many ways to do so. Indeed, this book is a criticism of how standards are being implemented if they lead to less time for play. We firmly believe play complements standards rather than competes with them. To discourage the use of standards is not the answer. We believe standards might actually provide a reason to play more and engage in more hands-on learning experiences.

STANDARDS AS GOALS

One way to think about the implementation of standards is to recognize that they provide teachers with an agreed-upon set of learning goals. Goals give us direction. They shape the purposes for everything that goes on. What connects goals to practice is intentionality. Ann Epstein (2014) explains:

> To be intentional is to act purposefully, with a goal in mind and a plan for accomplishing it. Intentional acts originate from careful thought and are accompanied by consideration of their potential effects. Thus, an intentional teacher aims at clearly defined learning objectives for children, employs instructional strategies likely to help children achieve the objectives and continually assesses progress and adjusts the strategies based on that assessment. The teacher who can explain why she is doing what she is doing is acting intentionally—whether she is using a strategy tentatively for the first time or automatically from long practice, and whether it is used as part of a deliberate plan or spontaneously in a teachable moment. (Epstein 2014, 5)

To determine how best to use standards as goals, teachers can look at how the standards are layered. Both early learning and Common Core standards resemble a wedding cake, where the bottom layer is broad, and each subsequent layer is smaller. Most standards include at least three layers. Let's look at these layers with examples taken from Early Childhood Iowa's Early Learning Standards (ECI 2012):

1. A domain layer—the general area of knowledge or skills. Examples: Communication, Language and Literacy, or Physical Well-Being and Motor Development.
2. The standards layer—a broad statement about what children should know and be able to do. Examples: Children understand and use communication and language for a variety of purposes; or, Children develop large-motor skills.
3. The benchmark or indicator layer—a more refined or detailed list of specific things children need to know or be able to do. Examples: In the domain of Communication, Language and Literacy is the standard that reads, "Children understand and use communication and language for a variety of purposes" and the following more specific benchmarks:

- Demonstrates a steady increase in listening (receptive language) and speaking (expressive language) vocabulary.
- Initiates, listens, and responds in relationship to the topics of conversations with peers and adults.
- Speaks in phrases and sentences of increasing length and complexity.
- Follows oral directions that involve several actions.
- Asks and answers a variety of questions.
- Demonstrates knowledge of the rules of conversations such as taking turns while speaking.

The Common Core State Standards also have layers. These layers are labeled in different ways for English Language Arts and Mathematics. For English Language Arts for grades K–5, the following strands are identified:

- Reading
- Writing
- Speaking and Listening
- Language

"Each strand is headed by a strand-specific set of College and Career Readiness Anchor Standards that is identical across all grades and content areas. . . . Each CCR anchor standard has an accompanying grade-specific standard translating the broader CCR statement into grade-appropriate end-of-year expectations" (CCSS 2015b). For example, under the Reading: Literature strand for kindergarten there are four anchor standards:

1. Key Ideas and Details
2. Craft and Structure
3. Integration of Knowledge and Ideas
4. Range of Reading and Level of Text Complexity

The actual kindergarten standards are grouped under the appropriate anchor standard. So, the following standards are listed for Key Ideas and Details:

- With prompting and support, ask and answer questions about key details in a text.
- With prompting and support, retell familiar stories, including key details.
- With prompting and support, identify characters, settings, and major events in a story.

For Mathematics, the standards are labeled and organized in a different way. Domains are identified to describe related groups of standards. Clusters summarize the group of standards. The standards themselves "define what students should understand and be able to do" (CCSS 2015c). Here is an example for kindergarten.

In the domain of Counting and Cardinality, there are three clusters:

1. Know number names and the count sequence.
2. Count to tell the number of objects.
3. Compare numbers.

The kindergarten standards under the first cluster in the preceding list are as follows:

- Count to 100 by ones and by tens.
- Count forward beginning from a given number within the known sequence (instead of having to begin at 1).
- Write numbers from 0 to 20. Represent a number of objects with a written numeral 0–20 (with 0 representing a count of no objects).

Some criticisms of early learning or Common Core standards do not consider the complexity of the layers within the standards. Teachers who use standards to inform their teaching and assessment practices must spend time with all of the layers to understand how each fits into the other.

PLAY IN THE EARLY LEARNING STANDARDS

A few states include play in their early learning standards. Many include descriptions of how benchmarks might look in everyday circumstances in preschool classrooms, including those demonstrated during play experiences.

The section titled "Essential Considerations" in the Iowa Early Learning Standards is devoted to explaining the importance of play. Specifically, it reads:

The Iowa Early Learning Standards emphasize the importance of play in learning by integrating play into every content area of development using examples of both indoor and outdoor play to illustrate how caring adults can support children's natural inclinations, motivations, joy, and learning. Play is natural. Play is meaningful. Play is joyful. Play is essential as we engage and prepare our young children for the 21st century. (ECI 2012, 18)

Iowa went even so far as to write a standard about play— "Children engage in play to learn"—under the domain of Approaches to Learning. To cite some recent examples from other states:

- Wyoming's standards include a "Digging Deeper" section that frequently shows the connections between the learning benchmarks and how they might be manifested in play activities (Wyoming Early Childhood State Advisory Council 2013).
- Vermont, in its revision from August 2015, writes in the beginning of its standards: "Play was featured prominently in every domain of the VELS [Vermont Early Learning Standards], and we all came together around the belief that young children's play was the foundation upon which to foster learning across all development and content area domains. We continue to hold this belief" (Vermont Agency for Education and Agency for Human Services 2015, 4).
- For nearly every standard, Washington State Early Learning and Development Guidelines (Washington State Department of Early Learning 2012) include ways children can manifest the standards ("Children may. . .") during play and play suggestions for adults ("Ideas to try with children . . ."), even for the early elementary grade guidelines.
- Kentucky includes examples of skills demonstrations in a play context under each of its standards for three- and four-year-olds (Kentucky Governor's Office of Early Childhood 2013).

It's important for teachers and administrators to look carefully at their state's early learning standards, as well as introductions, appendixes, and other material, to find ways the state explains and clarifies how play and the standards can be integrated in curricular practices.

COMMON CORE AND PLAY

The Common Core State Standards were developed to promote critical thinking, problem solving, and analytical skills: "The fundamental goal of the Common Core State Standards . . . is to develop deeper understanding of a core set of content and skills" (Conley 2014, 7). The key words here are "deeper understanding." This does not mean rote learning only. Instead, the Common Core standards ask students to analyze, synthesize, and apply what they know and have learned to new situations and experiences.

Play is exactly about that deeper understanding. Murphy and her colleagues (2014) argue that the best way to promote critical thinking is by addressing precursor skills, namely, language and social-emotional skills. Play provides ample opportunities to exercise and practice these skills. Even more it promotes flexible thinking and situations that require solving problems in multiple ways (Pepler and Ross, 1981). Pretend play increases engagement and motivation to solve the problem when the solution is highly relevant to the pretend scenario (Weisberg, Hirsh-Pasek, and Golinkoff, 2013). Kindergarten teachers can plan for playful experiences to promote the skills related to the Common Core State Standards. They can develop fun and engaging ways to link pictures to words on a page or sequence a favorite story's illustrations on a flannel board. They can model counting out loud when moving a playing piece along a game board. We believe there are many ways to integrate these standards with play-based learning experiences.

> Nothing in Common Core—not one blessed thing—precludes schools and teachers from creating safe, warm, nurturing classrooms that are play-based, engaging, and cognitively enriching. If teachers are turning their kindergarten classrooms into joyless grinding mills and claiming they are forced to do so under Common Core . . . something has clearly gone wrong. Common Core demands no such thing, and research as well as good sense supports exposing children to early . . . concepts through games and songs. (Pondiscio 2015, 1)

One Common Core Caveat

There is one aspect of the Common Core that troubles us as early childhood professionals. When the Common Core was drafted, the developers began with the knowledge and skills they wanted to see in students when they graduated from high school. Then they asked, "If this is what is needed by the end of grade 12, what needs to happen in grade 11? And if this needs to happen in grade 11, what about grade 10?" And so on. It was all perfectly logical, but when you get down to lower elementary grades, especially kindergarten, those expectations may not be reasonable or even appropriate for a five-year-old. The approach ignored developmentally appropriate expectations for children.

For example, one standard for kindergarten is "Read emergent-reader texts with purpose and understanding." Should children really be reading by the end of kindergarten? More importantly, what are teachers supposed to do when they are not? (Heitin 2015). The answer lies in the application of the standards. If the standard exposes children to more books and pre-reading experiences, that is all well and good. If it means a teacher feels obligated to push for reading fluency, it is not good. No one has ever said that standards replace what we know about good teaching. Instead, they should point us to higher expectations.

Every teacher should know at what level her or his children are performing and encourage them to take the next step toward more knowledge and skill mastery. In some cases, that journey may be a few steps, and in other cases, it may require many, many steps. It is a matter of meeting children at their level and doing what you can to move them forward.

CONCLUSION

Standards are important and useful in defining goals for children's learning. Problems arise when figuring out how they should be used. Standards are, as we said earlier, the blueprint for education. But in architecture there is no building without cement and dozens of workers. Effectively keeping play in preschool and kindergarten classrooms and integrating it with standards is our next challenge.

We leave "anticipation" and move toward "wonder and surprise." The next chapter shows how to address standards as children play. We think you may be surprised to learn that it involves far more than "just play."

Implementation Ideas for Teachers:
EARLY LEARNING AND KINDERGARTEN STANDARDS

Something you can do right now is spend time reviewing your state's early learning standards and the Common Core State Standards for Kindergarten. This is a good exercise for both preschool and kindergarten teachers to do to familiarize themselves with not only the expectations for the age group with whom they work but also the preceding or following level. As you review the standards, look for the following:

- The domains that are included
- The ways the standards are organized
- The specific language of each standard (for example, does it say "beginning to" or "with prompting and support"?) These are very different expectations than the mastery of a skill or concept.

Implementation Ideas for Administrators:
EARLY LEARNING AND KINDERGARTEN STANDARDS

Sometimes administrators look at standards as the yardstick for how well their students have achieved a certain score on a district- or state-required assessment. Take one step back from that and really look at the standards themselves. Select a couple of standards from your state early learning standards or from the Common Core State Standards for Kindergarten. Choose at least one from each domain. Read them slowly and carefully with the following considerations in mind:

(cont.)

- What would it look like if a student were demonstrating proficiency in this standard? What would he be doing? What would she be saying? What work samples or evidence might a student create that would impress you with his or her competency in that standard?
- Imagine different students you know in your school demonstrating the standards. How do their performances differ?
- Think about what the standard looks like in action. Ask yourself: What is the core of this standard really about? Why is it a standard in the first place?
- Next time you visit a classroom, see if you can observe the standards coming alive in student performance.

SURPRISE AND PLEASURE

In chapters 4 and 5 we move to the next two steps in Scott Eberle's cycle of play: Surprise and Pleasure. Stuart Brown summarizes Eberle's description of these steps as follows:

> Surprise, the unexpected, a discovery, a new sensation or idea, or shifting perspective. This produces . . . pleasure, a good feeling, like the pleasure we feel at the unexpected twist in the punch line of a good joke. (Brown 2009, 19)

We assume that many teachers and administrators may be surprised by our thesis that teachers *can* address learning standards as children play, and we hope that teachers and administrators find delight and pleasure in the fact that it is actually possible!

We recognize that our thesis flies in the face of many approaches to standards-based education being implemented around the country. We are seeing more teacher-led and -directed activities in kindergartens as well as preschools. Children sit at tables or desks and complete worksheets related to isolated, discrete skills in the standards. They are required to listen to lessons with few opportunities for hands-on experiences or chances to apply and integrate what they are learning.

We do not believe direct instruction is the *only* way to incorporate standards. Instead, we recommend that play experiences that are well planned, carefully facilitated, and observed by teachers offer many opportunities to address early learning and Common Core standards. We both have witnessed that when teachers do so, they and the children enjoy the learning experience more fully:

- Learning becomes a fun and engaging process, not a grueling one.
- Laughter, smiles, and deep cognitive involvement replace boredom, tedium, and rote learning.
- Teachers teach in a different way.
- Children learn in a more meaningful way.
- Everyone benefits.

CHAPTER **4**

How Teachers Can Address Standards as Children Play

PROVOCATIVE QUESTION: **How can we be sure educators are addressing standards throughout their preschool and kindergarten curricula?**

Tom: The Administrator's Perspective

When an administrator sees children playing in classrooms, he may misunderstand and assume that this is downtime, not learning time. Some teachers may not be able to articulate clearly how they are integrating standards into play experiences. How can an administrator see something that is invisible, or at least invisible to him? Well, if the teacher is being intentional, and has clear lesson plans that detail the what, how, and why of what is going on in a classroom at any given time, then how the teacher is integrating standards into play experience is visible. The "why" is the connection to the standards. When a teacher ensures a connection, administrators will be a lot more confident that standards are being addressed and won't expect them to come only from didactic instruction.

Gaye: The Practitioner's Perspective

Excellent teachers identify goals for the activities they plan for their classroom, whether the activities are teacher led or child directed. They choose those goals from the standards they want to address (or from an assessment tool that is aligned with the standards). It may seem easier to see the goals in teacher-led activities, but in a high-quality preschool or kindergarten classroom, goals are embedded in every part of the day. Teachers who embrace play as filled with learning opportunities are skilled at integrating standards into play experiences both by planning for them and by being responsive to the different directions in which children take the play.

DIRECT INSTRUCTION VERSUS PLAY

As we work with educators across the country, we hear much confusion about the implementation of standards. The most prevalent assumption we run into is that teacher-led activities with direct instruction are the only surefire ways to guarantee that standards are being addressed. Therefore, in most kindergartens, and in more and more preschools, play is being replaced by large- and small-group activities designed to address explicit standards-based goals. Children are engaged in passive learning more than active as the teacher directs and monitors the activity.

We think there are a number of important questions to consider when determining ways to implement standards in preschool and kindergarten classrooms:

- What are the roles for direct instruction versus play in implementing standards?
- Is this really an either/or issue?
- Is one better than the other?
- Does either of the approaches replace the other, or can they coexist?
- What kind of learning does each foster?

We are not the only education professionals who are asking these questions. In an article titled "Why We Don't Need to Get Rid of Common Core to Have Play in Kindergarten," Shayna Cook (2015) writes:

> The case for more play in today's kindergarten classroom is legitimate, and school leaders need to know that there is a way to integrate intentional play back into the classroom while teaching the high-level literacy [and math] skills that are found in Common Core. Play is so important, particularly for young children, to develop long-term cognitive skills that will enable students to become "college and career ready," in the long term. Principals must be convinced that a print-rich kindergarten classroom that fosters language and literacy development is possible through play, rather than primarily through direct instruction.
>
> To reintegrate play back into the kindergarten classroom, we don't need to get rid of the Common Core. We need to explain to school leaders that teaching in the ways young children learn best will achieve better outcomes for children than any "Common Core" aligned worksheet ever could.

Notice that Ms. Cook says children learn "through play, rather than *primarily* [emphasis added] direct instruction." She is not saying that one must replace the other. And yet that is exactly what seems to be happening in many early childhood programs. We believe this is a terrible mistake and not the best way to address the standards. Instead, we suggest that teachers implement standards using a balanced approach with the balance heavier on the side of high-level play. There is a place for direct instruction in the preschool and kindergarten day—teachers choose what times to engage in direct instruction related to standards when they understand how to integrate standards into play. They make learning evident throughout everything they do.

In a research paper prepared for the National Association for the Education of Young Children (NAEYC), Kyle Snow (2015) addresses this balance:

> The tension between play and direct instruction during the preschool years is as puzzling as it is real. Many (including NAEYC) argue that it is a false dichotomy—that both direct instruction and play have roles to play in high-quality early childhood education. . . . Research is just beginning to show how best to balance play and instruction to nurture each child's development in all the ways that are important for them. What is clear is that maintaining the dichotomy between play and instruction is a distraction. We need to turn away from an either/or view, to the more complex challenge of balancing them together.

Snow challenges early educators "to think about the roles of teacher and child, and of play and instruction, in more complex and more intentional ways."

We certainly have no desire to throw out direct instruction entirely. Rather, we want to understand its value alongside the value of play in preschool and kindergarten classrooms. John Hattie (2009) describes the process of direct instruction. Based on the work of Adams and Engelmann (1996), he identified seven teacher actions. What we find particularly relevant is how the teacher actions necessary to plan for playful learning experiences parallel these seven steps:

1. Teacher establishes a clear idea of what is to be taught.
2. Teacher establishes "success criteria" (what children have to do to show they have successfully learned what was taught).
3. Teacher builds commitment and engagement in the learning task (a "hook" to capture students' attention).
4. Teacher presents the lesson, which should include providing the information, modeling its use, and then checking for understanding.
5. Teacher provides opportunity for guided practice.
6. Teacher closes the lesson by reviewing the key points and summarizing the point and purpose of the lesson.
7. Teacher provides time for reinforcement practice, to repeat and generalize skills or knowledge obtained during the lesson. (Hattie 2009, 205–6)

Notice a couple of things here. First, see the deliberateness and the intentionality. Really learning something requires focus and time. No one is rushing through this lesson. The teacher is slowly and steadily making sure learning takes place. The opportunities to practice could be constructed as play-like experiences. Under the steady hand of a good teacher, none of it has to be experienced as drill and kill, as boring or tedious.

Teacher-directed activities are perfectly appropriate some of the time. But if these are the sole methods, they would make for poor pedagogy indeed. A balance, as we have written earlier, between teacher-directed and child-directed activities is healthy. So before we go on to talk about the use of play to teach standards, let's give direct instruction its due. Properly understood, some of the key components of direct instruction—the directness and intentionality, the focus on a clear purpose and "success criteria," getting commitment up front, modeling, providing multiple opportunities for practice—can be applied to the use of play as a means to teach.

Learning Results

What are the different types of learning that result from direct instruction and from child-directed, open-ended play? Snow (2015) includes the following graphic to illustrate that it is not necessarily a two-sided question but rather that it involves consideration of both the child's and the teacher's level of activity.

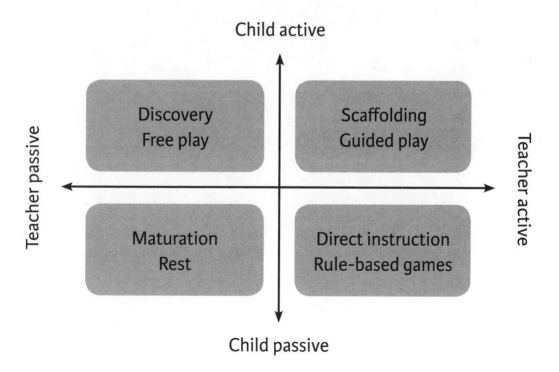

Note that both in play that is discovery oriented, or "free," and in play that is guided with scaffolding and facilitated by the teacher, the child is active. In direct instruction, the child is passively engaged—the child is not constructing his own understanding or actively applying skills and integrating knowledge. Rather, the child is taking in new information, is listening, is observing, or is following along rather than taking the lead. There is nothing wrong with the child being in such a learning mode. With young learners, however, the best results do not come from long periods of direct instruction or from using only this approach. Excellent teachers know to use a variety of teaching strategies and learning formats (Copple and Bredekamp 2009).

Another graphic represents teaching strategies related to child engagement (Gronlund and James 2008).

Teaching Continuum

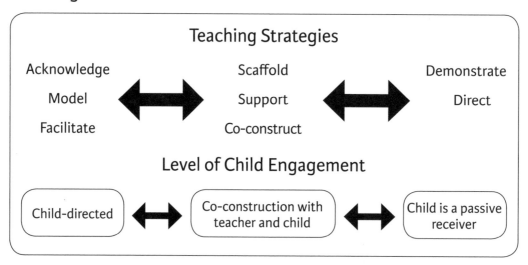

This continuum shows the many choices teachers have as they interact with children in classroom activities. It also shows the results of the different types of strategies regarding the child's level of engagement. As teachers consider ways to implement standards into their curriculum, they can plan for the level of child engagement as well. Why is this important? Judy Jablon and Michael Wilkinson offer the following observations concerning engagement:

Psychologically, engaged learners are intrinsically motivated by curiosity, interest, and enjoyment, and are likely to want to achieve their own intellectual or personal goals. In addition, the engaged child demonstrates the behaviors of concentration, investment, enthusiasm, and effort. . . .

Instruction that promotes passivity, rote learning, and routine tends to be the rule rather than the exception (Yair 2000; Goodlad 2004). Because children with low levels of engagement are at risk for disruptive behavior, absenteeism, and eventually dropping out of school (Roderick and Engle 2001), the need to increase engagement is critical to children's success in school. (Jablon and Wilkinson 2002, 1–2)

Teachers of young children are very aware when they lose the interest of the children. They report that behavior problems are more common and difficult to resolve. Children lose the joy in their learning. And teachers lose the joy in their teaching. True learning cannot take place in an environment where there are no "positive associations with learning" (Jablon and Wilkinson 2002, 2).

ADDRESSING STANDARDS IN PLAY

How do teachers plan wisely for play? How do they intentionally integrate standards without taking the joy and fun out of the experience? How do they make the learning evident to themselves and others without turning play into direct instruction? There are two ways to address standards in play:

1. Through reflection
2. Through intentional planning

Let's consider each of these in more depth.

Reflection

A knowledgeable teacher observes standards in action in her preschool and kindergarten classroom all the time. As she watches and engages with children in high-level play, she recognizes that they are demonstrating what they know and can do in multiple domains of development.

As she talks with children in the dramatic play area, asking about what they are cooking or inviting them to make a grocery list for shopping, she sees how they use oral language to communicate and what they know about writing. She learns how their abstract thinking is developing as she sees whether they can pretend that a red cup is an apple, or if they can proceed only if they have a plastic apple in their basket.

As she sits near children who are playing at the water table, she observes how they engage their senses to explore the properties of water, what their understanding of measurement is, and how they play alongside or with their classmates.

To make teacher observations meaningful and to identify the specific standards that have been observed, a teacher must plan a time for reflection. That may happen at the end of the day in a debriefing session with a colleague or in a quiet moment when she can write down some of her observations of the play experiences.

> Thinking about standards naturalistically requires conscientious attention to what children are doing and familiarity with your early learning standards. It also requires some form of reflection—whether in discussion with your colleagues or in written observations and recording. (Gronlund 2014, 14)

The link to standards is made in the debriefing or the documentation of the observation. The more that teachers are familiar with the standards, the easier this linking process will be. That does not mean they need to memorize every single indicator or benchmark. Rather, they need to have a clear idea of the broader goals within the standards. Then, as they observe children at play, they can ask, "What am I seeing related to the broad goals of the standards?" For example, when a teacher observes children working with puzzles, he can recognize that deconstructing and reconstructing puzzles involves geometric knowledge and spatial reasoning, both areas included in math standards.

A caution: Reflective integration of standards is not the place to assess the number of alphabet letters a child can identify or the numerals a child can write between 0 and 20. Those very specific standards are better addressed in small-group work with children where the teacher can easily record their performance. Play lends itself to standards that are more application oriented. In the following tables, play areas are identified where early learning and Common Core standards might be readily observed.

		Addressing Language as Standards in Play Areas		
LANGUAGE ARTS STRANDS	**EARLY LEARNING STANDARD**	**COMMON CORE STATE STANDARDS FOR KINDERGARTEN**	**LOCATION**	**EXAMPLE OF SKILL/ KNOWLEDGE IN ACTION**
Oral or Expressive Language	"Use language for a variety of purposes." (Illinois Early Learning and Development Standards)	"Describe familiar people, places, things, and events and, with prompting and support, provide additional detail."	All play areas	• Conversing with other children • Conversing with teachers
Writing	"Write letters or letter-like shapes to represent words or ideas." (California Preschool Learning Foundations)	"Use a combination of drawing, dictating, and writing to compose pieces (including opinion, informative/ explanatory texts, or narratives) of a single event or several loosely linked events." (three in combination)	Writing center, art area, dramatic play, block center, sensory table	• Children write names • Children write names on art projects • Children write as part of dramatic play (menus, receipts, cards, letters, phone messages, grocery lists) • Children write as part of block play (signs, addresses, maps, blueprints) • Children make notes and observations as part of science experiments, sensory experiences. For kindergarteners especially, notes can help them remember what they observed or the order of steps of an experiment.

Addressing Math Standards in Play Areas

MATH DOMAINS	EARLY LEARNING STANDARD	COMMON CORE STATE STANDARDS FOR KINDERGARTEN	LOCATION	EXAMPLE OF SKILL/ KNOWLEDGE IN ACTION
Sorting and Classifying	"Shows increasing abilities to match, sort, put in a series, and regroup objects according to one or two attributes (shape, size, color, etc.)." (Alabama Performance Standards for 4-Year-Olds: Preparing Children "4" Lifelong Learning)	"Classify objects into given categories; count the numbers of objects in each category and sort the categories by count."	Manipulative play area, math games, and dramatic play	• Children sort and classify objects based on clear criteria. • Children use bowls or plates to organize objects as they are sorted and classified. • Children can imitate or create their own patterns as they string beads or create designs with the many items available.
Geometry	"The child will describe simple geometric shapes (circle, triangle, rectangle, and square) and indicate their position in relation to an individual and to other objects." (Virginia's Foundation Blocks for Early Learning: Comprehensive Standards for Four-Year-Olds)	"Analyze and compare two- and three-dimensional shapes, in different sizes and orientations, using informal language to describe their similarities, differences, parts (e.g., number of sides and vertices/"corners") and other attributes (e.g., having sides of equal length)."	Block area, art area, and manipulative play area	• Children describe different shapes of blocks with accurate vocabulary (square, triangle, etc.) • Children sort and categorize different kinds of blocks, noticing their differences and similarities. • Children show awareness of spatial relationships and position as they build with blocks. • Children create collages with shapes and paint or draw with shape templates.

Intentional Planning

Teachers can integrate both broad and specific standards into child-directed, open-ended play experiences by *intentionally* planning to do so. The result should be some kind of written document (for example, a lesson or activity plan) that provides the guidance of what the teacher will do.

The intentional planning process has four steps:

1. Identifying the standard(s) to be addressed
2. Considering the best materials to provide
3. Choosing possible teacher support strategies
4. Determining how to gather assessment information

Let's look at each of these steps in more depth.

Identifying the Standard(s) to Be Addressed

Teachers want to be practical and realistic as they choose which standards to address in play. They do not need to add to their busy to-do list by having to make special games or stretch their thinking to try to make a standard fit an activity. Teachers can help themselves determine the standards to target in specific play experiences by asking themselves the following questions:

- Does this standard occur naturally as children direct their own involvement in this play experience?
- In the play experience, are there many ways for a child to show what he can do related to the standard?

If the answer to either of these questions is no, the standard identified may not be the best match. Let's consider two examples from kindergarten classrooms. First, an unsuccessful one:

> On her weekly lesson plan, kindergarten teacher Anne noted that during the hour-long investigation time in her classroom, one of the Common Core State Standards that she planned to address involved phonics: "Demonstrate basic knowledge of one-to-one letter-sound correspondences by producing the primary sound or many of the most frequent sounds for each consonant."

(cont.)

She planned to interact with children in various centers of the classroom (blocks, dramatic play, manipulatives, and art) and converse with them about the primary sounds for the objects with which they were playing. At the end of the week, she turned to her assistant teacher and said, "I constantly felt like I was interrupting the children's engagement in what they were doing as I tried to get them to make letter-sound correspondence. A few children joined with me, but most seemed to run the other way! I think they saw it as a test rather than a learning experience integrated into their play."

Why didn't Anne's plan work? She chose a standard that did not naturally occur in the play experiences of the children. In addition, the kinds of questions she needed to ask regarding letter-sound correspondence were closed ended. They had one right answer. Either the child knew the sound of the primary letter or he did not. This standard is better addressed directly in small-group work involving reading and writing than addressed in play.

Now, a successful example:

In Mark's kindergarten classroom, he has writing materials available in a number of play areas and has encouraged the children to use them freely to enhance their play experiences. In addition, he invites children to write about their play by drawing a picture of their creations and describing them or writing about the scenario they created in their dramatic play. On his lesson plan for several weeks, he identified the following Common Core State Standards that he could observe for and interact with children about as they participated in writing during his center time:

Demonstrate command of the conventions of standard English grammar and usage when writing or speaking [including]:

- Print many upper- and lowercase letters.
- Use frequently occurring nouns and verbs.
- Produce and expand complete sentences in shared language activities.
- Demonstrate command of the conventions of standard English capitalization, punctuation, and spelling when writing [including]:

(cont.)

- Capitalize the first word in a sentence and the first-person pronoun.
- Recognize and name end punctuation.
- Write a letter or letters for most consonant and short-vowel sounds (phonemes).
- Spell simple words phonetically, drawing on knowledge of sound-letter relationships.

Not only did Mark find these standards easy to see and to facilitate as the children engaged in writing about their play, but he also ended up with writing samples to save as evidence in the children's portfolios.

Why did Mark's plan work? He considered ways to integrate these standards by creating a climate of writing throughout the play areas of the classroom. He did not limit himself to addressing only one specific standard (such as print many upper- and lowercase letters). He incorporated many standards related to writing so that even the child who only printed in uppercase was still successful in showing what she understands about writing related to the other standards included.

Teachers can plan to integrate many standards into an extended period of time devoted to child-directed, open-ended play. They can look at the play areas they have organized in their preschool or kindergarten classroom and consider where standards most naturally fit. Some teachers may say, "You should address *all* standards in *all* play areas." We recommend being selective. Do not force the match, but rather look at each play area carefully. Consider the play areas in your classroom and make your own matching lists to help with your intentional planning. Also consider activities that have a by-product like Mark's writing samples. They make terrific artifacts that show achievement with respect to the standards.

Considering the Best Materials to Provide

Once teachers have identified the standard(s) they will integrate into a specific play experience, they need to consider the materials to provide. For example, if the standard is related to measurement, then the teacher will add measurement tools such as rulers, tape measures, yard and meter sticks, and balance scales. These tools are appropriate when addressing measurement benchmarks related to standard units of measure. By inviting children to explore the various ways to measure, the teacher can introduce the vocabulary of standard measures: inches, feet, centimeters, meters, ounces, or pounds. However, if the goal is nonstandard measurement, such tools are not necessary. Children instead could be invited to measure items with pieces of string, with a set of connecting blocks or Unifix cubes, or even with their own bodies. The materials that a teacher provides are determined by the specifics of the standard or benchmark that is being addressed. It is a good idea to add different kinds of materials to provide for multiple means for children to show their abilities. New materials also create interest and engagement and provide a way to attract children to a desired center.

Choosing Possible Teacher Support Strategies

Intentional planning does not just involve choosing goals or materials. It also involves planning for teacher support. Certainly many decisions about teaching strategies are made in the moment as the play unfolds. However, thinking ahead of time about ways to facilitate and enhance the play experience helps teachers be prepared. Here are some questions to ask yourself when planning for possible teacher support strategies:

- Is this a familiar experience for the children? What do they already know about it? Where have they been successful in the past? What are they ready for next?
- Is this a new experience for the children? What do I need to introduce and explain to them? Where might they need my assistance? How will I know when I can step back and be nearby, ready to offer guidance or help?

As we address meeting standards in specific domains in later chapters, we will describe effective teaching strategies to consider.

Determining How to Gather Assessment Information

The final step in the intentional planning process is determining how to gather assessment information about how each child is performing related to the standards. How do teachers gather this information? By observing as children play, documenting those observations in some way, and relating the observations to the standards. This is authentic assessment, the most reliable and informative method when determining what young children know, understand, and can do.

As learners, preschoolers and kindergartners vary in their acquisition of skills and knowledge, and vary even more in their day-to-day performance. Therefore, professional recommendations in early childhood education endorse sound assessment practices that are "ongoing, strategic, and purposeful" and "include results of teachers' observations of children, clinical interviews, collections of children's work samples, and their performance on authentic activities" (Copple and Bredekamp 2009, 22). Neisworth and Bagnato (2004) contrast authentic assessment with conventional assessment:

At the heart of authentic assessment is the issue of sampling behavior. In authentic assessment, we observe and/or obtain reports about the child's performances in and across natural settings and occasions. Appraisal of the child's developmental skills as practiced in the child's real environments cannot be done through "testing" by a stranger at a table with flashcards, blocks, and beads. Clearly, such conventional testing ignores the crucial requirement for valid sampling of behavior that enables inferences about the presence, absence, fluency, and utility of skills. Use of psychometrically selected items administered in decontextualized settings results in biased samples of the child's functioning—samples that often yield results far different from how the child really behaves. (Neisworth and Bagnato 2004, 201)

As teachers intentionally plan to address standards in child-directed, open-ended play, they also ask themselves these questions:

- What will I observe children doing that will tell me what they know and can do related to the standard(s)?
- Are there questioning techniques or conversations that I can plan with the children to help me learn more about their understanding?
- How will I document my observations? In observation notes alone? Will there be a reason to take a photograph or make a video or audio recording?
- Will this play experience lend itself to the child producing a work sample that I can collect?

Thinking about assessment as a teacher plans can make the assessment process much easier. The activity or play supports can be designed with a particular approach to assessment in mind. For example, collecting the menus children write while playing restaurant can provide information about prewriting skills.

CONCLUSION

Addressing standards as children play is a challenging task, but it can be accomplished through both reflection and careful planning. Teachers must be knowledgeable of the standards they are implementing and continually observe and reflect to determine the best ways to integrate them into play experiences. Many components must be taken into consideration to do so effectively.

The next chapter gives suggestions for ensuring that play is part of the classroom experience for *all* children.

ADDRESSING STANDARDS IN PLAY

Something you can do right now is engage in reflection and planning related to play and standards:

- Think back over the week and remember play experiences in which your children engaged. What broad standards can you relate to those play experiences?
- Look at your lesson plans and consider the ways in which you could intentionally plan to integrate standards into children's play experiences.

ADDRESSING STANDARDS IN PLAY

Next time you are observing teachers and children, ask yourself whether each teacher is equally adept at both teacher-directed and child-directed instructional approaches. If you sense teachers struggling with either approach do the following:

- Check in with teachers to see if they agree about strengths and weaknesses related to these two approaches.
- Review your professional development calendar for the coming months or for next year. Are you providing opportunities to learn and share the skills you think are important?
- What about skills needed to be effective "reflectors"? Effective intentional planners?

CHAPTER 5

Ensuring That Play Is Part of the Classroom Experience for *All* Young Children

PROVOCATIVE QUESTION: How should teachers and administrators address the different needs of each and every child?

Tom: The Administrator's Perspective

The increasing diversity of student populations puts pressure on teachers and on the educational system as a whole. Children from varying backgrounds and life experiences have different needs and respond to different instructional approaches. Jamie Vollmer (2002) makes a helpful point in his "Blueberry Story." He compares a school to an ice-cream-making business. The business can reject a shipment when an order of blueberries is too small or too bruised. Unlike a business, a school has to accept all of its ingredients exactly as they come. In education, each blueberry has to be used to make the next batch of ice cream. Educators have to do what is necessary to help each and every child succeed. We need to reject the idea that diversity is a problem for teachers and see it as an opportunity and a reason for celebration. Every child can be successful.

Gaye: The Practitioner's Perspective

Teachers often report feeling pulled in many directions as they attempt to meet the varied needs of the children in their preschool or kindergarten classrooms. Even among a group of typically developing children, there is a broad range of developmental capabilities, variation in life experiences, and differences in learning styles and personalities. Challenges come with the integration of young children with special needs as teachers attempt to meet Individualized Educational Program (IEP) goals and do so in an inclusive way. In addition, many communities in the United States include children from multiple cultures and who may speak languages other than English. And special attention must be given to individual differences so that all learners benefit from their early educational experiences.

BEING INCLUSIVE OF *ALL* CHILDREN

Today's classrooms bring new challenges and opportunities as they serve increasingly diverse populations. Teachers are expected to address the needs of many kinds of learners. We are certain that the implications of integrating play and standards will help preschool and kindergarten teachers with these challenges. In this chapter, we provide ideas for being inclusive so that children with different abilities, cultural and linguistic backgrounds, and life experiences can be supported in their learning.

While adaptations for individual differences are necessary, integrating play and standards is a strategy that can work for *all* children. The better teachers are at engaging children in deep and authentic play, the better they will be at addressing the unique needs each child brings. When teachers implement an approach to play that is child directed and open ended, they find that it carries with it an inherent potential for individualization. First and foremost, all children benefit from good teaching. So, being the best teacher possible is an important place to start in meeting the needs of every child. And knowing how to integrate play and standards will be the best basis for addressing the special needs of individual children.

Teachers and administrators would do well to make some important accommodations to ensure the effectiveness of the strategies offered. What kind of accommodations are necessary? How should they be implemented? We provide some answers to these questions with the focus on

- children with identified special needs,
- culturally diverse learners,
- dual-language learners, and
- other individual differences that may present impediments to play.

Children with Identified Special Needs

Let's first explore the push for full inclusion of children with identified special needs in general education classrooms. Inclusion is addressed in the federal Individuals with Disabilities Education Improvement Act:

> To the maximum extent appropriate, children with disabilities, including children in public or private institutions or other care facilities, are educated with children who are nondisabled; and (ii) Special classes, separate schooling, or other removal of children with disabilities from the regular educational environment occurs only if the nature or severity of the disability is such that education in regular classes with the use of supplementary aids and services cannot be achieved satisfactorily. (IDEA 2004, sec. 300.114)

For a government regulation, this is stated in remarkably clear language. All children should be included, and the burden of proof rests with those who don't want to include children.

While the issue of inclusion is not new, in recent years it has received increased attention. In 2009 the Division for Early Childhood of the Council for Exceptional Children and the National Association for the Education of Young Children issued a far-reaching and passionate position statement titled *Early Childhood Inclusion* (DEC/NAEYC 2009), which says that inclusion is the way all early childhood programs should operate. The statement describes inclusion as driven by three principles: access, participation, and supports. These principles should be the benchmarks by which teachers assess whether they are truly including all children in their classroom. The principles can be used to evaluate play in preschools and kindergartens. Teachers can ask themselves these questions:

- Do all children have access to all play opportunities?
- Do all children fully participate in play opportunities?
- What additional supports are needed to ensure access and full participation?

If play is an important part of the activities all children experience, then supporting participation by all children is necessary. Play benefits every child without regard to ability.

With inclusion, many early childhood settings are blended classrooms and "least restrictive environments" for children on IEPs. Teachers must plan ways to fully include children with special needs in classroom activities and to provide children with the "special education" to which they are entitled. The following are some important considerations as teachers support children with identified special needs:

1. Creating an inclusive classroom climate
2. Designing supports and adaptations for full participation
3. Following the Division for Early Childhood of the Council for Exceptional Children Recommended Practices for Early Intervention/Early Childhood Special Education (DEC 2014)

We believe that by taking these steps, teachers can implement the suggestions relating to play and standards that we discuss in this book. Let's look at each separately.

Creating an Inclusive Classroom Climate

Creating an inclusive environment means taking time to build a classroom community where all children are welcomed and supported regardless of their abilities. This means not only in teachers' actions and planning but also in the climate they create among the children. Teachers create a feeling of community and shared group identity within the classroom. Throughout every day, they emphasize that children

- look out for one another,
- practice making friends, and
- take responsibility for each other's success.

Approaches like these help all children benefit, whether they have a disability or not.

Designing Supports and Adaptations for Full Participation

When thinking about play experiences, teachers pay attention to whether children with special needs are playing as much and in as many ways as other children. Teachers may need to design supports and adaptations to make each child's participation as full as possible. Here is an example:

A child with autism has trouble communicating effectively with her peers. She watches other children engaged in dramatic play but does not join in. Observing this, the teacher identifies a goal for the child: joining in play with others. She and her colleagues work with both the child and her peers to support more and greater participation in play experiences. They may need to try any or all of the following strategies:

- Coach the child in how to join in play.
- Coach typically developing peers about how to invite and include the child in play experiences.
- Provide scaffolding and assistance to the child so that her participation is successful.
- Model for all of the children ways to interact with each other when differences in communication skills and styles are present.

Research has shown great benefit to using peers in play situations to increase the skills of children with special needs (Strain and Hoyson 2000).

Following DEC Recommended Practices

Teachers can turn to the guidelines for working with young children with special needs developed by the Division for Early Childhood, Council for Exceptional Children:

The DEC Recommended Practices were developed to provide guidance to practitioners and families about the most effective ways to improve the learning outcomes and promote the development of young children, birth through five years of age, who have or are at-risk for developmental delays or disabilities. (DEC 2014, 2)

Using the DEC Recommended Practices begins with the IEP:

> An Individualized Education Program (IEP) is a written statement of the educational program designed to meet a child's individual needs. Every child who receives special education services must have an IEP. (Center for Parent Information and Resources, 2013)

Everything we have said about the connection between play and standards might equally be said about play and IEPs. Most states require that IEPs be written using goals that reflect standards so that children with special needs can access the same curriculum and standards that typically developing children do. Teachers can connect play to the IEP goals of children in the same way they connect play with specific or targeted standards. They can look at the IEP and think about how to address its goals by adding materials, changing the environment, and using grouping strategies. Teachers can provide support during play experiences for young children with special needs.

Culturally Diverse Learners

Besides a renewed focus on full-inclusion or blended classrooms, demographic changes are altering the populations of preschool and kindergarten classrooms. The United States is becoming more racially and ethnically diverse. Demographers point out that in 2045 the population of the country will shift from a white majority to a nonwhite majority (Colby and Ortman 2015). That major switch will happen a full five years earlier if you just look at the population of young children under the age of eight, and even sooner if the age range under consideration is five and younger. Young children are the leading edge of the increase in America's racial and ethnic diversity. The changes will be felt first in early childhood classrooms in every part of the nation.

The challenges of culturally diverse classrooms call for cultural responsiveness and competence. This is true for implementing play-based learning strategies as much as any other aspect of an educator's responsibility. Play exists in all cultures, so teachers should be sensitive to how culturally relative play is. Legos or playdough may not be familiar to all children. Sociodramatic play, in which children reenact experiences from their lives, may require settings, dress-up clothes, and furnishings that are different from what is currently in a classroom.

Terry Cross and his colleagues (1989) describe five key competencies that all individuals and organizations need if they are to be effective working in cross-cultural situations:

1. The ability to value diversity
2. The ability to conduct an individual cultural self-assessment

3. The ability to manage the dynamics of difference
4. The ability to acquire and use cultural knowledge
5. The ability to adapt to diversity and the cultural contexts of the communities being served

These five competencies, strengthened and adhered to through training and practice, provide an invaluable foundation for working with children from diverse cultures.

Value Diversity

The first competency is a call to enter more deeply into the complexity of the human family. It is about changing assumptions from seeing differences as problems to seeing them as good things. Culturally competent people enjoy differences. They appreciate the uniqueness of each child. They embrace differences as opportunities to learn more and to be better educators. Think of the image of a mosaic: it takes thousands of broken pieces, fitted together, to make a beautiful picture. Each teacher and administrator can look at a classroom as a beautiful work of art. They can allow difference to become a reason to celebrate, marvel, wonder, and enjoy all the ways of being there are.

When it comes to play, valuing diversity means learning to appreciate the different approaches children take in using materials and engaging in play opportunities. This is far more evident when play is truly child directed and open ended. A child-directed activity can go in as many different directions as there are children in the classroom. It's exciting to watch something unexpected. Learn to cherish what each child brings to the play experience. The shift toward greater valuing of diversity is a shift not in strategy but in attitude. Orient to that attitude—forgoing the natural tendency we all have to judge and discriminate and hold on to expectations—and we promise you that the experiences of your children will take on new power and value.

Conduct an Individual Cultural Self-Assessment

Developing the second competency means learning about yourself. Do some self-reflection and consider the following:

- What is your cultural background?
- Where were you raised? Who raised you?
- How has your upbringing shaped your values, beliefs, linguistics, customs, practices, expressions, patterns of thinking, and styles of communication?

Educators can truly appreciate the culture of students and families only after they come to understand and appreciate their own culture.

This competency has two dimensions:

- embracing and valuing your own culture and background
- understanding the limits and relative nature of your own perspective

Not everyone has had your experiences. Not everyone shares your values or beliefs. Not everyone understands your language and customs. Not everyone appreciates your customs, practices, and expressions. Not everyone thinks like you. One thing to consider is your own thinking about play. Ask yourself the following questions:

- What do I value about play?
- Where did my ideas come from?
- What earlier experiences shaped my current attitude toward play?
- How does my current attitude influence what I see in my classroom?
- How does it influence my interpretations of what I see?

Knowing how you feel about things makes it easier to adopt the open-mindedness necessary to be a keen observer. You see the play of children through a wider and less critical lens.

Manage the Dynamics of Difference

The third competency is the ability to manage the inevitable conflict that comes from difference. Most of us avoid conflict. Culturally competent individuals expect conflict and know how to use it as an opportunity to grow intellectually, emotionally, and socially. Effectively dealing with conflict requires special skills of clear communication, thinking rationally at emotionally charged moments, and taking the perspective of the other. Unless you can manage conflicts well, they can get out of hand and derail your efforts. Like all skills, managing conflict has to be practiced if it is to be learned and perfected.

Culturally competent teachers and administrators know how to manage the dynamics of difference and recognize that conflict can occur during play. This competency includes conflict resolution and reframing the situation so that a win-win resolution is possible. These skills are essential in situations of cultural difference even between adults and children.

Acquire and Use Cultural Knowledge

This competency is about making intentional efforts to learn about the different cultures in your classrooms. This knowledge can be invaluable in helping you make accommodations so play experiences are more appropriate for the children in your program. For example, some families may have known times of extreme hunger. If children see a sensory table full of rice to be poured or scooped like sand, they might be troubled or confused.

Only by learning about the history and experiences of children and their families can we be sensitive to how ordinary aspects of the classroom appear to different children.

Culturally competent individuals intentionally seek out information about the cultures represented in their classrooms. They take time to get to know every family member. What do they enjoy about their child? How do their families have fun together? Teachers know that they are better teachers with such knowledge. While it may be helpful to find out about specific racial or ethnic cultures through research or on the Internet, the best source of information is the families themselves.

Equally important to acquiring knowledge is using it. That knowledge should change practices and plans. It should inform how you determine learning goals, set up play areas, design challenging play experiences for children, and reflect on their play. It should help administrators rethink program policy so that it is flexible enough to meet the needs of diverse families.

Adapt to Diversity and the Cultural Contexts of the Communities Being Served

As teachers and administrators use the knowledge acquired in relationships with children and families, they are making changes and adapting their practices. This competency begins with being open to change and prioritizing practices that are congruent with the needs of the children and their families in the program. Administrators may invite families to participate in planning or advisory groups, signaling the value of their opinions and a willingness to listen and take their suggestions seriously.

Within the context of play, adapting to diversity may mean specific efforts to learn about the play experiences of families. Teachers can send home surveys or engage in conversations with families, asking the following questions:

- What kind of play does the child enjoy at home?
- What are popular games in the family?
- How did the parents or other family members play as children?

Such information can be useful when planning play areas and activities that reflect different cultures. Families can be invited to recommend or lend specific play objects that are unique to them. Children appreciate familiar objects and enjoy sharing with other children about how to use them.

Here are more suggestions for incorporating aspects of various cultures into play experiences:

- Include items or objects parents or other family members are willing to share that represent their culture. Don't assume what those are. Let families decide, telling them you want their child to see familiar objects so that they feel at home and the classroom provides a reflection of their background.

- If you find a good game or play material that is part of the culture of some of the children in your classroom, take a moment to learn the correct names for the materials or the games and use those terms so children can connect their play at home with their play in the classroom.

- Play activities can easily lend themselves to being organized into thematic studies or projects that can involve books, traditional centers with new materials added, special art projects, and field trips. Studies provide lots of opportunities for children to make connections using vocabulary in both English and a home language. Consider selecting topics that are usually of universal interest to children, such as hats, rain, houses, and emotions. For example, there are many different kinds of hats across different cultures. That study could be expanded by using books with photographs such as the one by well-known author Ann Morris called *Hats, Hats, Hats* (1993). A collection of interesting hats can be added to the dress-up area and stimulate different kinds of play.

Dual-Language Learners

Linguistic diversity adds the challenge of communication to the other dynamics of cultural diversity. Dual-language learners may come into the classroom speaking only their home language. Or they may speak a little, some, or a lot of English. Because preschoolers and kindergartners are so young, there is much to learn in their home language and, at the same time, they may also be learning English. The good news is that this is the best time in their lives to become bilingual because their brains will never be better prepared to absorb and collect what they need to know to be fluent in two (or more) languages (Brynie 2010).

Play can be an important strategy for learning languages. However, these new speakers are obviously less fluent in English than their peers whose home language is English. So communication can become a barrier in play. Dual-language learners may be excluded from English-speaking playgroups or may not be able to interact as fully because of language constraints. They may need teachers who speak their home language to help them. Here are some recommendations for addressing the unique needs of dual-language learners even if a teacher does not speak the child's language:

- The best way to support the development of English for dual-language learners is to use the literacy instruction you provide to all children. When you use play to promote both expressive and receptive language, reading and writing skills, such practices will benefit dual-language learners.

- Make sure family members understand the importance of children maintaining their home language. Encourage them to use their home language with their child, share stories, sing songs, and talk to their child about how they played as children. Encourage them to keep using the home language even after the child gains proficiency in, and even prefers, speaking English.
- Encourage family members to play with their children and use their home language as they interact during play. Especially emphasize play that uses songs, chants, or expressions because they involve language.
- Be sure to expose children to individuals who speak English clearly and correctly. Every opportunity to play alongside, model, scaffold, or support is an opportunity to support English-language communication.
- Make sure environmental print (labels, signs, posters) you have in the classroom is in English as well as other dominant home languages used by children in the classroom. As much as possible, augment the print with photographs or drawings that illustrate the message of the label, sign, or poster.
- Having a consistent schedule with predictable transition rituals can help children who do not understand the common language learn how the classroom functions. Creating clear time in the schedule for play activities, with routine transitions in and out of play, will help dual-language learners to better engage and participate. If necessary, have the schedule clearly explained in the home language to children and their family members.
- Support the engagement of dual-language learners in play activities as much as possible. Such activities provide many opportunities for children to hear and use rich and varied language related to a subject of interest to the child and in a meaningful context.

Play benefits all children regardless of their home language. Evidence-based strategies that support dual-language learners can be combined effortlessly with all the suggestions in this book about linking play and standards. Understanding the basics of the challenge, putting a strong emphasis on good instruction regardless of the home language of the child, acknowledging the home language and incorporating it into daily activities as much as possible, and working hard to ensure the full engagement of children are the key approaches to making these practices work for dual-language learners.

Individual Differences as Impediments to Play

As we have stated repeatedly in this chapter, the central issue to address is how to ensure that all children are able to participate in play experiences. Some children's lives are filled with challenges that may interfere with their ability to engage in successful play. To link play and standards, and to use play-based curricular approaches, teachers need to recognize and address problems for individual children.

Some children have not had experiences with child-directed, open-ended play. They may not have access to a wide variety of toys or toys of quality in their homes. They may not be sure how best to use the block area in their preschool or kindergarten classroom. Building and constructing will be a new experience and may require some coaching and modeling on the teacher's part. Some children have not had the opportunity to travel, to go on vacations, to visit museums or libraries, or to go to plays or concerts. Their lack of experiences may be reflected in limited story lines as they attempt to engage in dramatic play scenarios. Again, teachers will need to be ready to help them build on their home experiences and expand their horizons through investigations and thematic studies.

For such children, the answer is to replace those missing experiences with new experiences. Here are some recommended teaching strategies:

- Treat play as a new experience to be introduced in stages, teaching explicitly how to use different objects and how to engage with materials.
- The play may be more teacher than child directed until children have the skill and confidence to engage in play independently.
- Support children by pairing them with more experienced players to serve as models. A simple invitation may be all that is needed: "Pablo, would you show Caleb what you are doing with those cars?"

Some children live in home situations where they experience chronic stress. When parents are overworked, distracted, or emotionally absent, children may lack a sense of security, attachment, and love. Some children spend every day in the midst of family chaos. They may be victims of or witnesses to physical or emotional abuse, chronic neglect, severe and enduring maternal depression, persistent parental substance abuse, or repeated exposure to violence within the family or community. The resulting stress can actually change the architecture of a child's brain. Its development emphasizes fight-or-flight responses and deemphasizes growth in the areas of the brain that control learning, memory, and self-regulation (National Scientific Council on the Developing Child 2007). Children who are living with such experiences often find it harder to enter into or sustain high-level play experiences. They lack the ability to concentrate and lose themselves in play. They become moody and unable to manage emotions. They can overreact to situations of frustration or conflict, sometimes throwing, hitting, or biting. That makes them poor playmates.

Children exhibiting challenging behaviors, whatever their origins, will have a hard time entering into play. Sadly, not being able to participate fully robs these children of the calm and pleasure play provides. In other words, they can't get the very things they need the most.

Teachers (with the help of administrators) should take immediate and concrete steps to address such issues. A team that includes the teacher and others should analyze the circumstances of the challenging behavior to arrive at a clear understanding of what is motivating the behavior that prevents successful play engagement. The team can begin by focusing on recurring moments when they have observed a child struggling to enter into a play experience. It may be because he cannot focus or she is in a bad mood. Then the team can develop strategies for developing alternative behaviors or "replacement skills," and teach these skills so that the child can engage successfully (Fox and Duda accessed 2017, 19). It's important to discover and articulate what the child needs to make successful play possible. Such solutions are never easy, and administrators play an important role in making sure teachers are supported by outside experts in finding successful solutions.

Moving children toward effective management of their feelings and behaviors requires constant support, encouragement, and patience. The important thing is not to let behavioral barriers keep children from playing. Make the goal full participation. Act quickly to reduce the time not involved in play to a minimum. Any barrier that prevents children from engaging in child-directed, open-ended play—whether it is misguided policies that take play out of the classroom or children's circumstances and behavior—should be addressed if play is to benefit children's learning. Play needs to be for all children if its benefits are to be shared equitably across the classroom.

CONCLUSION

Being inclusive and ensuring universal access to and participation in play means paying attention to all the differences children bring into the classroom. The key to responding to those differences is to acknowledge them, understand them, and embrace them while intentionally working at removing the barriers to play those differences may create. Teachers and administrators must work together to create an inclusive culture where every child is welcomed and supported to be successful.

Implementation Ideas for Teachers:
INCLUSIVITY AND PLAY

Something you can do right now is to consider the inclusiveness of your class-room and the successful participation of the children in child-directed, open-ended play experiences:

- How do you create a climate of welcome and acceptance for all children?
- How do you support children's full participation in child-directed, open-ended play?
- What ideas from this chapter will you try in relation to young children with identified special needs, culturally diverse backgrounds, home languages other than English, and individual differences that sometimes create impediments to successful play?

Implementation Ideas for Administrators:
INCLUSIVITY AND PLAY

An old adage says that management is about doing things right; leadership is about doing the right things. Inclusion is the right thing to do, and therefore it requires administrators to lead more than administer. Strengthen your leader-ship skills by doing the following:

- Read a book on leadership.
- Review your district's or program's policies about inclusion and equity. Are they strong and unequivocal about the importance of considering the needs of every child before decisions are made? Do they address a commitment to a diverse workforce? Are there model policies you can access that provide a strong foundation for equity and inclusion?
- Look at your child outcome data that has been disaggregated by race, ethnicity, English-language learner status, and IEPs. Are clear disparities present? Do all your teachers know about this? What are you going to do differently?
- Reinforce your own knowledge and skills about cultural competence by getting additional training or taking a class.

PART 3

UNDERSTANDING AND STRENGTH

With chapters 6 through 12, we move to two new steps in Eberle's cycle of play: *Understanding* and *Strength*. Brown summarizes Eberle's description of understanding as follows:

- the acquisition of new knowledge
- the synthesizing of concepts
- the incorporation of new ideas (Brown 2009, 19)

Understanding is a key payoff for play because it yields both emotional and intellectual benefits. Play helps us understand many things about ourselves, our capabilities, and how the world around us works. When children have rote knowledge without understanding, they are not able to use and apply that knowledge effectively. If there is no understanding, the entire educational enterprise is a failure. Eberle says that understanding, then, leads to strength, and he includes the following qualities in his description of that step in the cycle of play:

- the mastery that comes from constructive experience and understanding
- the empowerment of knowing more about how the world works (Brown 2009, 19)

Strength is the increased capacity we gain with new knowledge. Play makes us more capable by giving us opportunities to repeat our past experiences where we practice skills and solidify understanding or to do something new and different that brings about new learning.

In these chapters, we move from engaging in general conversations about play and standards to sharing practical implementation ideas. We want to empower teachers, and we believe that knowledge is power. Ralph Waldo Emerson wrote, "Skill to do comes of doing; knowledge comes by eyes always open, and working hands; and there is no knowledge that is not power" (Emerson 2007, 162).

In chapters 6 through 12 we emphasize "working hands." We provide hands-on and practical applications for the suggestions from earlier chapters. Each chapter focuses on a specific domain: Approaches to Learning (chapter 6), Language and Literacy (chapter 7), Mathematics (chapter 8), Science (chapter 9), Social Studies (chapter 10), Physical and Motor Development (chapter 11), and Social-Emotional Development (chapter 12).

To go along with Emerson's notion of "eyes always open," we encourage the reader to look at these chapters with openness and awareness, understanding that when teaching, each moment is a chance to teach *and* to learn. When teachers are alert and aware, their capacity to reach each child increases. They become stronger and more competent teachers. They learn a lot about the children they teach and about the mysterious process of learning. They gain the ability to make split-second decisions, to ask the right questions, and to understand exactly what a child needs so he can learn more.

We hope the ideas we share in these chapters also assist administrators in seeing more clearly the benefits of play-based approaches when combined with standards. We are confident they will see teachers who can engage young learners successfully and young learners who demonstrate improved learning outcomes.

GENERAL CONSIDERATIONS IN CHAPTERS 6 THROUGH 12

While each of the chapters offers ideas for linking play and standards related to a specific domain, some general considerations should be kept in mind for *all* of the chapters:

- the recognition that play addresses many standards from across multiple domains at the same time
- the value of learning the organizational structure and language of the standards
- the importance of avoiding narrow and rigid curricular approaches

Play Addresses Many Standards at Once

While we present standards as separate collections of content from domains, we recognize that in child-directed, open-ended play experiences, teachers rarely observe standards in isolation. Instead, as children play, teachers see them demonstrate standards from multiple domains. Here's an example:

Two children are working with playdough. As they pull, pinch, roll, and shape the dough into what they call "cookies," they are talking together. They pass a roller and cookie cutters back and forth, sharing the materials. They name the shapes they create. They count the number of finished cookies and compare who has more or less. They laugh and giggle as they socialize throughout the play experience.

The following domains and standards can be observed in this play experience:

- Fine motor: eye-hand coordination
- Language: communicating with others, vocabulary
- Social-emotional: sharing and cooperating, building friendship
- Mathematics: identification of shapes, counting, and quantitative comparison

We recognize that children integrate their skills and capabilities as they play. In fact, their ability to generalize the use of their skills and knowledge signals important and sophisticated growth. We organized the following chapters by domains merely as a matter of convenience. We hope by focusing on separate domains, teachers will be able to note precisely in what ways children are growing and learning. But we also hope teachers recognize that children are actually growing and learning in many ways at the same time.

It may be overwhelming to see multiple standards when they all happen at once. Our advice is not to fight the complexity. Rather, treat it as a benefit.

Play provides teachers with many opportunities to observe children showing what they know and can do. As teachers watch children play, intervene in play, and support and provoke new play, they can think of how many domains can be addressed at once rather than thinking of only one domain or one standard. Standards should not drive play. Rather, the play should drive the realization of the standards in action, or as Gaye says, "making standards come alive."

If standards are truly alive in curricular planning and implementation, administrators will be able to observe them more clearly too. Appropriate assessment that is imbedded in daily curriculum will show that children are learning. Administrators will not have to rely on inappropriate assessment to determine that standards are being addressed.

Learn the Standards

One way to make the whole process easier is to become as familiar with the standards as possible. By doing so a teacher can label children's experiences and easily link them to specific standards. But learning the standards is not always easy. Early learning and the Common Core standards include many items. Keeping track of all of them at the same time is clearly impossible. What we recommend is studying them to learn the logic of how they are organized by asking the following questions:

- What are the domains?
- What are the strands and clusters?
- What are the specific benchmarks?

We have found that it helps to focus as much on the structure of the standards as on the standards themselves. Many state early learning standards include introductory chapters that describe how they are organized and how best to understand them. The Common Core State Standards for both Language Arts and Mathematics have introductory pieces as well. Don't ignore them. When teachers read these carefully, they are digging deeper into the standards and will understand the organizing principles behind them.

Some states have created posters or condensed documents that summarize and present the early learning standards for at-a-glance convenience. Get these aids and use them. Put them on display, tape them to a computer or tablet, or make a miniature copy to put on the back cover of a planning book. When teachers do so, they are, in effect, creating a mental map so they can visualize where different standards fit and how they relate to each other. They are making the standards their own. We are not suggesting that teachers memorize every standard. But the clearer the mental map is, and the more content it includes, the easier it will be to link play and standards while keeping play authentic, child directed, and open ended.

Avoid Narrow and Rigid Curricular Approaches

It can be tempting to think that the only way to address standards is by planning activities, even playful ones, that focus on isolated, discrete benchmarks. Implementing standards in play does not mean narrowing or rigidly compartmentalizing the curriculum or the teaching approach. In contrast, play experiences offer opportunities to provide complex and multileveled experiences. Rather than making activities more constrained or shallow, or making an activity so simple it fails to engage the children, we recommend that teachers plan for experiences that can grow in complexity and richness. The identified benchmark(s) can still be the focus, but in a good play experience, children have many ways to demonstrate the benchmark as they dive deeply into the play activity. In this way, teachers can observe what is being learned—both what they expected and did not expect to see! The examples in the next chapters offer planning ideas for such rich play experiences.

MAKING THE BEST USE OF THE EXAMPLES IN THE NEXT CHAPTERS

In chapters 6 through 12, we do not attempt to address all of the standards and benchmarks in early learning or Common Core standards. Instead, we take four standards randomly selected from various state early learning standards, from the Common Core State Standards for Language Arts and Mathematics, and from other sets of standards for kindergarten. We hope teachers and administrators recognize that the examples can be applied to additional standards and benchmarks. We remind readers that standards need to be considered for the appropriate age group:

- For preschoolers: refer to the early learning standards.
- For kindergartners: refer to the Common Core State Standards or the other kindergarten standards we have chosen.

The examples we provide for integrating standards into play experiences can apply to both preschool and kindergarten children when appropriate. We trust that teachers and administrators will look at these examples and make adjustments to them so that they are well matched to the children in their classrooms. Perhaps they need to be simplified. Perhaps they need to be more complex or challenging. Teaching young children is a continual act of adaptation. We hope our ideas can stimulate your thinking about ways to address standards in play.

At the end of each of the chapters, we also provide a scenario of a play experience from either a preschool or a kindergarten classroom. We do so to show the richness of what can typically occur during high-quality play by telling a story of successful implementation. Both the examples provided in the tables and in the play scenarios are intended to give ideas of how specific types of standards can be addressed through play. They are meant to inspire and encourage the creativity of teachers to create their own ways of linking play and standards. We are interested in building the capacity of teachers to consider standards and pair them with play settings or contexts to promote authentic play experiences.

The most important task for teachers and administrators will be integrating play and standards in their own settings. They can do so with the knowledge they already possess about their own teaching strengths, their physical environment, and the strengths and needs of the children they teach.

CHAPTER **6**

Addressing Approaches to Learning Standards in Play

We begin our series of chapters on specific domains with the one that is the very foundation for children's success in school: Approaches to Learning. As we have pointed out, child-directed, open-ended play helps develop children's executive functions and approaches to learning. This is one of the most significant benefits of rich play experiences for children. Everyone agrees that in preschool and kindergarten, children are learning many concepts and skills. But most importantly, they are learning how to learn. Research shows that if the skills in this domain are not well developed, children may not have academic success as they move into the primary grades.

> There is research that suggests strong links between positive approaches to learning and children's success in school. For example, one study found that children with higher levels of attentiveness, task persistence, eagerness to learn, learning independence, flexibility, and organization, generally did better in literacy and math at the end of the kindergarten school year and the beginning of their first grade year. In addition, children who approach learning tasks or novel situations with these positive approaches to learning are better able to regulate their learning experiences, and more quickly acquire general knowledge and cognitive skills. (Conn-Powers 2006, 2)

How does play support and develop children's approaches to learning?

- High-level play fully engages children's attention.
- It invites them to follow their own curiosity and wonderings and to investigate further. They ask themselves, "How does this work? What can I do to figure this out?"
- Because the play is enjoyable and rewarding, they want to continue it. Therefore, they work to overcome problems that arise, whether the problems are with the materials themselves or with their coplayers.
- They develop persistence in the face of challenges, overcoming frustration and creating new strategies to make the play successful.

The early learning standards from most states include this domain. It either stands alone or is embedded into the standards in the social-emotional domain. In Kentucky's Early Childhood Standards, rather than identify specific standards, approaches to learning are identified as an important dimension of school readiness.

> Approaches to Learning recognizes that all children have different interests and attitudes toward learning experiences. Some children are more confident in exploring and exhibit more curiosity or natural engagement in play activities. Any individual child must have learning opportunities that match his or her interests and allow him or her to feel comfortable and safe in order to explore, try, ask for assistance and eventually master any new skill or concept. (Kentucky Governor's Office of Early Childhood 2013, 5)

We found some documents that address approaches to learning for kindergarten as well. We were especially delighted to see that in two sets of state standards, play and approaches to learning are linked. The Massachusetts Standards for Preschool and Kindergarten name this domain "Approaches to Play and Learning." The second edition of the Pennsylvania Learning Standards for Early Childhood calls it "Approaches to Learning through Play."

In this chapter, we focus on the strands we found most frequently included in this domain:

- Curiosity/Initiative
- Persistence
- Attention and Engagement
- Problem Solving and Creative Thinking

We firmly believe any high-level play experience has the potential for children to use and further develop their approaches to learning. However, we do not think it's helpful simply to say "all play" does so. Instead, we offer specific ideas and suggestions related to the different play areas in preschool and kindergarten classrooms and tie them to standards in each of the preceding four strands. These strands also overlap. In some state standards, attention and persistence are grouped together. In others, problem solving is put with curiosity and initiative. We felt these four strands were strong enough that they should be looked at separately in the context of play.

In the remainder of this chapter, we include sample standards from both preschool and kindergarten for each strand. For each, we also consider ways to integrate it in child-directed, open-ended play experiences. First, we suggest that you observe children in play throughout your classroom and reflect on your observations related to the specific standard. Then we offer ideas for intentionally planning to address the standard in these play areas and experiences by adding materials, making changes in the environment, or considering grouping strategies. Throughout, we ask you to consider additional ways you might observe for, support, and intentionally address the standard. We recognize that each classroom and group of children is different and that your knowledge of your students and setting will be important considerations.

At the end of the chapter, we share a story of how a teacher planned for play with many standards from this domain and others in mind. Realistically, many standards are integrated in children's play experiences, especially when they are foundational skills such as curiosity, persistence, or engagement. It's impossible to address only one standard at a time in play. That is precisely why it is such a rich and exciting curricular approach for preschool and kindergarten children! We encourage you to read through our specific examples in the tables on the following pages, think about your classroom and group of children, and come up with your own ideas. We also suggest that you look at the ways children demonstrate multiple standards from a variety of domains when teachers plan for integrated play activities such as the one shared at the end of the chapter.

DOMAIN: APPROACHES TO LEARNING
STRAND: CURIOSITY/INITIATIVE

Louisiana's Birth to Five Early Learning & Development Standards (ELDS)

Standard AL 1: Engage in play-based learning to explore, investigate, and acquire knowledge about themselves and their world.

AL 1 Indicator:

- Show curiosity, interest, and a willingness to learn new things and try new experiences. (4.1)

Massachusetts Standards for Preschool and Kindergarten

SOCIAL AND EMOTIONAL LEARNING, AND APPROACHES TO PLAY AND LEARNING

Standard APL2: The child will demonstrate eagerness and curiosity as a learner.

By the end of kindergarten, a child may:

- ask "why" questions about unknown future events and phenomena, as well as about the here and now (e.g., how, what if).
- try a wide range of new experiences (e.g., materials, tasks, academic or physical skills), both independently and with peers or adults.

- with support, seek information from a variety of sources, such as books, the Internet, experts, and observations.
- describe or demonstrate how he/she likes to learn best (observing, imitating, asking questions, hands-on investigation).

≈ Ways This Standard Occurs Naturally as Children Play

EXAMPLES:

Block area: Children explore and investigate principles of physics as they build and construct, asking "why" questions throughout.

Sensory table: Children engage in exploration with a variety of materials (e.g., sand, water, dirt, seeds, shaving cream), exploring textures and ways to manipulate with a variety of tools (e.g., strainers, shovels, scoops, waterwheels, measuring cups).

Outdoors: Children observe natural phenomena, such as wind, clouds, heat from the sun, and leaves changing colors, and ask questions to learn more.

- Where else might you see this standard occurring naturally in children's play?
- What other standards might children also demonstrate?

POSSIBLE TEACHER SUPPORT STRATEGIES:

Play alongside children, trying new experiences yourself.

Model ways to be curious, wondering aloud, asking questions, and seeking information from a variety of sources.

Provide scaffolding for children who are reluctant to try new things. Can they fingerpaint with tongue depressors instead of their hands? Can you pair them with a friend who is more of a risk taker?

What other support strategies might you try?

≈ Ways to Intentionally Plan to Address This Standard in Play Experiences

POSSIBLE MATERIALS, ENVIRONMENTAL CHANGES, OR GROUPING STRATEGIES	TEACHER SUPPORT STRATEGIES
Provide new objects, toys, and materials in various play areas to keep them interesting and intriguing to the children (e.g., pieces of fabric in the block area, magazines and newspapers in the dramatic play area, different types of brushes and rollers at the paint easel).	*Scaffold by providing some suggestions to children* for ways to use the new materials in their play.
Create a classroom museum and invite children to figure out things to display there. Let them take turns being the curators who design an exhibit and the ways that "museum visitors" can explore that exhibit.	*Challenge children* to think about museums that have hands-on exploration areas and assist them in designing their own exploratory exhibits.
Invite children to work in pairs and go on indoor and outdoor scavenger hunts.	*As a provocation,* make scavenger hunt cards that guide the children (e.g., find things that you never noticed before; find things that reflect the sunlight; find things that are changing each day). Invite children to design their own scavenger hunts.
Create "I wonder" books with the children.	*Reflect with children* about the things they want to know more about, the why questions they want answered. Then research with them to find the answers and put them in the book.
What other materials, environmental changes, or grouping strategies might you provide?	*What other support strategies might you try?*

DOMAIN: APPROACHES TO LEARNING
STRAND: PERSISTENCE

Mississippi Early Learning Standards for Classrooms Serving Four-Year-Old Children

CURIOSITY AND INITIATIVE DOMAIN: Demonstrate curiosity and initiative.

1. Demonstrate interest in new experiences by interacting with peers, using familiar materials in creative ways, and investigating new environments.

PERSISTENCE AND ATTENTIVENESS DOMAIN: Demonstrate persistence and attentiveness.

1. Follow through to complete a task or activity.

Arizona's College and Career Ready Standards—Mathematics—Kindergarten

Mathematical Practices (MP)

1. Make sense of problems and persevere in solving them.

≋ Ways This Standard Occurs Naturally as Children Play

EXAMPLES:

Manipulatives: Children connect and construct items, designs, and patterns, persevering as they work with the manipulative materials (e.g., getting the beads to snap together, the Lego construction to stand, or the marbles to roll down the run).

Art: Children use a variety of materials to express themselves, investing in the process with persistence and attentiveness more so than worrying about the product (e.g., mixing the paints to get just the right color, or using enough glue to hold the collage pieces in place).

Dramatic play: Children identify scenarios and organize materials and players to enact them, staying with the play even when problems arise with the "script," "scenery," or "props," or among the "actors."

- Where else might you see this standard occurring naturally in children's play?

- What other standards might children also demonstrate?

POSSIBLE TEACHER SUPPORT STRATEGIES:

Play alongside children—your presence often extends their attention to play experiences.

Model your own persistence in the face of problems, stating your frustration and identifying ways you can make what you are trying to do work.

Provide scaffolding to children who do not persist. Offer assistance, ideas, suggestions, or peer helpers.

Ways to Intentionally Plan to Address This Standard in Play Experiences

POSSIBLE MATERIALS, ENVIRONMENTAL CHANGES, OR GROUPING STRATEGIES	TEACHER SUPPORT STRATEGIES
Provide signs that say "Under Construction" and a place to leave partially finished creations so that children are encouraged to become deeply engaged, persist in problem solving, and finish what they started at a later time or on another day.	*Scaffold by being ready to support children* to save partially completed creations and to remind them later or on the next day to return to them.
Pair children who are more consistently persistent to play with those who are not.	*Challenge the pairs* to set a goal for their play experience and to work together to meet that goal (e.g., to build a road or bridge, to draw and paint a mural, or to do a science experiment).
Offer to time children's play with timers or stopwatches to see how long they work and play at different areas.	*As a provocation,* record their times and challenge them to see if they can beat their own "world records."
Create "I'm Trying to Get Better at . . ." books.	*Reflect with children* about things that are challenging for them, and talk through what strategies they can try to address the challenges.
What other materials, environmental changes, or grouping strategies might you provide?	*What other support strategies might you try?*

DOMAIN: APPROACHES TO LEARNING
STRAND: ATTENTION AND ENGAGEMENT

North Carolina Foundations for Early Learning and Development

Attentiveness, Effort, and Persistence

Goal APL-8: Children maintain attentiveness and focus.

Pennsylvania Learning Standards for Early Childhood (Continuum from Infant/Toddler through Kindergarten)

AL.2 Organizing and Understanding Information

A. Engagement and Attention

The learner will: Ignore distractions to complete a task.

≋ Ways This Standard Occurs Naturally as Children Play

EXAMPLES:

Class library: Children look at books, talking with each other, retelling stories, and making sense of print, even as other children go in and out of the library area.

Science area: Children follow investigations across time (e.g., trying out a number of items to see what sinks or floats, waiting for water to boil or for snow to melt, revisiting seeds planted to assess their growth).

Music/listening area: Children listen to stories on CDs, staying and attending to the end.

- Where else might you see this standard occurring naturally in children's play?
- What other standards might children also demonstrate?

POSSIBLE TEACHER SUPPORT STRATEGIES:

Play alongside children for increasing lengths of time.

Model ways to focus even in the face of interruptions and disruptions.

Provide scaffolding for children who have trouble concentrating. Ask what would help them—moving to a less busy area of the room? Playing with a different partner?

Ways to Intentionally Plan to Address This Standard in Play Experiences

POSSIBLE MATERIALS, ENVIRONMENTAL CHANGES, OR GROUPING STRATEGIES	TEACHER SUPPORT STRATEGIES
Arrange the classroom so that noisy play areas are grouped together and quieter ones are placed far from the noise.	*Scaffold by helping children make good choices* about where to engage in more active play (the noisy areas) and where to find peace and quiet.
Make clear that children are free to stay in play areas when they are deeply engaged. Do not set arbitrary time limits (such as ringing a bell and rotating after fifteen minutes). Such limits are limiting—children will not develop focus and attention when worrying about when the bell will ring.	*Challenge children* to come up with ways to handle situations in which children want to play in an area where others are deeply engaged. Suggest creating waiting lists, determining agreed upon time restrictions, or alternating days for playing in that area. Ask children for their suggestions.
Provide places in the classroom for individuals or pairs to "get away" and work and play on their own.	*As a provocation,* invite the children to help create private spaces for one or two children with beanbag chairs, pillows, a small table, stuffed animals, items to manipulate, drawing materials, and books to look at. Discuss the how, what, when, and why of using these spaces.
Recognize and celebrate children's focus and attention. Describe what you see to validate their concentration.	*Reflect with children* about times they have been interrupted and discuss how that felt. Strategize ways to overcome interruptions and deepen engagement.
What other materials, environmental changes, or grouping strategies might you provide?	*What other support strategies might you try?*

DOMAIN: APPROACHES TO LEARNING
STRAND: PROBLEM SOLVING AND CREATIVE THINKING

Wisconsin Model Early Learning Standards

B. Creativity and Imagination

Performance Standard B. EL. 1 Engages in imaginative play and inventive thinking through interactions with people, materials, and the environment.

Ohio's New Learning Standards: Kindergarten through Grade 3

STRAND: CREATIVITY

Standard Statements by the end of Grade 1 (no kindergarten level identified):

- Interact with a wide variety of objects and materials without concern of product or outcome.
- Identify differences between problem types and adapt strategies based on the type of problem.

≈ Ways This Standard Occurs Naturally as Children Play

EXAMPLES:

Block area: Children figure out inventive ways to use the blocks and combine them with other materials (e.g., PVC pipes, found objects, small people and animal figures, vehicles, household items).

Writing area: Children explore writing tools to draw and write with no concern for product or outcome, but rather to experiment with emergent writing and phonetic spelling.

Dramatic play: Children weave their own life experiences, plots, and characters from stories read and movies and television and create imaginative and unique dramatic play scenarios.

- Where else might you see this standard occurring naturally in children's play?
- What other standards might children also demonstrate?

POSSIBLE TEACHER SUPPORT STRATEGIES:

Play alongside children, ready to provide interesting materials and support problem-solving efforts.

Model new kinds of thinking with open-ended questions and comments: "I wonder what would happen if we . . . ?"

Provide scaffolding for children who are reluctant to use materials in new ways. Give permission, suggestions, ideas, and encouragement.

≈ Ways to Intentionally Plan to Address This Standard in Play Experiences	
POSSIBLE MATERIALS, ENVIRONMENTAL CHANGES, OR GROUPING STRATEGIES	**TEACHER SUPPORT STRATEGIES**
Provide loose parts throughout the classroom to encourage inventiveness (e.g., cardboard tubes and boxes, swatches of cloth in a variety of textures and sizes, PVC pipes, baskets and containers, items from nature such as a collection of pine cones, collections of keys, screws, nuts and bolts, shells, and stones).	*Scaffold by encouraging children* to use the loose parts in their creations and play and providing assistance in getting started.
Provide discarded appliances and tools for children to take apart.	*Challenge children* to come up with ways to dismantle the objects and use the tools. Help them figure out the purposes of the different parts. Challenge them to design new ways to use the pieces.
Put away the plastic toys, wooden puzzles, and premade games and only provide open-ended materials.	*As a provocation,* do not give directions other than "I wonder what you will do with these items in dramatic play. In the block area. At the art area."
Be the scribe and write down descriptive observations (like a story) about children's problem solving, dramatic play, and inventive thinking.	*Reflect with children* by reading the stories aloud at group times and letting the children tell more about their involvement in that play experience.
What other materials, environmental changes, or grouping strategies might you provide?	*What other support strategies might you try?*

A PLAY STORY FROM A PRESCHOOL CLASSROOM: LEARNING TO BE LEARNERS

As a teacher in a half-day mixed-age preschool program, Terri wanted to be clear to the children's families that she was addressing kindergarten readiness. She knew this was especially a concern for the families whose children were four turning five. But she even heard family members with three-year-olds raising the issue. Early in the fall, she decided to write a newsletter article about how she was helping the children in her program. She titled it "Learning to Be Learners."

In the article, Terri shared what she knew about children's approaches to learning. From all of her own education in early childhood development, from the professional reading she had done, and from the conference presentations she had attended, she had learned that kindergarten readiness was far more than just knowing letters and numbers. Children's curiosity, initiative, attentiveness, and ability to focus were critical to their later academic success. Their persistence in the face of challenges, problem-solving strategies, and creative innovations were all skills that would help them be successful in kindergarten, in elementary school, and throughout their lives. She was pleased to see that her state's early learning standards included the domain of Approaches to Learning and even linked the development of these approaches to play. For her family newsletter, Terri wrote about how she set up play in her preschool classroom so that this important area was being addressed every single day. She was confident she could communicate with her families about how she was truly helping her children be more successful learners and, therefore, ready for kindergarten.

Terri and her coteacher, Sue, were committed to offering ample time for play each day. They scheduled one hour for what they called "Investigation Time." They felt the name was far more descriptive of what they expected children to do than "Free Play." They did want children to play freely, to follow their own interests, and to make choices about what they would do and with whom. The choices were not "free," however. Terri and Sue carefully organized the play areas and available materials. And they interacted with children in a variety of ways as they played. Doing so made it possible for them to provide support for learning in all domains, and especially in Approaches to Learning.

Attention and Focus

The one-hour time period allowed children to become deeply engaged. But sometimes that took time. Some children needed to watch and see what other children were doing. Some needed to try something for a little while and then move on to another activity. Each child was figuring out where he wanted to focus his attention, what grabbed his interest. Terri and Sue were ready to help. They observed as children made choices and settled in. For those who did not, they made suggestions, offered new materials, and helped children find playmates. Sometimes she and Sue were the coplayers themselves!

Curiosity and Initiative

Materials and play opportunities changed as children's interests changed. Terri and Sue paid attention to what children were curious about. They listened closely for children's questions and wonderings. They followed children's lead as they initiated a new play experience. They took advantage of teachable moments and followed up with experiences and information to build on them. The sighting of a rainbow outdoors one day led to multiple play experiences related to rainbows—creating paintings and drawings, reading and making up stories, singing songs, engaging in color mixing, and investigating prisms.

Persistence

During play, Terri and Sue did not do things *for* children. Rather, they acted as quiet nearby presences or as facilitators and guides. They let the children try to figure things out for themselves, knowing that learning to stick with a task even when it's challenging is an important approach for learning anything in life. They knew that kindergarten teachers appreciate children who are able to persist when things are hard. They knew that children need to figure out how to handle frustration in appropriate ways. Terri and Sue were always close by to offer a helping hand, when need be.

Creative Problem Solving

Finally, there were many opportunities for this important approach to learning in the play areas of Terri's classroom. As children built structures in the block area, they had to figure out where to place the larger, heavier blocks so that their construction would be stable. As they engaged in dramatic play, they problem solved as they tried to build a pretend campfire from the materials available in the house corner. The tent was no problem. A piece of fabric thrown over a table provided the perfect solution. As children put puzzles together, they used their geometric and spatial thinking to place the pieces in just the right spot. As children chose materials to create a collage in the art area, they had to strategize on how to make the various items stick. Terri loved to watch, feeling as if she could see the wheels turning in each child's head as he or she puzzled out solutions to problems.

Yes, Terri and Sue addressed approaches to learning every day as children played. Children showed incredible curiosity about the world, developed longer attention spans, coped with frustration more easily, and came up with inventive solutions to problems. Indeed, they were getting ready to tackle kindergarten, elementary school, and life!

What Standards Were Addressed?

In addition to the approaches to learning standards listed above, the following were among the standards addressed:

- social-emotional skills, including taking turns, sharing, and cooperating
- language as children listened and conversed with their teachers and with each other
- reading and writing as children visited the class library, reading books about rainbows and other topics of interest, and wrote and drew at the writing and art areas
- fine-motor skills as children worked with puzzles and manipulatives
- math concepts of spatial relationships and geometry as children built with blocks and completed puzzles

CHAPTER 7

Addressing Language and Literacy Standards in Play

Language and literacy or language arts is a foundational domain of development for learning. The infant is raised in a home language that surrounds him from the moment of birth. As he is loved and cared for, he hears words and phrases that help him form an organizational structure for his thinking. His vocabulary grows as he connects words to the people and things in the world around him and acts on them. And as he is exposed to books and print, he starts to connect the spoken word to the written, giving him new ways to communicate with others and to learn about the world. By the preschool years, most children are fluent in their home language, show interest in books and stories, and play with making marks and writing. By kindergarten, they start honing skills that will lead them to reading and writing as they continue to grow and develop. Reading and writing will be the way they move into the academic world, gaining knowledge in other content areas such as math, science, history, and social studies.

Most state early learning standards and the Common Core standards for kindergarten include the following broad topics or strands for Language and Literacy or English Language Arts:

- Speaking and Listening
- Reading
- Phonological Awareness
- Writing

EMERGENT LITERACY AND PLAY

Language and literacy receives a primary focus in the Common Core State Standards and in every state's early learning standards. In fact, George W. Bush's early childhood initiative, Good Start, Grow Smart, required that early learning standards include literacy, math, and science, but not other developmental domains. The argument for its central importance was that reading at grade level by third grade is one of the more reliable predictors of academic success (AECF 2010; Hernandez 2011). We know that when teachers and administrators are pressured to accentuate academic learning, the emphasis is on literacy skills. But we want to stress that learning the fundamentals of emergent literacy in early childhood does not mean abandoning play.

In fact, some of the strongest research about the benefits of play focuses on its impact on language and literacy skills. The evidence cited by a variety of research studies shows that play benefits extend to each of the four strands of this domain. Let's look more closely at research about play related to each of the literacy strands.

Speaking and Listening

- Studies examined the use of language during sociodramatic play and showed that children greatly increased their expressive language use during role play and make-believe (Christie and Roskos 2006).
- In a review of research about children's language development, Hirsh-Pasek, Golinkoff, Berk, and Singer (2009, 31) declare, "Children demonstrate their most advanced language skills in playful environments, and these language skills are strongly related to literacy development."
- Teachers know that play often involves children talking with one another and can involve a variety of new vocabulary words (for example, when children play hospital, they use the vocabulary related to that setting). Dickinson and Moreton (1991) found that the amount of time three-year-olds spent talking to peers was associated with vocabulary size in kindergarten. The more they talked, the larger their vocabulary!

Reading and Writing

- When teachers provided books within play areas, the amount of time children spent pretending to read to other children, dolls, or stuffed animals increased. And play centers that included theme-related reading and writing materials promoted more engagement of children in reading and writing experiences (Christie and Roskos 2006, 65; Neuman and Roskos 1992).
- Strong effects were found when teachers added literacy materials to the environment. Children increased their use of the materials, frequency in pretending to read, creation of written labels, and inclusion of literacy activities as part of their pretend play (Neuman and Roskos 1992).

Phonological Awareness

- Connections between children's knowledge of nursery rhymes and engagement in word play were associated with greater phonological awareness (Fernandez-Fein and Baker 1997).
- Rhyming games, making shopping lists, and reading storybooks predicted greater development of phonological awareness for young children (Bergen and Mauer 2000).

One of the approaches recommended to promote development in literacy and language arts is to use literacy-enriched play interventions (Justice and Pullen 2003). These authors suggest adding literacy props and materials to the dramatic play area and engaging in adult mediation (teacher involvement in literacy play). As they observed these interventions in action, they noted an increase in children's alphabet knowledge and environmental print recognition.

In this chapter, we provide one example of a standard in each of the strands and consider ways to integrate it in child-directed, open-ended play experiences. First, we suggest that you observe children in play throughout your classroom and reflect on your observations related to the specific standard.

In addition, we offer ideas for intentionally planning to address the standard in these play areas and experiences by adding materials, making changes in the environment, or considering grouping strategies. Throughout, we ask you to consider additional ways you might observe for, support, and intentionally address the standard. We recognize that each classroom and group of children is different and that your knowledge of your students and setting will be important considerations.

At the end of the chapter, we share a story of how a teacher planned for play with many standards from this domain and others in mind. Realistically, many standards are integrated in children's play experiences. It's impossible to address only one standard at a time in play. That is why it is such a rich and exciting curricular approach for preschool and kindergarten children. We encourage you to read through our specific examples in the following tables, think about your classroom and group of children, and come up with your own ideas. We also suggest that you look at the ways children demonstrate multiple standards from a variety of domains when teachers plan for integrated play activities such as the one shared at the end of the chapter.

DOMAIN: LANGUAGE AND LITERACY
STRAND: SPEAKING AND LISTENING

Pennsylvania Early Learning Standards for Early Childhood Pre-Kindergarten

CC.1: English Language Arts

Standard Area—CC.1.5: Speaking and Listening

Participate in collaborative conversations with peers and adults in small and larger groups.

Common Core for Kindergarten

Speaking and Listening

Comprehension and Collaboration

CCSS.ELA-LITERACY.SL.K.1: Participate in collaborative conversations with diverse partners about kindergarten topics and texts with peers and adults in small and larger groups.

≋ Ways This Standard Occurs Naturally as Children Play

EXAMPLES:

Dramatic play: Children invent dialogue in a scenario (family home, restaurant, hospital, grocery store).

Blocks: Children converse in order to work together to build a structure.

Outdoors: Children develop and agree on rules during outdoor play.

- Where else might you see this standard occurring naturally in children's play?
- What other standards might children also demonstrate?

POSSIBLE TEACHER SUPPORT STRATEGIES:

Play alongside children and engage in conversations about what you are doing together.

Model by announcing that you are waiting for the other person's response; then follow up with a related question or comment.

Provide scaffolding by supporting a child in expressing himself. Give him some words or phrases to help him communicate more clearly, and then gently remind him to wait for the response so that give-and-take occurs.

What other support strategies might you try?

≈ Ways to Intentionally Plan to Address This Standard in Play Experiences

POSSIBLE MATERIALS, ENVIRONMENTAL CHANGES, OR GROUPING STRATEGIES	TEACHER SUPPORT STRATEGIES
Provide tape recorders and record what children say to each other as they play in any area.	*Scaffold by assisting children* in creating recordings. Then *listen and review* with them.
Take dictation about children's drawings, paintings, or constructions.	*Provide a challenge* to children by *reading their dictation back* to them and *engaging* in a conversation about what they liked and what they might do differently next time.
Video children engaged in pretend play or construction with blocks or manipulatives.	*Use the videos as provocations. Review* with the children. *Discuss* ways they communicated and identify questions they could have asked each other.
Pair children after play experiences and have them describe to each other what they did, what they liked, and what they might do differently next time.	*Reflect with children, supporting and encouraging* them in their pair conversations.
What other materials, environmental changes, or grouping strategies might you provide?	*What other support strategies might you try?*

DOMAIN: LANGUAGE AND LITERACY
STRAND: READING

Illinois Early Learning and Development Standards

Goal 2: Demonstrate understanding and enjoyment of literature.

2.B Recognize key ideas and details in stories.

2.B.ECb: With teacher assistance, retell familiar stories with three or more key events.

Common Core for Kindergarten

Reading: Literature

Key Ideas & Details

CCSS.ELA-LITERACY.RL.K.2: With prompting and support, retell familiar stories, including key details.

≋ Ways This Standard Occurs Naturally as Children Play

EXAMPLES:

Art: Children draw, paint, or make creations related to familiar stories read.

Writing area: Children write, draw, and/or dictate related to familiar stories read.

Dramatic play: Using puppets or props, children act out familiar stories read.

- Where else might you see this standard occurring naturally in children's play?
- What other standards might children also demonstrate?

POSSIBLE TEACHER SUPPORT STRATEGIES:

Play alongside children and support their efforts to incorporate the key events and details of familiar stories read.

Model the way your creation, writing, or dramatic play reflects details of stories read.

Provide scaffolding by offering a key detail or event to help a child incorporate that into her creation, writing, or dramatic play.

What other support strategies might you try?

Ways to Intentionally Plan to Address This Standard in Play Experiences

POSSIBLE MATERIALS, ENVIRONMENTAL CHANGES, OR GROUPING STRATEGIES	TEACHER SUPPORT STRATEGIES
Place multiple copies of books already read in accessible places throughout the classroom so children can return to them again and again.	*Scaffold by being ready to assist children* in incorporating details from stories into block building, dramatic play, creative art, and other activities in the classroom.
Provide puppets and other props related to familiar stories.	*Challenge* children to reenact familiar stories with puppets and props. Set up a stage area. Help them rehearse and perform.
Offer art materials that match the illustrations in familiar books.	*As a provocation, invite children* to create their own illustrations (e.g., watercolors and collage for Eric Carle books) and retell a familiar story by that illustrator.
Video children's reenactments of familiar stories.	*Use the videos as provocations. Watch and review* with the children and compare with the original book to check on details included and those missed.
Create a display of children's drawings, writings, and creations related to familiar stories.	*Reflect with children as you create the display.* Take children's dictation about their creation or invite them to write about it for the display.
What other materials, environmental changes, or grouping strategies might you provide?	*What other support strategies might you try?*

DOMAIN: LANGUAGE AND LITERACY
STRAND: PHONOLOGICAL AWARENESS

Foundations to the Indiana Academic Standards for Young Children from Birth to Age 5

ELA.1.15: Imitate simple rhymes.

Common Core for Kindergarten

Reading: Foundational Skills

Phonological Awareness—CCSS.ELA-LITERACY.RF.K.2: Demonstrate understanding of spoken words, syllables, and sounds (phonemes).

CCSS.ELA-LITERACY.RF.K.2A: Recognize and produce rhyming words.

≋ Ways This Standard Occurs Naturally as Children Play

EXAMPLES:

Class library: Children choose favorite rhyming books (in English or other languages) and look at and retell it in their own words.

Manipulatives: Children make up silly words that rhyme (in English or other languages) as they use connecting manipulatives, complete puzzles, or play with sorting items.

Music area: Children listen to, dance to, and sing along with rhyming songs and chants (in English or other languages).

- Where else might you see this standard occurring naturally in children's play?
- What other standards might children also demonstrate?

POSSIBLE TEACHER SUPPORT STRATEGIES:

Read and play alongside children pointing out rhymes.

Model substituting initial sounds to make rhymes in a name game or in a song or chant. Make up silly rhyming word combinations together.

Provide scaffolding to help children make successful rhymes or encourage them to sing along with songs and chants when in the music area alone.

What other support strategies might you try?

≋ Ways to Intentionally Plan to Address This Standard in Play Experiences

POSSIBLE MATERIALS, ENVIRONMENTAL CHANGES, OR GROUPING STRATEGIES	TEACHER SUPPORT STRATEGIES
Supply the library with many rhyming books (in English or other languages).	*Scaffold by assisting children* in reading and identifying rhymes.
Use rhymes (in English or other languages) at transition times.	*Challenge children* to come up with their own rhymes.
Introduce rhyming name games and rhyming songs (in English or other languages) with CDs in the music area.	*Invite children* to make up their own rhyming games and songs.
Create a series of rhyming books (in English or other languages) with the children and place in the class library.	*Reflect with children by revisiting the* rhyming books periodically in small and large groups.
What other materials, environmental changes, or grouping strategies might you provide?	*What other support strategies might you try?*

DOMAIN: LANGUAGE AND LITERACY
STRAND: WRITING

Washington State Early Learning and Development Guidelines Birth through 3rd Grade

Communicating (Literacy)

Writing

Use letter-like symbols to make lists, letters and stories or to label pictures.

Common Core for Kindergarten

Writing

Text Types and Purposes

CCSS.ELA-LITERACY.W.K.2: Use a combination of drawing, dictating, and writing to compose informative/explanatory texts in which the children name what they are writing about and supply some information about the topic.

≋ Ways This Standard Occurs Naturally as Children Play

EXAMPLES:

Blocks: Children create signs for their structures or write/draw about their construction.

Sensory table: Children record the results of experimentation with sinking/floating or measurement of sand.

Science area: Children document explorations and experiments with drawings and descriptions of things observed.

- Where else might you see this standard occurring naturally in children's play?
- What other standards might children also demonstrate?

POSSIBLE TEACHER SUPPORT STRATEGIES:

Write and play alongside children.

Model by writing in their style (not necessarily in adult writing), showing acceptance of their efforts at scribble writing, letter-like shapes, and phonetic spelling.

Provide scaffolding to children as they attempt to write.

What other support strategies might you try?

Ways to Intentionally Plan to Address This Standard in Play Experiences

POSSIBLE MATERIALS, ENVIRONMENTAL CHANGES, OR GROUPING STRATEGIES	TEACHER SUPPORT STRATEGIES
Provide a variety of writing materials in all of the areas of the classroom.	*Scaffold by giving children reasons for writing* as they play (signs for block buildings, adding their names to creations, pretending to write in dramatic play scenarios).
Provide clipboards with paper and markers or pens for children to draw and write on as they participate in different experiences.	*Challenge children by adding the expectation of writing* to their explorations.
Invite children to record their investigations at the science area or sensory table.	*Ask provocative questions for them to respond to through drawing/writing* (e.g., What did you notice as you poured the water over the waterwheel? How did the sand feel when it was dry? When it was wet? What was the same or different?).
Encourage children to share their writing and journals with others (in pairs, or in small or large groups).	*Reflect with children by reviewing their drawing/writing with them.* Note the way they are communicating, using letters, and/or beginning to spell. Celebrate their efforts.
What other materials, environmental changes, or grouping strategies might you provide?	*What other support strategies might you try?*

A PLAY STORY FROM A KINDERGARTEN CLASSROOM: CLASS POST OFFICE

Ms. Kenworth and her colleague, Ms. Anders, wanted to encourage children to write in more areas of their kindergarten classroom than just the writing center. They decided to set up a class post office. They gathered donations of different types of stationery, envelopes, and stickers (for the children to use as stamps). They set aside an area for these materials and added pens, pencils, markers, and crayons as well as a mailbox. In addition, they provided an address book with children's names and addresses (one on each page for easy reference). They introduced the post office idea to the children and discussed the writing of letters and the process of sending and receiving mail. The children's initial response was enthusiastic. At the end of each day, at the closing group meeting, a child was designated as the mail carrier and delivered the "letters" to the children to whom they were addressed. This involved being able to read what was written on the envelope and get the letter to the right person. Teachers and other children helped the recipients "read" their letters. Again, this encouraged writing in ways that were clear and readable.

Children showed strong interest and participation in the class post office from the beginning. At first, children mostly wrote their own names on the letter and the recipient's name on the envelope. Over time, Ms. Kenworth and Ms. Anders encouraged children to begin writing the address correctly on the envelope. This took more time and effort on the part of the children. The interest of some children waned with this stricter requirement. The teachers decided to waive that requirement every time and provide other incentives to write letters to friends. They began by writing letters themselves (especially to the children who had not received as many from other children). They did not always put the child's home address on the envelope themselves. Sometimes they did. Their messages to the children were simple sentences they knew the children could figure out, such as these:

(cont.)

- "I like you."
- "Thank you for helping today."
- "You are learning at our school."
- "You are a good friend."

Sometimes they wrote in the child's home language and other times in English. As they hoped, their letters became models for children to copy for their own letters to their friends. Discussions about how to write certain words were common. Identification of letters and sounding out of words occurred. As time went by, the teachers made word cards for children with words they asked for. The cards were placed on key rings so children could easily find the word they needed. Letters became more detailed as children's writing skills improved and their interest was continually stimulated and supported.

What Standards Were Addressed?

- All four strands of Language Arts were addressed: Speaking and Listening, Reading, Phonological Awareness, and Writing.
- Fine-motor skills were developed as children used the writing tools, folded stationery, and sealed envelopes.
- Social-emotional development was addressed as children communicated with friends through writing and reading and felt pride and confidence in their accomplishments.
- As children chose their words, other domains such as science, math, and social studies were incorporated.

CHAPTER 8

Addressing Mathematics Standards in Play

I n the preschool and kindergarten years, children are building the foundations of their mathematical understanding by exploring the world around them. They are not ready for paper-and-pencil computations until they have had many hands-on opportunities to work with real objects. They sort and categorize, match one-on-one, create groups of objects to build understanding of quantity, explore and construct with geometrical shapes, investigate spatial relationships, make comparisons between sizes and weights of objects, and learn the vocabulary related to counting, quantity, measurement, and geometry. Math is everywhere in children's lives and can be easily integrated into multiple play experiences. Yet supporting growth in this kind of learning at a young age is often neglected (Baroody, Lai, and Mix 2006). In this chapter, we will share ideas to help teachers and administrators in preschool and kindergarten classrooms recognize and enhance the possibilities for addressing mathematical concepts as children play.

Children use a number of key concepts of mathematics in high-level play to move the play along or to provide the player with needed information. They may

- tally scores in a chase game outdoors;
- combine blocks of different sizes in the block area;
- use a timing device to aid taking turns at the listening or computer areas; and
- with table games, count spaces on the board or dots on a dice, or identify numerals on a spinner.

The mathematical skills and knowledge involved in child-directed, open-ended play serve a functional purpose and thus increase learning (Gelman 2006). Moreover, research confirms a clear connection between play and development of mathematical understanding. We have organized the findings in the following table:

WHAT CHILDREN DO	MATH THEY LEARN	REFERENCE
Block play Model building Carpentry	Spatial knowledge	Baenninger and Newcombe (1995)
Blocks Construction toys	Spatial relations Measurement	Clements et al. (1999)
Playing with blocks, Legos, tracks	Geometry, architecture	Ness and Farenga (2007)
Number and color board games	Numerical magnitude Number line estimation Counting Numerical identification	Ramani and Siegler (2008)
Miscellaneous play (including sociodramatic play)	Patterns Shapes Enumeration	Seo and Ginsburg (2004)

Most state early learning standards and the Common Core standards for kindergarten include the following broad topics or strands for Mathematics:

- Number Sense, Quantity, and Counting
- Operations and Algebraic Thinking
- Measurement
- Geometry and Spatial Relationships

In this chapter, we provide one example of a standard in each of the four strands and consider ways to integrate it in child-directed, open-ended play experiences. First, we suggest that you observe children in play throughout your classroom and reflect on your observations related to the specific standard.

Then we offer ideas for intentionally planning to address the standard in these play areas and experiences by adding materials, making changes in the environment, or considering grouping strategies. Throughout, we ask you to consider additional ways you might observe for, support, and intentionally address the standard. We recognize that each classroom and group of children is different and that your knowledge of your students and setting will be important considerations.

At the end of the chapter, we share a story of how a teacher planned for play with many standards from this domain and others in mind. Realistically, many standards are integrated in children's play experiences. It's impossible to address only one standard at a time in play, which is why it is such a rich and exciting curricular approach for preschool and kindergarten children. We encourage you to read through our examples in the tables on the following pages, think about your classroom and group of children, and come up with your own ideas. We also suggest you look at the ways children demonstrate multiple standards from a variety of domains when teachers plan for integrated play activities such as the one shared at the end of the chapter.

DOMAIN: MATHEMATICS
STRAND: NUMBER SENSE, QUANTITY, AND COUNTING

Florida Early Learning and Developmental Standards for Four-Year-Olds

V. Cognitive Development and General Knowledge

A. Mathematical Thinking

2. Shows understanding of how to count and construct sets

Benchmark a: Child counts sets in the range of 10 to 15 objects.

Common Core for Kindergarten

Counting & Cardinality

B. Count to tell the number of objects

CCSS.Math.Content.K.CC.B.4: Understand the relationship between numbers and quantities; connect counting to cardinality

---

≈ Ways This Standard Occurs Naturally as Children Play

EXAMPLES:

Manipulatives: Children count out objects as they put them into containers or sort them into piles.

Science area: Children describe objects collected outdoors (leaves, nuts, rocks, sticks) using quantity and numbers.

Class library: Children look at a variety of counting books and count the items pictured on the pages.

- Where else might you see this standard occurring naturally in children's play?
- What other standards might children also demonstrate?

(cont.)

POSSIBLE TEACHER SUPPORT STRATEGIES:

Play alongside children and make inquiries and comments about quantities.

Model counting out loud as you manipulate objects. Wonder about what the next number will be. Model one-to-one correspondence.

Provide scaffolding by assisting children as they count higher quantities of objects used in the play activity.

What other support strategies might you try?

≈ Ways to Intentionally Plan to Address This Standard in Play Experiences

POSSIBLE MATERIALS, ENVIRONMENTAL CHANGES, OR GROUPING STRATEGIES	TEACHER SUPPORT STRATEGIES
Add numeral cards and/or dice and encourage children to use them to determine how many manipulatives to count. Increase the number of dice to get higher totals to practice counting beyond 6 or 12.	*Scaffold by assisting children* in recognizing the quantity on the card or die and counting out that many items. For children who are ready, facilitate addition problems by combining the quantities on each of the die or cards.
Provide baskets with numeral cards for the sorting and counting of items collected outdoors.	*Challenge* children to catalog what they have collected on a tally sheet on a clipboard, in a photograph album, or in a display to share with other children.
Set up a math area with number lines and charts, playing cards, dice, dominoes, magnetic numbers, and math games. Add writing materials for recording purposes.	*As a provocation, invite children* to figure out ways to use the items in the math area. Challenge them to see how high they can count, if they can match up equivalent numbers of dots on dominoes, ways they can record their math play, and ways to work together to make up their own math games and explorations with the materials.
Encourage counting throughout all play areas and daily experiences.	*Reflect with children by conversing about counting in their play and other daily experiences.* (How many blocks did you use to build your bridge? How many other children were playing with you?)
What other materials, environmental changes, or grouping strategies might you provide?	*What other support strategies might you try?*

DOMAIN: MATHEMATICS
STRAND: OPERATIONS AND ALGEBRAIC THINKING

Revised Texas Prekindergarten Guidelines

V. MATHEMATIC DOMAIN

B. Adding To/Taking Away Skills

VB1: Child uses concrete models or makes a verbal word problem for adding up to five objects.

Common Core for Kindergarten

Operations & Algebraic Thinking

A. Understand addition as putting together and adding to, and understand subtraction as taking apart and taking from.

CCSS.Math.Content.K.OA.A.1: Represent addition and subtraction with objects, fingers, mental images, drawings, sounds (such as claps), acting out situations, verbal explanations, expressions, or equations.

≋ Ways This Standard Occurs Naturally as Children Play

EXAMPLES:

Dramatic play: Children engage in discussions as they plan for pretend play, identifying how many more children they need for their family, their train trip, their pet store, and so on.

Music area: Children do addition (and subtraction) as they chant and act out familiar fingerplays ("Three Little Monkeys Jumping on the Bed," "Five Little Monkeys Swinging in a Tree," "Five Little Ducks Went Out to Play," "Ten in the Bed").

Blocks: Children figure out how many blocks need to be added or taken away to complete their structures, roads, and other projects.

- Where else might you see this standard occurring naturally in children's play?
- What other standards might children also demonstrate?

POSSIBLE TEACHER SUPPORT STRATEGIES:

Play alongside children, pointing out instances where addition or subtraction is happening.

Model ways to represent addition and subtraction problems with objects and in writing equations.

Provide scaffolding by assisting children in acting out addition or subtraction situations.

What other support strategies might you try?

≈ Ways to Intentionally Plan to Address This Standard in Play Experiences	
POSSIBLE MATERIALS, ENVIRONMENTAL CHANGES, OR GROUPING STRATEGIES	**TEACHER SUPPORT STRATEGIES**
As children transition from activity to activity, encourage them to form groups by demonstrating addition and subtraction.	*Scaffold by assisting children* in creating groups of students waiting in line to wash hands or getting ready to go outdoors. (Can you add two more children—how many will that be? What happens if we take away three children?)
In the manipulatives area, provide numeral cards as well as cards with equal signs, plus signs, and minus signs.	*Challenge* children to use the manipulatives and the cards to create addition and subtraction problems.
Set up a number books station with premade stapled books of blank paper, stickers, and writing materials.	*As a provocation, invite children* to create their own number books using the stickers or creating drawings that show differing combinations (e.g., for a "5" book, each page might have a combination, such as $5 = 1 + 4$ or $5 = 2 + 3$ or $5 = 5 + 0$ or $5 = 6-1$).
Converse with children about addition and subtraction as it arises in play and daily experiences.	*Reflect with children* by pointing out when addition and subtraction arise in play and daily experiences.
What other materials, environmental changes, or grouping strategies might you provide?	*What other support strategies might you try?*

DOMAIN: MATHEMATICS
STRAND: MEASUREMENT

Iowa Early Learning Standards

Area 12: Mathematics and Science (12.6 Measurement)

Standard: Children understand comparisons and measurement.

Benchmark 2: The child makes comparisons between several objects based on one or more attributes, such as length, height, weight, and area, using words such as *taller, shorter, longer, bigger, smaller, heavier, lighter, full, empty, length, height,* and *weight.*

Common Core for Kindergarten

Measurement & Data

  A. Describe and compare measurable attributes

CCSS.Math.Content.K.MD.A.1: Describe measurable attributes of objects, such as length or weight. Describe several measurable attributes of a single object.

≋ Ways This Standard Occurs Naturally as Children Play

EXAMPLES:

Blocks: Children make comparisons related to height, length, and weight (e.g., constructing a tower to a specified height in relation to another object, such as the seat of a chair or up to a child's waist).

Sensory table: Children use measuring cups to add sand to a bowl, noting how many cups are being poured.

Art: Children make collages with items of different lengths and widths (e.g., paper strips, yarn, and ribbons) and items of differing weights (i.e., feathers, twigs, and beads).

- Where else might you see this standard occurring naturally in children's play?
- What other standards might children also demonstrate?

POSSIBLE TEACHER SUPPORT STRATEGIES:

Play alongside children using comparative language.

Model ways to measure and compare different items, lining blocks up next to each other, counting how many cups of sand fill the bowl, feeling the weight of different items in your hands.

Provide scaffolding by giving children the vocabulary words to describe measurable attributes.

What other support strategies might you try?

≋ Ways to Intentionally Plan to Address This Standard in Play Experiences

POSSIBLE MATERIALS, ENVIRONMENTAL CHANGES, OR GROUPING STRATEGIES	TEACHER SUPPORT STRATEGIES
Add a variety of measuring tools to different play areas in the classroom (different kinds of measuring cups, rulers and tape measures, scales).	*Scaffold by assisting children* in figuring out ways to use the tools in their play.
Encourage children to work with a partner and measure items in the classroom with nonstandard tools, such as string, connecting blocks, or their bodies. (Is it as long as your arm? Your finger? Your foot?).	*Challenge* children to measure the room with a partner in the areas where they are playing. Ask how they can keep a record of what they learned as they measured. Help them document their explorations through drawings, photographs, and writing. Make the challenge greater by comparing nonstandard measurement with that done with standard measuring tools.
With the children, measure off and mark indoor and outdoor spaces with tape and label with the appropriate measurement (e.g., 5, 10, 15, 20 feet).	*As a provocation, invite children* to help you measure off and mark spaces. Determine what tools you will use and at what increments you will place the labels. Then encourage children to walk, hop, jump, or run on the measured paths, calling out the measurements as they reach each one.
Recognize when children use comparative language or measurement strategies in play and daily experiences.	*Reflect with children* by commenting on their natural use of comparative language and measurement strategies. Help them do so in appropriate and meaningful ways.
What other materials, environmental changes, or grouping strategies might you provide?	*What other support strategies might you try?*

DOMAIN: MATHEMATICS
STRAND: GEOMETRY AND SPATIAL RELATIONSHIPS

Vermont Early Learning Standards

III Learning about the World

Domain: Mathematics

4. Geometry and Spatial Reasoning

4b. Geometry

1. Children recognize, describe and characterize shapes by their components and properties, compose and decompose geometric shapes, and discuss spatial structures and relations.

Common Core for Kindergarten

Geometry

B. Analyze, compare, create, and compose shapes.

CCSS.Math.Content.K.G.B.4: Analyze and compare two- and three-dimensional shapes, in different sizes and orientations, using informal language to describe their similarities, differences, parts (for example, number of sides and vertices/"corners"), and other attributes (such as having sides of equal length).

≋ Ways This Standard Occurs Naturally as Children Play

EXAMPLES:

Manipulatives: Children create shapes with pattern and connecting blocks and construct shapes in puzzles.

Outdoors: Children recognize shapes in nature and on the playground or fill baskets or tubs with rocks and objects found outdoors.

Writing area: Children draw shapes and letter-like shapes, and if writing letters, they note their shapes.

- Where else might you see this standard occurring naturally in children's play?

- What other standards might children also demonstrate?

POSSIBLE TEACHER SUPPORT STRATEGIES:

Play alongside children, naming shapes in the materials of the play area.

Model comparing shapes, counting the sides, using language about straight lines, angles, rounded edges, and other characteristics.

Provide scaffolding by providing shape names as children attempt to identify them.

What other support strategies might you try?

≈ Ways to Intentionally Plan to Address This Standard in Play Experiences	
POSSIBLE MATERIALS, ENVIRONMENTAL CHANGES, OR GROUPING STRATEGIES	**TEACHER SUPPORT STRATEGIES**
Provide sidewalk chalk and spray bottles with water outdoors and encourage children to create shapes on the pavement.	*Scaffold by assisting children* to create shapes, name them, compare and contrast them, and combine them.
Encourage children to find ways to create different shapes in the block area.	*Challenge children* to figure out how to combine triangles to make a square or squares to make a rectangle; how to create a cube or a rectangular prism.
Encourage children to work with a partner or small group and go on a shape hunt in the classroom.	*As a provocation, invite children* to work with others and search for specific shapes in the classroom. Provide a way of documenting (iPad? Camera? Premade shape list on a clipboard?) and have children share what they found with others.
Converse with children about geometric shapes in their play and daily experiences.	*Reflect with children by* discussing geometric shapes in various play materials and in daily experiences.
What other materials, environmental changes, or grouping strategies might you provide?	*What other support strategies might you try?*

A PLAY STORY FROM A PRESCHOOL CLASSROOM: MATH WHEN LINING UP

Janet's preschool classroom was located in an elementary school building. Unfortunately, the restrooms were down one hallway and the playground down another. Janet needed to help her preschoolers understand how to move in an organized way throughout the school. Therefore, she had to teach them about lining up. She decided to make the most of this necessary task by infusing math learning into the process. Near the children's cubbies, she created a lining-up area with twelve-inch by twelve-inch squares of contact paper, one for each child. Into each square she affixed six different items cut from various colors of construction paper:

- two different numerals (between 1 and 10)
- two different geometric shapes
- two animal figures in different sizes

Initially, she also created a second set of all of the items she affixed in the squares. As she called out children's names to go to the line-up area, she held up one of the items and the child needed to find that item and stand on the appropriate square. She was ready to assist as children learned the placement of the items, but soon no assistance was needed. Children relished the hunt for their item. After some time, she did not show the children the model, but merely said, "Jamal, please go to the red circle. Ayana, please go to the green number 3. Pedro, please go to the large dog. Missy, please go to the medium-sized chicken."

Janet felt the time she spent in transitioning children to getting ready to go down the hallways was well spent. Even as children waited at the squares, they discussed the items there, using mathematical vocabulary and demonstrating mathematical understanding.

What Standards Were Addressed?

- Three of the strands for the domain of mathematics were addressed: Number Sense, Quantity, and Counting; Measurement; and Geometry and Spatial Relationships.
- Language was addressed as children listened, followed directions, and talked with Janet and other children about the items on their squares.
- Social-emotional development was addressed as children demonstrated self-regulation in organizing themselves to leave the classroom.
- Gross-motor development was addressed as children moved themselves to the appropriate squares.

CHAPTER 9

Addressing Science Standards in Play

The domain of science is a vitally important one for our current lives and our future. In education, science and technology are linked in what are called "STEM" initiatives. STEM stands for science, technology, engineering, and mathematics. Some researchers and public and private leaders relate the very future of our country to STEM:

> The nation's capacity to innovate and thrive in the modern workforce depends on a foundation of math and science learning. . . . A sustained, vibrant democracy is dependent upon this foundation in STEM. (Sneiderman 2013, 1)

In 2014 the National Academy of Engineering and the Board on Science Education of the National Research Council released a report about the importance of integrating these disciplines in science education approaches (NAE and NRC 2014).

In early childhood education, STEM is recognized as an important way to look at scientific learning. Young children are scientists at heart. From birth, they explore their world to make sense of it, to find their place in it, to figure out how it works and how to manipulate and make changes to it. In preschool and kindergarten classrooms, children can be exposed to scientific thinking, practices, and basic concepts. Teachers can use the intrinsic motivation of young explorers so that science experiences are filled with learning opportunities that integrate skills from multiple domains.

> The most important thing to remember about teaching STEM to early learners is that they are perfectly adapted to learn STEM concepts. . . . The secret is to tap into their natural and innate curiosity about the living world. By simply allowing them to investigate, by encouraging them to ask questions about the real world, you are engaging children in STEM. (Sneiderman 2013, 1)

For the science domain, we look at early learning standards from a variety of states and the newly developed Next Generation Science Standards for kindergarten (www .nextgenscience.org). The latter are based on recommendations from the National Research Council and developed by stakeholders from a number of states. These standards integrate the four components of STEM and emphasize educational approaches across domains. In this chapter, we use six of the practices from the Next Generation Science Standards to guide our choices of standards. We think that teachers in preschool and kindergarten class-rooms will find young children already engaging in many of these practices as they play:

1. Asking questions and defining problems
2. Developing and using models
3. Planning and carrying out investigations
4. Analyzing and interpreting data
5. Constructing explanations and designing solutions
6. Obtaining, evaluating, and communicating information

We recognize that the domain of science is full of many discrete pieces of knowledge. For example, children learn that birds build nests, that bears hibernate, that gravity causes blocks to fall to the ground, that when heated, water turns to steam, and when frozen, to ice. We also recognize, however, that science is much more than discrete facts. Children already have the core foundational inclinations for scientific inquiry in their innate and seemingly insatiable curiosity, which causes them to ask questions, experiment, make predictions, and draw conclusions. Our emphasis will be to capitalize on these traits of young learners and mesh them with the six practices.

One other point of explanation for the tables in this chapter is needed. The structure of the Next Generation Science Standards is such that the practices are listed as foundational to specific standards in different scientific and engineering areas. As you look at the tables describing science standards in play, you will see that the kindergarten ones from the Next Generation Science Standards address specific content, including the following areas:

- Motion and Stability: Forces and Interactions
- From Molecules to Organisms: Structures and Processes
- Energy
- Engineering Design

As in previous domain chapters, we provide one or two examples of a standard in each of these strands and consider ways to integrate them in child-directed, open-ended play experiences. First, we suggest that you observe children in play throughout your classroom and reflect on your observations related to the specific standard.

Then we offer ideas for intentionally planning to address the standard in these play areas and experiences by adding materials, making changes in the environment, or considering grouping strategies. Throughout, we ask you to consider additional ways that you might observe for, support, and intentionally address the standard. We recognize that each classroom and group of children is different and that your knowledge of your students and setting will be important considerations.

At the end of the chapter, we share a story of how a teacher planned for play with many standards from this domain and others in mind. Realistically, many standards are integrated in children's play experiences. It's impossible to address only one standard at a time in play. That is why it is such a rich and exciting curricular approach for preschool and kindergarten children. We encourage you to read through our specific examples in the tables on the next pages, think about your classroom and group of children, and come up with your own ideas. We also suggest that you look at the ways children demonstrate multiple standards from a variety of domains when teachers plan for integrated play activities such as the one shared at the end of the chapter.

DOMAIN: SCIENCE
PRACTICE: ASKING QUESTIONS (FOR SCIENCE) AND DEFINING PROBLEMS (FOR ENGINEERING) AND PLANNING AND CARRYING OUT INVESTIGATIONS

Arizona Early Learning Standards

Science Standard for Young Children from Three to Five Years Old, Strand 1: Inquiry and Application

Concept 1: Exploration, Observations, and Hypotheses

The child asks questions and makes predictions while exploring and observing in the environment.

Next Generation Science Standards for Kindergarten

Motion and Stability: Forces and Interaction

- K-PS2-1. Plan and conduct an investigation to compare the effects of different strengths or different directions of pushes and pulls on the motion of an object.
- K-PS2-2. Analyze data to determine if a design solution works as intended to change the speed or direction of an object with a push or a pull.

≈ Ways This Standard Occurs Naturally as Children Play

EXAMPLES:

Blocks: Children explore and observe as they make structures and build ramps, asking questions, identifying problems, and making predictions as they construct.

Outdoors: Children observe swings going back and forth, teeter-totters going up and down, and other aspects of force and motion as they run, jump, climb, and play.

Manipulatives: Children try out different ways to use manipulatives (creating a marble run, connecting Legos into a tall tower that stands, interlocking gears so they turn).

- Where else might you see this standard occurring naturally in children's play?
- What other standards might children also demonstrate?

(cont.)

POSSIBLE TEACHER SUPPORT STRATEGIES:

Play alongside children and encourage observing, questioning, and hypothesizing.

Model wondering aloud about what will happen if . . . and trying it out to see the result.

Provide scaffolding by assisting children as they set up ways to test out their own hypotheses.

What other support strategies might you try?

≈ Ways to Intentionally Plan to Address This Standard in Play Experiences

POSSIBLE MATERIALS, ENVIRONMENTAL CHANGES, OR GROUPING STRATEGIES	TEACHER SUPPORT STRATEGIES
Record children's questions and hypotheses as they explore pushes and pulls as well as other scientific concepts in their play.	*Scaffold by assisting children* as they state their questions and determine what they must do to observe and predict. Record through audio or video or written documentation.
Provide a space and materials for investigation of pushing and pulling objects. Invite children to use different sized blocks to push objects. Provide a variety of ropes, elastic bands, fabrics, and string for pulling objects.	*Challenge* children to plan and conduct an investigation comparing the strength of different tools to push and pull a variety of objects.
Suggest that children work in teams of 2–3 to create ramps and roll a variety of items at different inclines, noting the speed and distance rolled.	*As a provocation, invite children* to compare the differences between inclines as well as between objects rolled.
Encourage children to record the results of their investigations through photographs, videotapes, drawings, and written documentation.	*Reflect with children by helping them record the results of their investigations in whatever way is most appropriate for them.* Encourage sharing recorded results with the large group.
What other materials, environmental changes, or grouping strategies might you provide?	*What other support strategies might you try?*

DOMAIN: SCIENCE
STRAND: ANALYZING AND INTERPRETING DATA

Maine's Early Learning and Development Standards

Standards for Science: Life Science

Observes and describes animals in his/her immediate environment to learn what they need to live

Next Generation Science Standards for Kindergarten

From Molecules to Organisms: Structures and Processes

- K-LS1-1. Use observations to describe patterns of what plants and animals (including humans) need to survive.
- K-ESS3-1. Use a model to represent the relationship between the needs of different plants and animals (including humans) and the places they live.

≋ Ways This Standard Occurs Naturally as Children Play

EXAMPLES:

Science area: Children observe, care for, and play with classroom pets.

Class library: Children look at, read, and listen to nonfiction books about animals.

Dramatic play: Children pretend to be animals, relating accurate information about what animals actually need to live.

- Where else might you see this standard occurring naturally in children's play?
- What other standards might children also demonstrate?

POSSIBLE TEACHER SUPPORT STRATEGIES:

Play alongside children, describing traits of animals and their needs.

Model ways to get more information about animals by turning to books or online research.

Provide scaffolding by assisting children in accurately representing animal traits and needs in their play.

What other support strategies might you try?

Ways to Intentionally Plan to Address This Standard in Play Experiences

POSSIBLE MATERIALS, ENVIRONMENTAL CHANGES, OR GROUPING STRATEGIES	TEACHER SUPPORT STRATEGIES
Provide animal figures in the blocks and manipulatives areas. Include a variety of land and sea animals as well as birds and insects.	*Scaffold by assisting children* as they play with the figures to identify animals by name, comparing habitats and what they need to live.
Organize a special library area with books, posters, magazines, and online sources for investigating plants and animals.	*Challenge* children to learn more about the traits and needs of classroom and family pets, of animals seen on the playground and in other places in the local community.
Invite children to help grow and tend to plants in a classroom garden (indoors or outdoors).	*As a provocation, invite children* to figure out what plants need to grow and compare that with the needs of animals and themselves.
Encourage children to write stories or act out plays about plants and animals and their needs.	*Reflect with children* by having them share their stories or perform their plays.
What other materials, environmental changes, or grouping strategies might you provide?	*What other support strategies might you try?*

DOMAIN: SCIENCE
STRAND: CONSTRUCTING EXPLANATIONS AND DESIGNING SOLUTIONS

Montana Early Learning Standards 2014

Core Domain 4: Cognition

Subdomain: Science

Physical Science Standard 4.17: Children develop an understanding of the physical world (the nature and properties of energy, nonliving matter and the forces that give order to the natural world).

Next Generation Science Standards for Kindergarten

Energy

K-PS3-2. Use tools and materials provided to design and build a structure that will reduce the warming effect of sunlight on Earth's surface.

≋ Ways This Standard Occurs Naturally as Children Play

EXAMPLES:

Outdoors: Children observe the properties of the sun, wind, and other physical phenomena as they play.

Science area: Children investigate heat from a sunny window or a heat lamp.

Sensory table: Children experiment with the force of water as they pour water on various objects.

- Where else might you see this standard occurring naturally in children's play?
- What other standards might children also demonstrate?

POSSIBLE TEACHER SUPPORT STRATEGIES:

Play alongside children, making comments about the nature and properties of energy (light, sound, force).

Model ways to investigate energy, such as feeling the warmth of the sunlight or the force of the wind or observing the force of water.

Provide scaffolding by helping children recognize the effects of energy and forces around them.

What other support strategies might you try?

≋ Ways to Intentionally Plan to Address This Standard in Play Experiences

POSSIBLE MATERIALS, ENVIRONMENTAL CHANGES, OR GROUPING STRATEGIES	TEACHER SUPPORT STRATEGIES
Provide streamers (crepe paper, fabric strips) to play with outdoors on a windy day.	*Scaffold by assisting children* to observe the effects of the wind on their streamers, trying different positions and locations on the playground.
Provide waterwheels and different sized cups and pitchers in the sensory table or in a tub outdoors.	*Challenge* children to figure out ways to increase and decrease the force of water on the waterwheel.
Invite small groups of children to create structures that reduce the effect of heat or light from a source (the sun, a heat lamp).	*As a provocation, invite children* to reduce the effect of heat or light from a source. Provide materials such as fabrics, tents, or umbrellas. Be nearby for safety monitoring and guidance.
Converse with children about the nature and properties of energy and forces in the world.	*Reflect with children* by recognizing when the effects of energy or the results of forces are evident.
What other materials, environmental changes, or grouping strategies might you provide?	*What other support strategies might you try?*

DOMAIN: SCIENCE
STRANDS: DEVELOPING AND USING MODELS AND OBTAINING, EVALUATING, AND COMMUNICATING INFORMATION

Revised Tennessee Early Learning Developmental Standards

Science: Scientific Thinking

S.PK.3. Record and organize data using graphs, charts, science journals, etc., to communicate conclusions regarding experiments and explorations.

Next Generation Science Standards for Kindergarten

Engineering Design

K-2-ETS1-2. Develop a simple sketch, drawing, or physical model to illustrate how the shape of an object helps it function as needed to solve a given problem.

≋ Ways This Standard Occurs Naturally as Children Play

EXAMPLES:

Writing area: Children draw and write about observations from their explorations and investigations.

Art area: Children create models and drawings to illustrate results of an experiment or exploration.

Music area: Children explore the sounds of various instruments and represent the differences through mimicking or verbal description.

- Where else might you see this standard occurring naturally in children's play?
- What other standards might children also demonstrate?

POSSIBLE TEACHER SUPPORT STRATEGIES:

Play alongside children and converse about ways to record and organize data and conclusions.

Model making charts, graphs, sketches, drawings, or models to document results of investigations.

Provide scaffolding by helping children choose and create a method for documenting their findings.

What other support strategies might you try?

Ways to Intentionally Plan to Address This Standard in Play Experiences

POSSIBLE MATERIALS, ENVIRONMENTAL CHANGES, OR GROUPING STRATEGIES	TEACHER SUPPORT STRATEGIES
Provide writing and drawing materials and paper, clipboards, and prestapled blank journals for children in all play areas.	*Scaffold by assisting children* to figure out ways to document their observations and explorations.
Provide playdough, clay, paints, and diorama materials for model making.	*Challenge children* to create three-dimensional models to document their observations (e.g., make a smaller copy of a bridge constructed in blocks; paint pictures of a plant's growth from a seed over time).
Invite small groups of children to explore the ways that musical instruments produce sound.	*As a provocation, invite children* to sort, categorize, and graph the differences in production (categories might include instruments that are struck or pounded, those that are plucked, those that are shaken, those that require air to be blown through them). Graphs can be floor graphs on which instruments are organized, or they can be written or drawn on charts or papers.
Encourage children to revisit their documentation of observations over time.	*Reflect with children* by reviewing their documented observations. Have they learned anything new? Would they add something different? Could they represent their learning in a different way?
What other materials, environmental changes, or grouping strategies might you provide?	*What other support strategies might you try?*

A PLAY STORY FROM A KINDERGARTEN CLASSROOM:

Pete noticed that his kindergartners were showing a lot of interest in setting up the tubes for the marble run in such a way that the marbles gained speed as they rolled down the inclines. He began to interact with the children who were especially engaged, discussing the angles at which they were setting up the inclines and

encouraging them to observe what was happening as the angles were steepened. The initial group of interested students got very excited as they began to predict successfully which angles produced more speed. Their excitement led to more children showing interest. Pete and his coteacher decided to engage the children in a full-blown study of inclined planes. Initially, they provided more materials for building ramps. Luckily, his classroom sat next to an isolated hallway in the building where large materials could be set out for

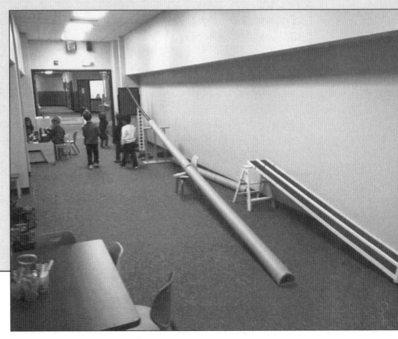

EXPLORING INCLINED PLANES

exploration. Children set up inclined planes and ramps with the plastic marble runs, long cardboard tubes, and long wooden planks. First they used the various materials in isolation. Then they figured out that they could combine them. They rolled different types of balls and vehicles down the ramps and measured distances and speeds with their teachers' assistance. They went on explorations around the school building, looking for inclined planes in their environment and found ramps that connected one level of the building with another. They created inclined planes in snowbanks outdoors and rolled snowballs down the icy surfaces. Pete and his colleague photographed children's investigations and encouraged children to write about their experiences, creating bulletin board displays, class books, and individual science journals. The study went on for weeks as children continued to explore ways to increase speed and distance with a variety of materials.

What Standards Were Addressed?

The following scientific practices were incorporated into the study of inclined planes:

- asking questions (for science) and defining problems (for engineering)
- developing and using models
- planning and carrying out investigations
- analyzing and interpreting data
- constructing explanations (for science) and designing solutions (for engineering)
- obtaining, evaluating, and communicating information

In addition, in their study of inclined planes, children explored the scientific concepts of motion, gravity, and force and the following standards from other domains:

- geometry and spatial relationships as children built the ramps and measured both speed and distance
- vocabulary development as they conversed while working together
- emerging writing skills as they documented their observations
- a variety of approaches to learning as they showed curiosity and initiative, problem solving, and persistence

CHAPTER 10

Addressing Social Studies Standards in Play

Social studies is a broad domain that encompasses areas such as geography, history, economics, political science, anthropology, sociology, ecology, and transportation. It is not surprising that state and national standards for preschool and kindergarten that relate to social studies follow varying approaches. Take the study of culture, for example. Some sets of social studies standards cluster communities and culture as part of a general understanding of the individual and his role in society. Others put it with history. Still others place culture under geography. The idea of the individual living in community is a category in and of itself in Montana's Early Learning Standards, beginning with the community all children know first and best: the family. But Maryland's Early Learning Standards emphasize the need to learn the importance of rules and controlling mechanisms within communities, paving the way to a foundational knowledge of political science and governance.

These approaches are neither right nor wrong. Rather, they are testimony to how broad the study of humans and society is. It seems appropriate at this time to remember that all standards are unique expressions of cultures and communities and what they value and want to pass along to the children of that community and culture.

So just what does the domain of social studies consist of in the early childhood years? Educational philosopher John Dewey thought social studies should be the foundation for activity-based learning that followed children's initiative and interest (Mindes 2005). Where we see social studies ideas first presented to young children is as part of "background knowledge," a key part of vocabulary and comprehension in early literacy. Education scholar Robert Marzano writes, "Researchers and theorists refer to what a person already knows about a topic as 'background knowledge'" (Marzano 2004). It is the "already knows" part that makes it both important for future learning and yet perhaps confusing for teachers. The more children know, the more they are able to know.

A recent study found that students from lower-income backgrounds who often do worse academically than their middle-income peers also, as a result, seem to have lower vocabulary and comprehension skills (Kaefer, Neumann, and Pinkham 2015). This is one reason why children who come from conditions of poverty begin from a deficit position. Our point here is simply to show that background knowledge is incredibly important, and the social studies content area intended for the preschool and kindergarten levels is largely learned by the children simply from living in society.

But how does one teach knowledge that children are supposed to "already know"? Simply put, the role of the teacher is to expand background knowledge with many rich and varied experiences and thus enhance children's vocabulary so that they can describe their experiences. Given the broadness of the social studies subject area and its connection to many experiences that are part of the daily life of young children, we are not including all of the possible topics for this domain. And we may not organize the ones we do address in the way some states do. In fact, some early learning standards do not even identify a "social studies" domain. We have selected four broad strands from a number of state and national standards:

- Geography
- History
- Community, Civics, and Government
- Economics

We will look at these strands with the young learner in mind. This will not involve children memorizing world capitals or examining charts about varying economic systems. Rather, it will focus on the foundational skills necessary so that children will come to understand more about the world and be ready to learn the many topics of social studies in their later schooling. Let's consider each strand in more detail:

- **Geography** is about understanding our place in the world, both within human or social space (community) and physical space (where am I?). It begins with the notions of people living, working, and playing together. Young children are most familiar with the family; then they learn more about their classroom and school, and then the town or city where they live. Geography also is about location, which is why it is helpful for preschoolers and kindergartners to be introduced to maps. Maps are how geographers explain the world.
- **History** is about how things change over time. For young children, history may begin with what they did yesterday. They can also learn more about their own history and that of their family (what I did as a baby; what my dad or mom did as a child). These topics are more meaningful when children think about both the past and the present. Was my day yesterday like today? If not, how was it different? Were my dad's favorite games like mine or different? This skill of comparing and contrasting can also be found in science and mathematics standards.

- The strand of **Community, Civics, and Government** is about human relations. For young children, the nuts and bolts of human relations are about how to make friends, get along with others, and follow basic rules to function in a community of learners. In this chapter, the focus is helping children understand who they are in the context of the wider world. It includes the conventions of community living, such as roles and functions of individuals in a community. It also includes how communities are structured and their patterns of relationships. In the words of HighScope, it is about moving from me to we (Neill 2015).
- **Economics** begins with wants and needs, and the allocation of scarce resources. When two children want the same toy, the knowledge or skills needed to resolve the problem may include learning how to share, which is a topic that is usually found in the social-emotional domain. In the social studies domain, the topic is about understanding sharing as a necessary skill to maintain social equilibrium because there is rarely enough of any desired object for everyone to get what they want immediately. The topic also includes understanding what a "want" is in the first place and how it is different from a need. Such topics are never far away from the daily experiences of young children.

In this chapter, we provide one example of a standard in each of these strands and consider ways to integrate it in child-directed, open-ended play experiences. First, we suggest that you observe children in play throughout your classroom and reflect on your observations related to the specific standard.

In addition, we offer ideas for intentionally planning to address the standard in these play areas and experiences by adding materials, making changes in the environment, or considering grouping strategies. Throughout, we ask you to consider additional ways you might observe for, support, and intentionally address the standard. We recognize that each classroom and group of children is different and that your knowledge of your students and setting will be important considerations.

At the end of the chapter, we share a story of how a teacher planned for play with many standards from this domain and others in mind. Realistically, many standards are integrated in children's play experiences. It's impossible to address only one standard at a time in play, which is why it is such a rich and exciting curricular approach for preschool and kindergarten children. We encourage you to read through our specific examples in the tables on the next pages, think about your classroom and group of children, and come up with your own ideas. We also suggest that you look at the ways children demonstrate multiple standards from a variety of domains when teachers plan for integrated play activities such as the one shared at the end of the chapter.

DOMAIN: SOCIAL STUDIES
STRAND: GEOGRAPHY

Colorado Preschool Social Studies Academic Standards: 2. Geography

Prepared Graduates: Develop spatial understanding, perspectives, and personal connections to the world.

Evidence Outcomes:

a. Use positional phrasing. Phrases to include but not limited to: "over and under," "here and there," "inside and outside," "up and down"

b. Identify common places to include but limited to home, school, cafeteria, and gymnasium

c. Describe surroundings

d. Use pictures to locate familiar places

e. Use nonlinguistic representations to show understanding of geographic terms

North Carolina Essential Standards: Kindergarten Social Studies

Geography and Environmental Literacy

Essential Standard: K.G.1: Use geographic representations and terms to describe surroundings

Clarifying Objectives:

- K.G.1.1 Use maps to locate places in the classroom, school and home
- K.G.1.2 Use globes and maps to locate land and water features
- K.G.1.3 Identify physical features (mountains, hills, rivers, lakes, roads, etc.)
- K.G.1.4 Identify locations in the classroom using positional words (*near/far*, *left/right*, *above/beneath*, etc.)
- K.G.1.1 Use maps to locate places in the classroom, school and home

---

≈ Ways This Standard Occurs Naturally as Children Play

EXAMPLES:

Block area: As children build with blocks, they talk about block positions in terms of *over* or *under*, *up* or *down*, or other positional vocabulary.

Sensory: Children play with water and sand together, creating ponds, lakes, streams, rivers, islands, and other features.

Dramatic play: Children enact scenarios with a specific geographic setting, such as pretending to be in a boat on the sea, hiking in the mountains or desert, or swimming at a beach.

- Where else might you see this standard occurring naturally in children's play?
- What other standards might children also demonstrate?

(cont.)

≋ Ways to Intentionally Plan to Address This Standard in Play Experiences

POSSIBLE MATERIALS, ENVIRONMENTAL CHANGES, OR GROUPING STRATEGIES	TEACHER SUPPORT STRATEGIES
Create a geography play area that includes maps, puzzle maps, globes, and photographs or books that feature mountains, rivers, oceans, roads, cities, and towns, along with art, playdough, and writing materials so children can describe nonverbally what they are learning.	*Scaffold* by helping children find places on the globe or supporting their efforts to represent locations or geographic features in maps, drawings, or playdough.
Add books to the library area that feature geographic terms and prepositions (e.g., *Rosie's Walk* by Pat Hutchins or *Where Am I Hiding?/¿Dónde me escondo?* by Pamela Zagarenski).	*Challenge* children to act out the positional descriptions (such as crawling under a table; standing up and sitting down, standing next to or behind).
Play a hide-and-seek game, but use a map to help identify where children or objects are hidden.	*As a provocation, invite children* to use a map to show where they are going to hide. Begin with a generic map of the classroom that children can draw on. Later let them draw the entire map themselves.
Ask children to bring in an object that represents a favorite place.	*Reflect with children* about the object and the place it represents: 1. Where is this place located? 2. What is the connection between the object and the place? 3. Why is this a "favorite" place?
What other materials, environmental changes, or grouping strategies might you provide?	*What other support strategies might you try?*

DOMAIN: SOCIAL STUDIES
STRAND: HISTORY

Virginia's Foundation Blocks for Early Learning: Comprehensive Standards for Four-Year-Olds

Virginia History and Social Science: Foundation Block 2

History/Change Over Time

The child will develop an awareness of change over time.
Young children become aware of time through events specific to themselves and to people in their immediate surroundings. Begin the focus with the child's own history, then when grandparents were children, and then to periods beyond living memory.

   a. Describe ways children have changed since they were babies.
   b. Express the difference between past and present using words such as *before, after, now,* and *then.*
   c. Order/sequence events and objects.
   d. Ask questions about artifacts from everyday life in the past.
   e. Recount episodes from stories about the past.
   f. Take on a role from a specific time, use symbols and props, and act out a story/narrative.
   g. Describe past times based on stories, pictures, visits, songs, and music.

Michigan—Grade Level Content Expectations: Social Studies. Kindergarten

History: Living and Working Together

Use historical thinking to understand the past.

   K – H2.0.1 Distinguish among yesterday, today, tomorrow.
   K – H2.0.2 Create a timeline using events from their own lives (e.g., birth, crawling, walking, loss of first tooth, first day of school).
   K – H2.0.3 Identify the beginning, middle, and end of historical narratives or stories.
   K – H2.0.4 Describe ways people learn about the past (e.g., photos, artifacts, diaries, stories, videos).

≋ Ways This Standard Occurs Naturally as Children Play

EXAMPLES:

Sensory table: Children uncover "fossils" buried in the sand and talk about them as objects from the past.

Library: After reading a story, children relate to memories of events in their past.

Art center: Children draw and paint about past events in their lives ("This is when we went to the zoo." "This is me when I was a baby").

- Where else might you see this standard occurring naturally in children's play?
- What other standards might children also demonstrate?

POSSIBLE TEACHER SUPPORT STRATEGIES:

Play alongside children and ask whether they have ever done previously what they are currently doing. Ask them when it was and how that experience was. Finally, ask how it was the same or different from their experiences doing it now.

Model talking about a past experience.

Provide scaffolding by assisting children with the language of sequencing and actions in the past. You might say, "So what happened first?" "Then what happened?"

What other support strategies might you try?

Ways to Intentionally Plan to Address This Standard in Play Experiences

POSSIBLE MATERIALS, ENVIRONMENTAL CHANGES, OR GROUPING STRATEGIES	TEACHER SUPPORT STRATEGIES
Add a wall calendar or a desk calendar with tear-off sheets for each day. Add a calendar to the dramatic play area so that children can use it to make appointments. In the math center, they can talk about what days come first and after one another.	*Scaffold* by plotting out on the calendars important dates, such as a birthday or holiday, and show how soon or far off it is from today by circling today's date and the important date.
Using children's baby pictures, laminate and turn into playing cards. Play a variety of matching and sorting games.	*Challenge* children by adding a second "deck" of cards with pictures of the children as they are today. Add more mix-and-match challenges.
Put some older artifacts in the science center. These could be old bones, antiques, or any other objects from the past. Talk about how long ago this was used and how it was used. Use older family members as reference ("When your grandma was a little girl, she used a hand beater to mix eggs").	*As a provocation, include a similar modern-day object.* Invite children to compare and contrast the two items as they play in the center.
Encourage children to engage in birthday party play and consider the different ways families celebrate birthdays.	*Reflect with children* about how old they are. Discuss past birthday celebrations in their families. Ask what they know from their parents about when they were babies.
What other materials, environmental changes, or grouping strategies might you provide?	*What other support strategies might you try?*

DOMAIN: SOCIAL STUDIES
STRAND: COMMUNITY, CIVICS, AND GOVERNMENT

Montana Early Learning Standards

Core Domain 1: Emotional/Social

Subdomain: Community

Standard 1.3—Community: Children develop an understanding of the basic principles of how communities function, including work roles and commerce.

- Watch other children
- Interact with other children
- Participate in parallel play next to another child
- Recognize and use the names of peers
- Play the role of different family or community members
- Demonstrate a beginning awareness of money and commerce
- Recognize community workers and describe their jobs
- Demonstrate community-building skills
- Describe what she wants to be when grown up

New Mexico Social Studies Standards: Grades K–4

Content Standard III: Students understand the ideals, rights, and responsibilities of citizenship and understand the content and history of the founding documents of the United States with particular emphasis on the United States and New Mexico constitutions and how governments function at local, state, tribal, and national levels.

K–4 Benchmark III-A: Know the fundamental purposes, concepts, structures, and functions of local, state, tribal, and national governments.

K 1. Identify authority figures and describe their roles (e.g., parents, teachers, principal, superintendent, police, public officials).

EXAMPLES:

Outdoor play: As children play a bouncing ball game, they take specific roles and follow rules.

Sensory table: Children are working together to accomplish a task, such as one pouring and the other holding the container. Or children are making a town or cityscape as they move sand around with a front-loader or dump trucks.

Manipulatives: Children play with small toy fire trucks, police cars, cement mixers, ambulances, tow trucks, and utility or moving vans and complete puzzles of various community helpers and authority figures.

- Where else might you see this standard occurring naturally in children's play?
- What other standards might children also demonstrate?

POSSIBLE TEACHER SUPPORT STRATEGIES:

Play alongside children and connect what they are doing with possible adult careers. (If the child is painting, discuss the work of artists; if building with blocks, talk about architects, engineers, and construction workers; if kicking a ball, talk about different kinds of athletes and coaches; if exploring in the science area, talk about the work of scientists and researchers.)

Model ways to create a sense of community in the classroom such as using children's names when playing together, clarifying rules and following them, and playing cooperatively.

Provide scaffolding by supporting children in being respectful, listening, helping each other, and playing cooperatively.

What other support strategies might you try?

Ways to Intentionally Plan to Address This Standard in Play Experiences

POSSIBLE MATERIALS, ENVIRONMENTAL CHANGES, OR GROUPING STRATEGIES	TEACHER SUPPORT STRATEGIES
Before center time, engage the children in a conversation about how to make playtime more fun for the whole class. Solicit ideas and then ask different children what they think of those ideas.	*Scaffold the conversation* by inviting conversations and suggestions about how to improve the play areas. Try to help the children make collaborative decisions together. Revisit the topic on a regular basis.
Add a variety of hats. Encourage children to use them to identify what role they want to play in the scenario. For example, include the hat of a firefighter, a policeman or policewoman, a chef, a professor (mortar board), an artist (a beret), and a nurse (a nurse's cap).	*Challenge children* by asking them to select a hat, discussing different aspects of that particular job, and engaging with them in role plays with those details in mind.
With the children, play cooperative games, such as adapted musical chairs (where children have to figure out how to make room for all the children to sit down with fewer chairs than children), working together to keep a balloon in the air, or making a human pretzel by randomly grabbing hands and trying to get untangled (unclasping hands is permitted).	*As a provocation,* remove one chair with each round, keep the balloon aloft only by blowing on it, or get untangled without letting go of each other's hands.
End play experiences with the established expectation that all children need to put away things. Make the focus on working together to make sure everything is cleaned up so that those who are done early help those who are not yet finished.	*Reflect with children* about how it feels to have the room tidy, and how working together makes the task go more quickly.
What other materials, environmental changes, or grouping strategies might you provide?	*What other support strategies might you try?*

DOMAIN: SOCIAL STUDIES
STRAND: ECONOMICS

Maryland Early Learning Standards: Birth–8 Years

Economics Standard: Students will identify the economic principles and processes that are helpful to producers and consumers when making good decisions

A. Scarcity and Economic Decision Making (4 Years)

1. Recognize that people have to make choices because of unlimited economic wants.
2. Identify that materials/resources are used to make products.
3. Explain how technology affects the way people live, work, and play.

Oregon Social Sciences Academic Content Standards (Kindergarten)

Economics/Financial Literacy

K.15. Identify various forms of money and explain how money is used.

K.16. Give examples of different jobs performed in neighborhoods.

K.17. Identify examples of ownership of different items, recognizing the difference between private and public ownership, and the need for sharing.

K.18. Explain how jobs provide income.

K.19. Distinguish between wants and needs.

≈ Ways This Standard Occurs Naturally as Children Play

EXAMPLES:

Manipulatives: Children are sorting coins by their proper denomination.

Outdoors: Children are faced with playing one or two things during playtime. Some activities have a line, like sliding down the slide or waiting a turn to kick a ball. Children make decisions about what to do given limited time and limited opportunity to play at certain activities.

Writing area: Children use receipts or invoice blanks to write up orders or document a transaction.

- Where else might you see this standard occurring naturally in children's play?
- What other standards might children also demonstrate?

(cont.)

POSSIBLE TEACHER SUPPORT STRATEGIES:

Play alongside children and ask if there are enough items to play with should another child want to join.

Model questioning how common objects they play with are made. If there is sufficient curiosity, show a Mister Rogers factory tour video. (Many are available on YouTube.)

Provide scaffolding by assisting children to understand the difference between wants and needs as they express the desire for something.

What other support strategies might you try?

Ways to Intentionally Plan to Address This Standard in Play Experiences

POSSIBLE MATERIALS, ENVIRONMENTAL CHANGES, OR GROUPING STRATEGIES	TEACHER SUPPORT STRATEGIES
Add play money (bills and coins), wallets and purses, blank checks, and pretend credit/debit cards to the dramatic play area. Incorporate the exchange of money as part of the roles families play. For example, if a plumber visits the house to pretend to fix the sink, pay her for her services.	*Scaffold* by assisting children in thinking about ways their families deal with cash, checks, or credit/debit cards in their lives.
Set up a dramatic play area as a store (grocery, shoes, garden shop). Add a toy cash register and play money, credit cards, checks, and receipts.	*Challenge children* to consider the various workers and jobs in different kinds of stores and to engage in dramatic play that reflects those roles accurately.
In the art area, provide models and materials so children can make their own money (bills and coins).	*As a provocation, invite children* to add some common features to their money, such as a picture of a person, numerals to match the denomination, seals, and other symbols.
Have children cut out pictures of objects in old magazines. Then ask them to glue them on a sheet of paper divided into "wants" and "needs."	*Reflect with children* about what makes something a want or a need (wants are things we would like to have; needs are things we must have to live). An example children understand is we need to drink water, but we *want* to drink soda.
What changes or grouping strategies might you provide?	*What other support strategies might you try?*

A PLAY STORY FROM A PRESCHOOL CLASSROOM: THE LAUNDROMAT PROJECT

Claire is a preschool teacher with a fervent dedication to "the project approach" (Chard 1994). She read aloud the popular children's story *A Pocket for Corduroy*, by Don Freeman, to her three- and four-year-olds. This story is about a lovable teddy bear named Corduroy who waits on a department store shelf until he is purchased and becomes the friend of a little girl. After Claire finished reading, her children had questions. They pointed out that during the story, Corduroy is washed in a washing machine at a Laundromat. They wanted to know what that was. Claire's classroom is in a rural community, and the children had never seen a Laundromat.

Claire recognized that she could expand the children's background knowledge by following up on their questions. She decided to organize a project investigation. For two weeks the class worked together to learn more about Laundromats. They took a field trip to one in a nearby town. They helped their teacher put clothes into a washing machine, add soap, load coins, and turn it on. They placed the wet clothes in wheeled carts and moved them to a dryer. They watched the clothes spinning around and around in the dryer, just like they had read about in the book. They saw how shirts could be placed on hangers and hung on the bar over the cart. They made comparisons to the ways their families washed and dried clothes at home and documented what they learned by drawing pictures and taking "notes" on clipboards. They also altered their play area back in the classroom to include coin-operated washing machines and dryers, as well as carts with hangers.

Claire and the children also talked about department stores and big cities. They located New York City on the globe and looked at photographs of Manhattan. They built skyscrapers and bridges in the block area based on their investigations. They created their own department store and "bought" and "sold" stuffed animals and other items from the classroom. The project went on for several weeks with much rich, engaged, child-directed and open-ended play. Claire realized she was addressing many of her state's early learning standards related to social studies and other domains.

What Standards Were Addressed?

- book knowledge by reading and attending to a story
- questioning skills
- oral communication skills as the children asked and answered their questions about *A Pocket for Corduroy*
- economics concepts such as the use of money in the Laundromat
- fine-motor skills by buttoning shirts
- writing skills by taking notes
- art skills by drawing pictures of the Laundromat
- science knowledge about movement as they wheeled around the cart
- geographic understanding of locations and cities and use of maps and globes

CHAPTER 11

Addressing Physical and Motor Development Standards in Play

Does anyone doubt that play can help children develop their physical skills? We assume not, but we want to consider more deeply all of the potential for fine- and gross-motor development that can be connected with child-directed, open-ended play. Compared to the high-stakes academic skills that are the cause of so much anxiety in schools, the need for children to master physical skills can sometimes seem "unnecessary." In fact, physical development is an important domain that needs attention in preschools and kindergartens. Children *do* need to be taught how to use their small muscles to accomplish fine-motor tasks, and how to use their large muscles to move, be fit, and exercise.

With childhood obesity at historically high rates, the role of educators in child care centers, preschools, and elementary schools in responding to this crisis is increasingly important (Harvard T. H. Chan School of Public Health 2016). The American Academy of Pediatrics has published position statements addressing the need for children to engage in active, physical play (Ginsburg 2007). Physical education is undergoing something of a revolution with more and more physical education teachers focusing on opportunities to increase children's moderate to vigorous activity levels as opposed to only emphasizing sports. Now the focus is on creating healthy activity and eating behaviors early in life so that they become lifelong habits.

National health experts are telling us that children need to be more active (www.cdc.gov /healthyschools/npao/strategies.htm). The Centers for Disease Control and Prevention, for example, recommends that all children get at least sixty minutes of physical activity every day (www.cdc.gov/physicalactivity/basics/children). That recommendation is echoed in the standards from the National Association of Sport and Physical Education and in the Nutrition and Physical Activity Self-Assessment for Child Care instrument (SHAPE 2009; https://gonapsacc.org). It is important for educators to recognize that even during recess (a time often viewed as nothing more than free time), children can have many opportunities to build not only their motor skills but also their social and language skills and meet the sixty-minute recommendation.

The motor or movement standards push children in other directions besides just being active. Young children are especially primed to learn movement skills because their brains and bodies are developing so rapidly. The standards identify skill areas such as coordination, balance, spatial and body awareness, physical fitness, and overall health awareness. Fine-motor skills, which involve manipulating and moving small objects with fingers and hands are also addressed. Fine-motor skills are essential for such tasks as putting on and taking off clothes, buttoning and zipping, or tying shoelaces. They are also important to school readiness skills. Children use fine-motor skills when they hold a pencil or marker to draw and write, and use scissors, hole punchers, and other tools. Play experiences can offer many opportunities to practice and master both gross- and fine-motor skills.

In state and national standards concerning physical motor development for preschoolers and kindergartners, there seem to be four common strands:

- Motor/Movement Skills—Gross
- Motor/Movement Skills—Fine
- Health and Well-Being
- Active Physical Play: Active Participation, Cardiovascular and Muscular Endurance, Muscular Strength, and Flexibility

The first and last strands may seem similar, but we want to emphasize a clear distinction between the two. On one hand, gross-motor development emphasizes moving large muscles in particular ways, such as climbing, running, hopping, and throwing, kicking, bouncing, and catching balls. The focus is on balance, coordination, and control in doing these activities. On the other hand, Active Physical Play (we pulled this descriptor from California's Foundations and will use it later in the chapter) is about the clear and consistent engagement in vigorous activities so that they can be considered aerobic exercise and contribute to cardiovascular health and the strengthening of muscles and bones. Both are important, but it seems that some standards have emphasized the importance of regular participation and engagement in highly physical activity because it has started to disappear from the lives of young children. The implication is that even though physical activity can be addressed through play it may require some teacher initiation and promotion (Brown et al. 2009).

Teachers and administrators should also be aware of how much their own attitudes toward physical exercise may be coloring their view of these standards. Perhaps we do not exercise as much as we want or have never been very good at sports, so we begin to undervalue the importance of exercise for children. Our professional responsibility as teachers and administrators is to ensure we address all the standards for all the children.

For each strand in the preceding list, this chapter includes sample standards for both preschool and kindergarten. For each strand, we also consider ways to integrate it in child-directed, open-ended play experiences. First, we suggest that you observe children in play throughout your classroom and reflect on your observations related to the physical and motor development standard.

Then, we offer ideas for intentionally planning to address the standard in these play areas and experiences by adding materials, making changes in the environment, or considering grouping strategies. Throughout, we ask you to consider additional ways you might observe for, support, and intentionally address the standard. We recognize that each classroom and group of children is different and that your knowledge of your students and setting will be important considerations.

At the end of the chapter, we share a story of how a teacher planned for play with many standards from this domain and others in mind. Realistically, many standards are integrated in children's play experiences. It's impossible to address only one standard at a time in play, which is why it is such a rich and exciting curricular approach for preschool and kindergarten children. We encourage you to read through our specific examples in the tables on the next pages, think about your classroom and group of children, and come up with your own ideas. We also suggest that you look at the ways children demonstrate multiple standards from a variety of domains when teachers plan for integrated play activities like the one shared at the end of the chapter.

DOMAIN: PHYSICAL AND MOTOR DEVELOPMENT
STRAND: MOTOR/MOVEMENT SKILLS—GROSS

Ohio Early Learning and Development Standards: Birth to Kindergarten Entry

Domain: Physical Well-Being and Motor Development

Strand: Large Muscle: Balance and Coordination

Standards:

- Demonstrate locomotor skills with control, coordination, and balance during active play (e.g., running, hopping, skipping).
- Demonstrate coordination in using objects during active play (e.g., throwing, catching, kicking balls, riding tricycle).
- Use non-locomotor skills with control, balance, and coordination during active play (e.g., bending, stretching, and twisting).
- Demonstrate spatial awareness in physical activity or movement.

National Association of Sport and Physical Education National Standards for Physical Education

Standard 1: The physically literate individual demonstrates competency in a variety of motor skills and movement patterns.

EXAMPLES:

Outdoors: Children are running, climbing on playground equipment, and throwing and kicking balls.

Music: Children listen, move, and dance to music, controlling and coordinating their movements and synchronizing with the beat.

Dramatic play: Children use gross-motor skills as they crawl under a table with a blanket thrown over the top as part of a scenario involving a cave or a camping tent. They climb in and out of a large box they have determined is a rocket ship going to Mars.

- Where else might you see this standard occurring naturally in children's play?
- What other standards might children also demonstrate?

POSSIBLE TEACHER SUPPORT STRATEGIES:

Play alongside children outdoors, dancing, and in physical dramatic play.

Model how to increase the difficulty of particular movements during outdoor play or dancing to music. The difficulty can be a more physically challenging movement or simply a more vigorous one. For example, add squats to a dance move or walk along a rope stretched across the floor.

Provide scaffolding by removing barriers to more vigorous play. For example, invite a child who is not active to join you in kicking or rolling a ball back and forth, or in hopping or skipping around the playground. Or assist a child struggling with climbing the ladder to the slide.

What other support strategies might you try?

Ways to Intentionally Plan to Address This Standard in Play Experiences	
POSSIBLE MATERIALS, ENVIRONMENTAL CHANGES, OR GROUPING STRATEGIES	**TEACHER SUPPORT STRATEGIES**
Add balls and a basket to a play area in the classroom and have children work in pairs taking turns throwing the balls into the basket and retrieving them. Make sure you have different sizes of balls.	*Scaffold by providing assistance to children as needed, then challenge* children by moving the basket closer or farther away.
Set up an obstacle course with tables to crawl under, masking tape "hurdles" to jump over, traffic cones to run around, a slide to slide down, and a plastic tunnel to crawl through.	*Challenge by timing children* using a stopwatch. See if each child can complete the course at a faster pace.
Dancing is better and more infectious with larger groups of children. Begin by putting on some lively music, and increase the interest by giving children scarves to dance with or rhythm sticks to play along with. Percussion is movement too!	*As a provocation,* set up a "magic" carpet. Use an ordinary carpet that you pretend has the power of making you dance. As soon as you step on it, you start to dance. Invite them to step on the carpet and see if it makes them dance too. As an alternative, turn music on and off, and see if children can stop ("Freeze!") when the music is off and begin dancing when it is on.
Groupings of at least two children are necessary for most play involving balls. Help children find partners to play with during outdoor active play. Try to ensure that all children are involved.	*Reflect with children* about their favorites when playing actively: • inside or outside • alone or with someone else • with or without adults • with objects, on wheeled toys, or on equipment • or playing and moving in open spaces Use these reflections to provide additional guidance and supports for active play.
What other materials, environmental changes, or grouping strategies might you provide?	*What other support strategies might you try?*

DOMAIN: PHYSICAL AND MOTOR DEVELOPMENT
STRAND: MOTOR/MOVEMENT SKILLS—FINE

Alabama Developmental Standards for Preschool Children

Physical Development

Goal 2: Children will develop fine-motor skills.

PD.P.2.1: Develop and demonstrate strength and coordination of small muscles.

Oklahoma Kindergarten Standards

Motor Skill and Lifetime Activity Development: Small Motor Development

Standard 1: The student will participate in activities that involve small-motor skills.

≋ Ways This Standard Occurs Naturally as Children Play

EXAMPLES:

Writing area: Children use different kinds and sizes of writing instruments and scissors.

Manipulatives: Children pick up small manipulative pieces to sort. They remove and place puzzle pieces. And they string beads, lace cards, and practice shoe tying.

Science area: Children handle and move around magnets or magnifying glasses.

- Where else might you see this standard occurring naturally in children's play?
- What other standards might children also demonstrate?

POSSIBLE TEACHER SUPPORT STRATEGIES:

Play alongside children and ask them to pass you things that will require that they pick up small objects or use fine-motor skills.

Model the use of various new items you might add to centers, such as magnifying glasses, tweezers, tongs, stringing beads, magnetic letters on a metal board, chopsticks, and clothespins.

Provide scaffolding by having children grab larger and fatter objects before smaller and thinner ones. Be sure to have various kinds of scissors or writing instruments (begin with fatter markers or sidewalk chalk before going to thin pencils or pens).

What other support strategies might you try?

Ways to Intentionally Plan to Address This Standard in Play Experiences

POSSIBLE MATERIALS, ENVIRONMENTAL CHANGES, OR GROUPING STRATEGIES	TEACHER SUPPORT STRATEGIES
Add items to centers that require small-muscle work. For example: • In the art center, add stickers, hole punchers, staplers, and clothespins to hang up art. • In the dramatic area, add doll clothes or dress-up clothes with snaps, zippers, and buttons. • In the play kitchen, add various kinds of eating and cooking utensils (e.g., tongs, chopsticks). • In the science or sensory area, add eyedroppers, plastic syringes, tweezers, and tongs.	*Scaffold* by introducing new items gradually. Show how each can be used.
In the music center, have CDs that include fingerplays. For example, "Itsy Bitsy Spider" requires moving and touching fingers. "Where Is Thumbkin?" requires hiding and revealing fingers.	*Challenge* individual children by having them lead others in the fingerplays.
Set up a playdough center. Use either purchased or homemade dough. Making the dough can be an activity in itself. Stock the center with rolling pins, cookie cutters, plastic knives, and molds. Squeezing, stretching, and kneading the dough develops small hand muscles.	*Challenge children* to combine two different colors of dough and make a new color (blue and yellow to make green; red and yellow to make orange). Combining dough requires hands to do a lot of squeezing and kneading.

(cont.)

In the art center, do fingerpainting or shaving cream painting. Combine paint with starch and let children smear and spread it around on a piece of paper. If that's too messy, put some shaving cream foam on a large baking sheet and let them create and write with their fingers.	*Reflect with children* about favorite activities. Here are some useful reflection questions: • What did you do today (in the fine-motor skill center [fingerpainting, playdough, fingerplays])? • What activity did you like the best? • Do you have something you did that you want to show me or Mommy and Daddy? • Shall we do this tomorrow? Write down the favorite activity and make a plan to do it again the next day during playtime.
What other materials, environmental changes, or grouping strategies might you provide?	*What other support strategies might you try?*

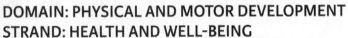

DOMAIN: PHYSICAL AND MOTOR DEVELOPMENT
STRAND: HEALTH AND WELL-BEING

Georgia Early Learning and Development Standards

Physical Development and Motor Skills (PDM)

Standard PDM1: The child will practice healthy and safe habits.

New Jersey Core Curriculum Content Standards for Comprehensive Health and Physical Education

Comprehensive Health and Physical Education

Standard 2.1 Wellness: All students will acquire health promotion concepts and skills to support a healthy, active lifestyle.

≋ Ways This Standard Occurs Naturally as Children Play

EXAMPLES:

Outdoors and other centers: Children observe safety by reminding other children to wear a helmet when using a tricycle. Children follow safety requirements in the classroom, such as putting on goggles when hammering or working with other tools.

Dramatic play: Children pretend to be helpers, such as doctors, nurses, police officers, or firefighters. They play the roles in ways that show their understanding of how and why these people help others (to get well, to be safe).

- Where else might you see this standard occurring naturally in children's play?

- What other standards might children also demonstrate?

POSSIBLE TEACHER SUPPORT STRATEGIES:

Play alongside children in areas where there are clear safety rules. Carefully observe all the safety rules yourself.

Model paying attention to safety and comment aloud: "I better put on these goggles. They will keep my eyes safe."

Provide scaffolding when children forget safety rules or are acting unsafe. These are opportunities to remind them about safety rules or wider behavioral expectations, such as being nice and not hurting others.

What other support strategies might you try?

Ways to Intentionally Plan to Address This Standard in Play Experiences

POSSIBLE MATERIALS, ENVIRONMENTAL CHANGES, OR GROUPING STRATEGIES	TEACHER SUPPORT STRATEGIES
Add materials to the science area that help children understand bones. For example, dried chicken bones, plastic skeletons, or old X-rays. Put out a life-size skeleton puzzle. This can be as simple as six large square pieces of paper that, when assembled, create a full child-size skeleton. Assemble on the floor and children can lie down on it. The puzzle helps show where the bones are in a child's body.	*Scaffold by assisting children* as they construct the skeleton puzzle; show them how to feel their own bones and then try to find ones like them on the puzzle pieces.
Add a "Dial 911" sign to the dramatic play area by the toy phone. Explain how if there is an emergency, children should dial 911.	*Challenge* children by moving into a dramatic play event and suggesting something bad has happened (someone gets a bad burn or falls down). Help them role-play calling for help by dialing 911. Encourage role playing of EMTs, police officers, or firefighters coming to the rescue.
During times of indoor or outdoor active play, make it a point to explain to children that being active makes their muscles and bones strong, makes their heart and lungs healthy, and helps their blood flow all around their bodies.	*As a provocation,* use a stethoscope to listen to children's heartbeats. Or have them place an ear on a friend's chest. Then have the children run around and listen again. Can they hear that their heart is beating faster?
Organize small groups of 4–5 and play a body parts game. Hold up a picture of a body part (leg, foot, elbow, face, knee, hand, nose, head) and the leader shouts out that body part. Everyone tries to touch that body part on herself or himself.	*Reflect with children* about what they do to be healthy. Connect all the things you do in the classroom (following safety rules, learning how to get help, engaging in active play, identifying body parts, brushing teeth, washing hands). Invite them to think about things they would like to play with tomorrow that help them learn about being healthy.
What other materials, environmental changes, or grouping strategies might you provide?	*What other support strategies might you try?*

DOMAIN: PHYSICAL AND MOTOR DEVELOPMENT
STRAND: ACTIVE PHYSICAL PLAY

California Preschool Learning Foundations

Foundations in Physical Development

Domain: Physical and Motor Development

Strand: Active Physical Play

2.0: Cardiovascular Endurance

2.1: Engage in frequent bursts of active play that involves the heart, the lungs, and the vascular system. Engage in active play activities that enhance leg and arm strength, muscular endurance, and flexibility.

National Physical Education Standards and Minnesota Benchmarks[1]

Standard 3: Participates regularly in physical activity. (Physical Activity)

---

[1] Minnesota has adopted the National Physical Education Standards, but the state developed its own benchmarks.

≋ Ways This Standard Occurs Naturally as Children Play

EXAMPLES:

Outdoors: Children ride tricycles or scooters, pull wagons, run, jump, climb on equipment, kick and chase after balls, bounce or sit on large bouncy balls, roll hoops. They are active in both structured and unstructured activities for sustained periods of time.

Music area: Using big movements, children stretch, twist, turn around, bend, and hop in response to music.

Transitions: When moving between play areas, children march by swinging their arms high and lifting their knees; they also can hop or tiptoe between play areas.

- Where else might you see this standard occurring naturally in children's play?
- What other standards might children also demonstrate?

POSSIBLE TEACHER SUPPORT STRATEGIES:

Play alongside children who are active and engage in active play yourself. Stretch. Do jumping jacks. Touch your toes. If you know how, you could do some Tai Chi moves or yoga poses, or simple exercises like sit-ups, knee bends, head rolls, arm twirls.

Model the use of active play that you do not see children doing (e.g., rolling a hula hoop, dancing vigorously, marching).

Provide scaffolding by observing how children are being active, noticing where they have trouble, and intervening quickly (you can suggest they do something less hard like walk quickly or jog instead of running, kick a larger ball, be pushed on the tricycle if pedaling is a challenge, engage in slower movements if balance is a problem).

What other support strategies might you try?

POSSIBLE MATERIALS, ENVIRONMENTAL CHANGES, OR GROUPING STRATEGIES	TEACHER SUPPORT STRATEGIES
Add new materials outdoors: Balls of all sizes, tricycles and other wheeled toys, Frisbees, and hoops. Use sidewalk chalk to make pathways, hopscotch squares, lines to jump over or bounce a ball across, circles to jump in and out of, or places to run between. Think about new materials that promote active outdoor play in all kinds of weather.	*Challenge children* who are less inclined to be actively engaged in using the materials. It may take a special invitation, extra modeling, or encouragement. Pair that child up with a more active buddy and encourage them to play a specific game together.
Set up an indoor gross-motor area. Possible items could include a chin-up bar to hang from, exercise posters, or CDs that suggest touching toes or doing jumping jacks, a masking tape outline or traffic cone obstacle course that is navigated by crab walking.	*Scaffold by assisting children* to use the materials and do the activities in the new gross-motor center. You may have to hold them up to the chin bar, lead them in the exercises, or make adaptations to the obstacle course.
Blow bubbles outdoors or in a gym and have children chase and catch the bubbles. Have the children take turns chasing the bubbles.	*As a provocation, tell children* to pop just two (or whatever number) bubbles, clapping their hands twice for each bubble they pop and then stopping and letting another child take a turn.
Create groups of children with different abilities. Create opportunities so all children become actively engaged in strenuous physical activity. For example, give the group the challenge of making sure each member of their group runs to a playground fence and back. Or set up a game of Blast Off! where one child in the group is the "launcher" and counts down from ten to zero and shouts "Blast off!" Then the rest of the children run from one side of the room or outdoor space to another. Children take turns being the launcher.	*Reflect with children about when* during their day they were really active so that they were breathing hard, their heart rate was up, and maybe they were sweating. Help them distinguish between just doing things outside or any other activity and "active play that involves the heart, the lungs, and the vascular system." Ask them when during their time at home they are active in such a way. Help them think about times with their families when they can be physically active.
What other materials, environmental changes, or grouping strategies might you provide?	*What other support strategies might you try?*

A PLAY STORY FROM A PRESCHOOL CLASSROOM: GETTING CHILDREN MOVING

Amanda's Head Start class had just finished its body mass index (BMI) screening. This was part of a number of key health assessments the program did on all of the children they served during the first months of the year. Amanda looked over the results and saw that eight of the students were classified as overweight and one as obese. At one level it seemed absurd to her that they would even be talking about a four-year-old as obese. But she also knew that childhood obesity rates were at historically high levels. She worried about what that meant for children's long-term health. Maybe this was a time for her to think seriously about the physical well-being of her children. No sooner had that thought crossed her mind than another came: she had noticed that healthier, fitter children were often the children who did better in school, in terms of both learning and behavior.

A few days later, with the BMI report still in mind, Amanda's attention latched on to this sentence from her state's early learning guidelines: "Children participate regularly in physical activity, equally in structured and unstructured play." Immediately her mind conjured up an image of the playground on a typical afternoon. Children were running around, climbing on equipment, and pedaling wheeled toys. But those children were not the eight on the BMI list. How could she address this standard with all of the children, she wondered.

She realized that this was not about the children's BMIs. It was about their lack of participation in physical activities. She recognized that she needed to provide support, encouragement, and meaningful conversation with children about physical development just as she did in relation to other domains such as language and literacy and math. She understood the importance of specially designed plans that met the needs of each child. "Why should gross-motor standards be any different?" She asked herself. "What can I do so that all children, especially these eight, are regularly participating in physical activities?"

That very afternoon, Amanda began careful observation of children in outdoor play. She noted what they were doing, what was engaging them and for how long. She vowed to take no action until she really knew what they were doing.

One week after her observations began, she reread her notes and asked herself a simple question: "What did I see?" Her conclusions were clear: these children were not participating outdoors in the same ways as others in the class. Some days they did nothing but sit and talk with other children, often with one another. What changes could she make in their experiences that would increase their participation rates?

Amanda selected three strategies. First, she added a "gross motor" center in the classroom where children could be physically active during playtime. Second, she added more dancing activities during large-group time. She played a variety of CDs and invited all of the children to move around, wave scarves and streamers, and respond to the beat and feel of the music. She increased the amount of dancing time as children's interest and participation grew. Her assistant teacher was amazed at the diverse moves children created and how each child participated in some way.

Third, she made a point of inviting the less active children to play with her each day. Some days they kicked a ball back and forth. Other days they did a "partners race" to the fence and back. She let the children take turns deciding whether they would run, walk backward, hop, or move sideways. At the end of the week, she set up an obstacle course through the play equipment—they climbed up the ladder; slid down the slide; ran around the far end of the playground; jumped over a line in the pea gravel; and raced across to the bars, climbed over the bars, and ended up back again at the foot of the ladder. She invited children (including the inactive ones) to run the course with her. Then she timed them as they went through. She encouraged them to rerun the path and see if they could do it faster. The other children were fascinated and watched

(cont.)

as each student ran. They all wanted to run the course too. Amanda made sure everyone got a turn.

The game became so popular that Amanda had to create rules to limit the number who could be involved at a time and give everyone a chance to run the course. She made sure her targeted children still got a chance on a daily basis to run the course. She was also careful to avoid any competition and focus only on improving each person's individual time. The direct engagement gave Amanda lots of chances to encourage children's efforts.

Amanda found that all of the children in the class benefited from the indoor gross-motor area, the dancing at group time, and the timed obstacle courses outdoors. With the children choosing activities and being involved, she could step back and observe as the children played. She was especially keen to see if the eight children who had originally not been very involved in the physical activity were, in fact, participating on a regular basis in physical activity. She watched their involvement in the center. She watched their play during outdoor time. All eight children were physically active far more frequently than before.

What Standards Were Addressed?

- physical and motor development by using large muscles, increasing balance and coordination, and engaging in active physical play
- math skills by reading numbers on the stop watch and recording times; determining which numbers are larger or smaller than others
- executive function, including impulse control and self-regulation, as children stopped and started dancing
- cognitive skills by remembering the sequence of events in the obstacle courses
- language skills as the children identified ways to "partner race"
- growth in self-esteem as children became more active and capable in using their bodies

CHAPTER 12

Addressing Social-Emotional Development Standards in Play

S ocial-emotional competence in young children is the most important foundation for future learning, yet it is also one of the most ignored (Raver and Knitzer 2002). In part, this
is because teachers and administrators assume all children have basic social skills to function
in school. But when children have difficulty regulating their emotions and behaviors, when
they struggle to establish and sustain relationships, and when they don't cooperate and con-
structively engage in classroom activities, learning is rarely possible. Social skills are so basic
that they tend to be taken for granted when they actually need to be made a priority.

The writers of many state early learning standards do acknowledge the importance of
social-emotional skills. They included them as desired milestones as children grow and
develop. That tells us two things:

1. Social and emotional development is an important expectation to have for young
   children.
2. Teachers can teach young children the skills necessary to promote their social and
   emotional development.

Social-emotional skills need to be learned like any other content. Teachers and administrators need to provide strategies and guidance when children

- don't know how to get along with others,
- struggle to manage strong emotions, or
- don't know how to resolve problems without hitting or pushing.

Controlling emotions and choosing alternative behaviors are hallmarks of growing up and
developing into our true selves. Social and emotional development is growth that lies at
the very foundation of identity.

Another important dimension of social-emotional development directly relates to play:
friendship skills. Children who know how to make friends are those who most easily enter
into play experiences with other children. The more successful they are in using these
skills, the more friends they have (Tremblay et al. 1981). And the more friends they have,

the more likely they are to spend time in rich and engaging play with their playmates. Early learning standards address social behaviors such as sharing, taking turns, helping others during play, giving compliments, and knowing how to give and receive apologies (Joseph et al. 2010). Children learn and practice these skills as they interact in play. Remember, peers can be some of their best teachers!

While social-emotional development is a common domain in many state early learning standards, it is rarely addressed in standards for grades K–12. Only six states (Idaho, Illinois, Kansas, Pennsylvania, Washington, and West Virginia) have comprehensive, freestanding standards that address social and emotional learning in K–12 (Bornfreund et al. 2015; CASEL 2015). Without clear guidelines, sometimes the responses of schools to children's disruptive and challenging behavior can be reactive and punitive. Children may be removed from classrooms and miss out on the learning taking place there. Sometimes they are even suspended or expelled. Increasingly, research is showing the importance of making social-emotional learning a focus throughout the elementary school years (Rimm-Kaufman and Hulleman 2015).

For kindergarten, there are no commonly used national standards like the Common Core for Math and English Language Arts. But we did find a few state standards for kindergarten that address social-emotional learning. Where social-emotional skills are addressed for both preschoolers and kindergartners, the standards tend to include the following strands:

- Relationships with Adults
- Names, Manages, and Expresses Emotions
- Self-Image
- Participates Cooperatively in Play

In this chapter, we have sample standards from both preschool and kindergarten for each strand. We show how to integrate each standard in child-directed, open-ended play experiences. First, we suggest that you observe children in play throughout your classroom and reflect on your observations related to the specific standard.

Then we offer ideas for intentionally planning to address the standard in these play areas and experiences by adding materials, making changes in the environment, or considering grouping strategies. Throughout, we ask you to consider additional ways that you might observe for, support, and intentionally address the standard. We recognize that each classroom and group of children is different and that your knowledge of your students and setting will be important considerations.

We recognize that when connecting social-emotional standards to play, it is hard to imagine any play-based experiences that do not have some connection to expressing emotions, developing relationships with others, reflecting on one's self-image, or playing cooperatively in groups. In this chapter, we focus on what to look for and target more directly in play opportunities related to specific social-emotional skills. We ask that teachers also keep in mind that play may not always be the best opportunity to teach social-emotional skills, but it is the perfect time to practice and refine those skills and to generalize them across a variety of situations and settings.

At the end of the chapter, we share a story of how a teacher planned for play with many standards from this domain and others in mind. Realistically, many standards are integrated in children's play experiences. It's impossible to address only one standard at a time in play, which is why it is such a rich and exciting curricular approach for preschool and kindergarten children. We encourage you to read through our specific examples in the tables on the next pages, think about your classroom and group of children, and come up with your own ideas. We also suggest that you look at the ways children demonstrate multiple standards from a variety of domains when teachers plan for integrated play activities like the one shared at the end of the chapter.

DOMAIN: SOCIAL-EMOTIONAL
STRAND: RELATIONSHIPS WITH ADULTS

Rhode Island Early Learning and Development Standards

Social and Emotional Development (SE)

Component 1: Relationships with Others

Learning Goal 1a: Children develop trust in and engage positively with adults who are familiar and consistently present in children's lives.

Pennsylvania Learning Standards for Early Childhood: Kindergarten

Key Learning Area: Social and Emotional Development: Learning about myself and others

Standard 25.3: Pro-Social Relationships with Adults

BIG IDEA: Children will learn to develop healthy relationships through positive adult interactions.

STANDARD STATEMENT:

- Solicit help from adults to accomplish challenging tasks.
- Respond, and appropriately question adults' directives for greater understanding.
- Engage in reciprocal conversation with familiar and unfamiliar adults when appropriate.

≋ Ways This Standard Occurs Naturally as Children Play

EXAMPLES:

Class library: Children look at, listen to, and read books with teachers and peers about special relationships (such as moms, dads, siblings, grandparents, uncles, aunts, and teachers).

Sensory table: Children play with objects at the sensory table (such as filling a spray bottle with water). They cannot screw on the top of the bottle, so they ask an adult for help. Another holds up a pail full of water and says, "Look how full I got this!" Children show teachers what they are doing.

Dramatic play: The children engage in a play scenario that involves playing adult roles like shopkeeper, mother or father, server or chef.

- Where else might you see this standard occurring naturally in children's play?
- What other standards might children also demonstrate?

POSSIBLE TEACHER SUPPORT STRATEGIES:

Play alongside children and see if just your presence makes them initiate a conversation with you or show you what they are doing.

Model how to join the play of others, narrating your strategy: "It looks like you are having fun playing with the water. Carly, may I play with you? It looks like you are filling that bowl. How can I help?"

Provide scaffolding to a child who is upset when a parent drops her off by reassuring the child that she is safe with you, making a clear connection with the parent, not rushing the drop-off and departure, and seeing if there is some object the parent could leave behind that might reassure the child that the parent will return.

What other support strategies might you try?

For specific ideas on how to promote positive relationships, see "Building Positive Teacher-Child Relationships" among the "What Works" briefs on the website of Vanderbilt University's Center on the Social Emotional Foundations for Early Learning (http://csefel .vanderbilt.edu).

Ways to Intentionally Plan to Address This Standard in Play Experiences

POSSIBLE MATERIALS, ENVIRONMENTAL CHANGES, OR GROUPING STRATEGIES	TEACHER SUPPORT STRATEGIES
Add adult men's and women's dress-up clothes to the dramatic play area and tell the children these are clothes mommies and daddies wear. Encourage adult role plays.	*Scaffold by prompting* a play scenario about Mom or Dad leaving for work or dropping the child off at the child care, preschool, or kindergarten class. Play might begin by you asking, "Where do you work?" or "What time are you leaving?" Further prompts could include: "Be sure to tell your little girl where you are going," or "I will take care of her while you're gone" (Family Communications 1995).
Include books in the library that tell stories of relationships children have with significant others (e.g., *The Grandma Book* by Todd Parr or *Off to School, Baby Duck* by Amy Hest).	*Challenge* children with questions about significant relationships they have with adults. What kinds of things do they do together?
Add paper, envelopes, and a mailbox to the writing center. Suggest that children write letters to a teacher, assistant teacher, or other adult helper in the classroom. The letter can be folded, put in an envelope, and "posted" in the mailbox.	*As a provocation,* model how you think about what you might write to that person. Assign a child to be the "mail carrier" to deliver the letters.
Identify children who push your buttons. Make a point to play with them so that you can better understand and relate to them. Be sure to do the following: • engage one-on-one, face-to-face • use a pleasant and calm voice • provide warm and responsive physical contact • follow the child's lead during play • emphasize redirection if challenging behavior occurs • acknowledge children for accomplishments and effort (CSEFEL, n.d.)	*Reflect with children* about what activities they most enjoy in the classroom. Look for ways the child can do those things or be the leader in the class in doing those things.
What other materials, environmental changes, or grouping strategies might you provide?	*What other support strategies might you try?*

DOMAIN: SOCIAL-EMOTIONAL
STRAND: NAMES, MANAGES, AND EXPRESSES EMOTIONS

North Carolina Foundations for Early Learning and Development

Domain: Emotional and Social Development (ESD)

Subdomain: Learning about Feelings

Goal ESD-6: Children identify, manage, and express their feelings

(Connecticut) The Kindergarten through Grade Three Social, Emotional, and Intellectual Habits Framework

Strand: Identify and understand emotions of self and others

Learning Progression: Identifying and Understanding Emotions

Kindergarten Indicators:

- Identify and appropriately label basic feelings in self and others (e.g., happy, sad, mad, scared).
- With adult support, discuss how some basic emotions impact behavior in self and others.

EXAMPLES:

Music area: Children listen to different kinds of music and identify different emotional tones: sad, happy, dramatic, calm.

Art: Children express emotions through various open-ended art projects.

Writing center: Children express emotions as they communicate in writing with others.

- Where else might you see this standard occurring naturally in children's play?

- What other standards might children also demonstrate?

POSSIBLE TEACHER SUPPORT STRATEGIES:

Play alongside children and hold up a mirror so they can see themselves. Ask about how they are feeling. Ask what expressions they see on their faces.

Model emotions with facial expressions as you read books and play with children. (For example, if playing restaurant, model both an angry and a happy customer. Be sure to explain: "Let's pretend that I am mad that you have not taken my order." Or, "Let's pretend I'm really enjoying the food you served me.")

Provide scaffolding by assisting children in acting out and expressing their own feelings in play.

What other support strategies might you try?

For a summary of the research and a list of suggestions about identifying and labeling emotions, see "Fostering Emotional Literacy in Young Children: Labeling Emotions" (available at http://csefel.vanderbilt.edu/briefs/wwb21.pdf).

Ways to Intentionally Plan to Address This Standard in Play Experiences	
POSSIBLE MATERIALS, ENVIRONMENTAL CHANGES, OR GROUPING STRATEGIES	**TEACHER SUPPORT STRATEGIES**
Add a mirror to one of the play areas along with some "feelings" cards that have photographs of children expressing feelings. Encourage children to express a variety of emotions in the mirror. Or pair children up, with one drawing cards and the other one showing the emotion in the mirror. Let them take turns.	*Scaffold* by offering to be the "dealer" of the feelings cards. Put a card face up and ask both children to express the emotion shown. Change the game by putting the card face down; then you make the face and see if the children can guess the emotion. Let them take turns doing that as well.
During outdoor play, organize a game of "feelings" tag. Select a feeling (fear, anger, happiness, sadness) and say that as long as a person expresses that emotion he is safe from being caught.	*Challenge* children by calling out the emotions while they are playing so they have to think fast.
Set up the science center with three experiments. Each experiment is matched to a feeling (the vinegar-and-baking-soda volcano for anger; pluck a rubber band strung between two nails for calm sounds; blow bubbles or a pinwheel for happy; or something else. Be creative). Let children choose which experiment to do based on which feeling (angry, calm, or happy) is most like how they feel right now.	*As a provocation, invite children* to describe how another child is feeling, and let that be the way they choose which experiment to do.
Whenever clear emotions are expressed during play, take time to notice them, describe them, and name them.	*Reflect with children* by reminding them that everyone has all kinds of feelings (everyone is sad sometimes or angry sometimes or happy sometimes), and the feelings are natural and okay. Talk about different ways to express feelings without hurting others.
What other materials, environmental changes, or grouping strategies might you provide?	*What other support strategies might you try?*

DOMAIN: SOCIAL-EMOTIONAL
STRAND: SELF-IMAGE

Missouri Early Learning Standards

Content Component: Knowledge of Self

Process Standard: Exhibits self-awareness

Indicators:

- Shows respect for self
- Develops personal preferences
- Knows personal information

Massachusetts Standards for Preschool and Kindergarten: Social and Emotional Learning, and Approaches to Play and Learning

Social and Emotional Learning, and Approaches to Play and Learning

Area: Self-Awareness

Standard SEL2: The child will demonstrate accurate self-perception.

Standard SEL3: The child will demonstrate self-efficacy (confidence/competence).

≈ Ways This Standard Occurs Naturally as Children Play

EXAMPLES:

Blocks: As children build with blocks, they express preferences as they choose blocks and build structures, stand up for themselves as they build with others, and show pride in their own competence.

Sensory table: As children pour, scoop, and measure at the sensory table, they overcome challenges in manipulating the materials and develop confidence.

Art: Children draw or paint pictures of themselves and their families, revealing personal information and self-perceptions.

- Where else might you see this standard occurring naturally in children's play?
- What other standards might children also demonstrate?

POSSIBLE TEACHER SUPPORT STRATEGIES:

Play alongside children and ask about what they are doing. Make it a point to encourage specific efforts or celebrate accomplishments.

Model ways to express pleasure in what you are doing and how you have made something.

Provide scaffolding when children are struggling to stand up for themselves and celebrate their own accomplishments.

What other support strategies might you try?

Ways to Intentionally Plan to Address This Standard in Play Experiences

POSSIBLE MATERIALS, ENVIRONMENTAL CHANGES, OR GROUPING STRATEGIES	TEACHER SUPPORT STRATEGIES
Organize playtimes so children can choose what they want to do within the planned play opportunities. As much as possible, try to let children do things for themselves. If they can't, identify the skill they lack and target that for teaching and practice. That approach will set the stage for more independent play in the future.	*Scaffold choice making by assisting* children in setting goals for the day. What are things they want to learn about? Let that be the reason for their choices. Follow up to see if they achieved their goals.
Add a mirror to a play area and encourage children to look at themselves. What do they see?	*Challenge* children by telling them they are unique and special, and that you like them exactly as they are—just the way they look in the mirror.
With the children, make a list of things they can do (put on a coat, put on shoes, comb their hair, brush their teeth, buckle a belt, do a somersault, run fast).	*As a provocation, invite children* to identify and demonstrate their skills to you and/or to one another. Make sure there is something each child can do. Use this as an opportunity to identify things they do well and express that to them.
Recognize during play when children accomplish something, especially something that connects with a standard you are targeting as a personal learning goal. Be specific about what they did that showed you that they did that thing well.	*Reflect with children* about how it feels to accomplish things. Remind them that that is part of the fun of learning, feeling satisfied about what we did and feeling good about ourselves.
What other materials, environmental changes, or grouping strategies might you provide?	*What other support strategies might you try?*

DOMAIN: SOCIAL-EMOTIONAL
STRAND: PARTICIPATES COOPERATIVELY IN PLAY

Nebraska Early Learning Guidelines for Ages 3 to 5

Social and Emotional Development

Cooperation (SE.03)

Widely Held Expectations

- Child increases ability to sustain relationships.
- Uses compromise and conflict resolution skills.
- Plays actively with other children.
- Attempts to solve problems with other children, independently by negotiation or other socially acceptable means.

Health Education Content Standards for California Public Schools Kindergarten through Grade Twelve

Content Area: Mental, Emotional, and Social Health

Kindergarten

Standard 4: Interpersonal Communication

- 4.1.M Show how to express personal needs and wants appropriately.
- 4.2.M Cooperate and share with others

EXAMPLES:

Manipulatives: Children engage in both solitary and group play and may share materials and ideas for using them.

Outdoors: Children form ever-changing groups for running and other types of games, for imaginary play, and for exploring nature.

Dramatic play: Children negotiate and compromise as they determine roles and work out actions in pretend scenarios.

- Where else might you see this standard occurring naturally in children's play?
- What other standards might children also demonstrate?

POSSIBLE TEACHER SUPPORT STRATEGIES:

Play alongside children and see if your presence encourages communication and cooperation between you and the children (even nonverbally). Ask if they would be willing to share a toy or object with you.

Model good interpersonal communication skills by using careful listening and serve-and-response verbal interactions, and by including pleasantries such as greetings. Or model how to resolve a conflict, perhaps using puppets to enact a scenario in which two puppets fight over a toy.

Provide scaffolding when children are in conflict during play. Work with both parties involved in the conflict to do the following:

- help children identify the problem (what exactly is wrong)
- ask about possible solutions
- think through the solution to see if it solves the problems and still makes everyone feel okay; commit to trying the solution

What other support strategies might you try?

≋ Ways to Intentionally Plan to Address This Standard in Play Experiences

POSSIBLE MATERIALS, ENVIRONMENTAL CHANGES, OR GROUPING STRATEGIES	TEACHER SUPPORT STRATEGIES
Provide toys and materials that encourage cooperative use, such as balls, toys, or used telephones, board games, and teeter-totters.	Encourage children to *scaffold* and *assist* each other as they find a partner and play with some of these items.
Set up a puppet area. Use purchased or homemade puppets or have materials available so children can make their own. Encourage children to have the puppets interact with each other and show how they cooperate and resolve conflicts.	*Challenge children* to reenact scenarios that show the puppets cooperating. It helps to model talking *to* the puppet, talking *for* the puppet, and having children talk *with* the puppet with you providing the voice of the puppet (see www .fredrogerscenter.org/category/enewsletters /what-we-can-continue-to-learn-from-fred -rogers).
Establish a buddy system that pairs children up for specific periods of the day or parts of the schedule. This will increase social interactions among students to build relationship skills in the context of daily play.	*Reflect with children* about how the time with peers went. Identify ways they cooperated with each other and what problems they needed to resolve to keep playing and working together.
Encourage children to work with new friends during playtime.	*As a provocation, invite children* to try playing with different playmates. For example, hand out colored necklaces and have those with blue, green, red, or purple beaded necklaces work at the same center together. Observe the new groups and how they function. Who helps organize the new people? Who struggles to be included? Who needs additional support to be a "team player"?
Designate a "reporter" during playtime. Supply that person with a fedora and a "press card" (inserted in the brim or attached to a lanyard around the neck) or a microphone (a real one or a toilet paper tube with foil ball on the top). That person's assignment is to report on what is happening at each play area.	*Reflect with children* by making time during large group or circle to report back on the most exciting and interesting things the children are doing in the centers with an emphasis on cooperation.
What other materials, environmental changes, or grouping strategies might you provide?	*What other support strategies might you try?*

A PLAY STORY FROM A KINDERGARTEN CLASSROOM: ADDRESSING CHALLENGING BEHAVIORS

Michael was an experienced teacher who got a lot of satisfaction from helping children learn, but this year he thought he would be lucky if he could just keep them from physically harming one another. Six children in his current class required something close to one-on-one support to control their tendencies to hit, yell, and throw things.

After two months of implementing careful classroom management strategies, some sense of order began to emerge. Michael made a special effort to keep to a consistent and regular schedule, providing daily reminders about the flow of activities each day. He established behavioral norms and spent precious classroom time directly teaching children what was expected of them during each period of the day—arrival, center time, group times, meals, outdoor recess, and time spent in the hallways going to music and art. Each day began with a "morning meeting" where he discussed with the children ways to be friends, to engage in activities successfully, and to resolve conflicts. And throughout, he made certain he was creating a unique connection with each child every day. He checked in to see how the child was doing, finding something each was doing well and commenting on it, and reminding the child how much he enjoyed having him or her in his classroom.

With the daily routines approaching normality, Michael turned his attention to the six children who presented almost daily challenges. He focused his observations of these children on how and when each of them tended to be at their best and their worst, noting every successful moment and every time they were not able to meet his classroom expectations. At the same time, he reviewed his state's social-emotional standards and documented how closely they met those skills. As he reviewed his observation notes, he saw clear patterns emerge:

- specific times of the day when children misbehaved
- which children they got along with and which they clearly did not
- intervention strategies he tried that worked and did not work

Armed with this critical information, he established behavioral goals and developed an intervention plan for each of the six children. As one of the most outspoken advocates at his school for the value of play as an important tool for learning and development, he made sure his plan meant more time for play (and practice of social skills) rather than less.

Michael recognized that most of the problems occurred at playtime. The children who were unsuccessful were moving from one center to another randomly, not settling in, and therefore disrupting the play of others. He identified two issues he wanted to work on with these children: (1) choosing a center in advance and spending at least five minutes at that center, and (2) being able to join other groups of children in a cooperative and nondisruptive way.

To address the first issue, he talked with each child at the start of center time, helping him plan how he was going to spend his time. Then he paired each child with a successful buddy to play with or alongside at the desired center. He chose the buddies carefully from among a group of students who seemed particularly mature and with whom he had seen positive interactions with his target children. He rotated them on a daily basis and was ready to support the buddies if challenging behavior should arise. He also provided the target children a script to follow when asking to join a center where children were already playing. Then he let them go . . . and watched.

The first day nothing worked. Some of the target children ran around as always, their buddies hopelessly following without ever getting a chance to actually play. Some joined centers where there were other children but went in without saying anything and began to grab toys or objects. The next day was pretty much the same. The third day, Michael himself, along with the buddies, stayed close to the target children, intervening immediately as necessary, providing verbal cues about asking to join a group or requesting a role. There was slight improvement: fewer disrupted centers, longer time at the centers selected,

(cont.)

and more interactions with the buddies at the centers. Michael repeated this for two weeks. There were certainly bad days, but most days he saw improvement or at least the maintenance of earlier improvement. He was committed to providing focused, individualized interventions for all children with the same idea of using his state's social-emotional standards as a guide. Engaging in play and using play to practice social skills was a common thread.

Over time Michael noticed that if he was called away to attend to other children's needs during those times when he was trying to stay close to the target children, those children did not usually return to their previously disruptive behavior. So he began to follow less closely and pull back more and more. The children were more and more successful in engaging in productive play with a variety of playmates. Michael was so relieved that he had taken a long view. As the children's behavior improved, his relationship with them improved and their relationships with other children blossomed into friendships. By the end of the year, he was really sorry to see them move on to first grade.

What Standards Were Addressed?

- social-emotional skills, including taking turns, sharing, and knowing how to engage others to get needs met (joining a group), cooperating, and resolving conflicts appropriately
- approaches to learning, including impulse control, self-regulation, planning, and decision making
- social studies, in getting along in a community of learners and working toward the common good of the group
- language as children listened, followed Michael's directions and explanations, and communicated with other children

PART 4

POISE

In the final two chapters, we move from *Understanding* and *Strength* to *Poise*, the last step in the play process. Stuart Brown uses four descriptors to define the poise phase:

- grace
- contentment
- composure
- a sense of balance in life (Brown 2009, 19)

This stage seems to us the natural end of all cycles of change. After the change has happened, we move into a new state of being where the change has been integrated. Equilibrium is restored, but we find ourselves in a new place and, perhaps, as new persons. Poise comes from an old French word that means weight, balance, or consideration. Balance and weight are connected, because in older times weights were carefully calibrated objects that weighed a specific amount so they could be put on a balance scale to determine an object's true weight. Having gained a deeper understanding and appreciation of play and standards, and how poise can apply to teaching young children, we are now weighted, grounded, deepened, and in balance. When we get to the *poise* level, we are ready to move on in our work in new ways with our new selves.

Poise gives us the ability to move into these new challenges. And it reminds us that it is not enough to do the right thing; we need to know that what we are doing is making a difference. We need to move into wider arenas to make change broader and more permanent.

CHAPTER 13

The Importance of Assessing Children's Progress toward Standards in Play

PROVOCATIVE QUESTION: What is the role of assessment in play-based classrooms?

Tom: The Administrator's Perspective

Anytime someone talks to me about assessment, I wait for him to talk about his goals. Is the assessment to inform teacher practice? To reflect on how well students are doing or how well an activity worked? If he is able to describe the purpose, I know he is talking about formative assessment. Is the purpose to determine if a child needs further evaluation? If so, the kind of assessment needed is a screening tool. Perhaps the assessment is being conducted for program evaluation to determine whether individual schools, programs, or school districts are showing improvement in the overall percentage of children who meet a certain level of proficiency on a standardized measure. It's important to clarify the kinds and purposes of assessments.

Gaye: The Practitioner's Perspective

It seems to me that the biggest misunderstanding related to standards-based approaches in early education is how to assess children's learning. Whether preschool and kindergarten teachers are using standards as their goals or identifying goals from other sources, they still need to be implementing the recommended practices of assessment for young children. And those practices resoundingly endorse authentic assessment based on teacher observations, not testing or on-demand tasks. Young children are not reliable test takers. Instead, they show teachers what they know and can do as they play, interact with materials and other children, and interact with their teachers in meaningful and interesting activities. Excellent early educators observe children throughout the day, document some of those observations, and then engage in reflection about those observations, determining where each child is performing in relation to the standards and using that determination to plan for the next steps to embed in child-directed, open-ended play experiences.

REFLECTION, OBSERVATION, AND ASSESSMENT IN PLAY

In this chapter, we look at the importance of reflection and observation in assessing children's learning related to standards. We want to emphasize the interrelatedness of these two processes in the assessment of young children and show how well they work with play-based approaches. We recognize, however, that there are many misunderstandings in the field of early education about assessment recommendations.

Assessment is a broad and controversial topic. Some educators and families are concerned that we are testing children to death. Too often we are seeing programs back away from play because teachers and administrators worry that children are not learning enough based on what kind of testing is looming in their future. Lessening time for play and increasing teacher-led academic activities is a common response. Just as we have been told that standards are the enemy of play, so, too, we are told that assessment can be a similar enemy.

In reality, the design for effective education is a triangle that integrates curriculum (what is to be taught), instruction (how it is to be taught), and assessment (how effectively it was taught).

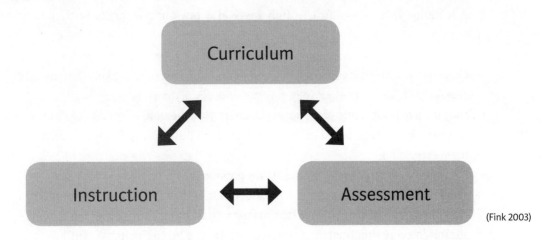

(Fink 2003)

Assessment is a critical and coequal component of all teaching, so avoiding assessment is not an option.

We have shown throughout this book that teachers need to take an active and engaged role even when play is child directed and open ended. We also believe that teachers and administrators' use of appropriate assessment for young learners, especially when integrated with standards, can actually make children's play even more beneficial. Through observation and reflection, teachers can determine the success of play experiences related to learning. They can make changes in approaches, materials, activities, and teacher support.

And they can observe and document how each child is showing progress in multiple domains as she plays.

Standards provide the expectations for what children know and can do. Teachers use standards to shape curriculum, and in preschools and kindergartens, they link curriculum with play. Then they use assessment to determine what worked. They engage in this process again and again.

AUTHENTIC ASSESSMENT

What are the right methods? What is the best way to assess preschool and kindergarten learning when implementing play-based curricular approaches? *Authentically*. Through teacher observation of children at play, through documentation of selected observations (what the teacher sees and what the children create), and through reflection related to standards. Tests do not give authentic information. Their reliability and validity for young learners need to be seriously questioned. Likewise, on-demand assessments—calling over a child to perform a task out of context—do not give the same kind of information that a teacher will learn watching and engaging with children in meaningful play experiences.

The trouble with assessing through tests and on-demand tasks is that they are *inauthentic*:

- They have inauthentic content (they do not assess knowledge or skills that directly pertain to children's lives, or they may not address all domains).
- They involve inauthentic procedures (teachers are collecting information about children's knowledge and skills in a way that is not how they typically demonstrate them in real life).
- They rely on an inauthentic process (they provide only discrete feedback at a very specific point in time, in a contrived context rather than the natural environment).
- They yield inauthentic evidence (they assume that the evidence collected is generalizable in every situation) (Bagnato, Neisworth, and Pretti-Frantczak 2010).

With these shortcomings in mind, it is safe to say that there are no really good standardized assessment instruments that work for young children. The use of tests and on-demand tasks in preschools and kindergartens should be limited. If they are used, the information gleaned from them needs to be treated with a critical eye. This is a strong caution against standardized tests for young children who are not good test takers.

Some assessment developers have actually tried to make their instruments more authentic so that they can be integrated into play. For example, the second edition of

Transdisciplinary Play-Based Assessment (Linder 2008) is a curriculum-based assessment that relies on careful observations of children for an hour or more as they play with toys and materials. Other observational assessments commonly used throughout the early childhood field also recommend that teachers observe as children play. They provide criteria for children's performance at different ages and then align those criteria with early learning standards from across the country. These assessments include:

- Early Learning Scale Preschool Assessment (Riley-Ayers, Boyd, and Frede 2008)
- Teaching Strategies GOLD (Berke et al. 2011)
- The Work Sampling System (Meisels et al. 2015)
- COR (Child Observation Record) Advantage (HighScope 2014)

In this chapter, we assume that preschool and kindergarten teachers are committed to following authentic assessment procedures whether they are using an assessment system or not. We provide concrete suggestions for how to do authentic assessment—observing, documenting, and reflecting—in the context of child-directed, open-ended play. We think our suggestions fit with the practices and tools that emphasize the importance of play and how it is a natural context for demonstrating a child's ability.

OBSERVING AND REFLECTING

As teachers integrate standards in play, they are continually observing. They observe not only for the children's performance but also for the success of their own efforts to integrate learning and play. Teachers are continually watching and taking in information throughout the classroom day. They pay special attention to how children address problems in their play, such as balancing blocks as they make a tower or working out how to share a toy. Based on what they see, teachers make adjustments and changes:

- They add new materials.
- They change part of the environment.
- They suggest different playgroups.
- They provide assistance.
- They pose challenging questions.

Sometimes adjustments and changes happen in the moment, sometimes a little later in the day, and sometimes they are made after the teacher has thought about them for a while, discussed them with colleagues, and determined a new plan of action.

In *Planning for Play, Observation, and Learning in Preschool and Kindergarten*, Gaye provides the following graphic to capture the many steps involved in teaching young children. Observation and reflection are key components of the planning process. Notice that all of the steps revolve around age-appropriate goals.

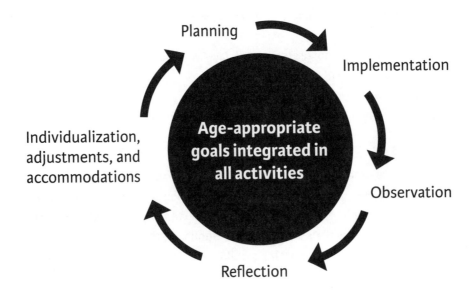

Reflective Questions about the Success of Play Experiences

Before determining exactly what to do next with children, teachers ask themselves questions that require them to think back over time, to review their internalized knowledge about the children, and to look at documentation they have collected that captures what children's strengths and challenges are. These reflective questions might include the following:

- What was the quality of the play? Are children moving toward deeper or richer play (engaging more and longer, exhibiting more imagination and improvisation)?
- What were the learning results? What skills or knowledge were evident?
- What has yet to be learned? What comes next in the learning trajectory for this standard?
- Were the play environment, materials, or grouping strategies effective? Did they promote the targeted learning goals?
- Were the teacher support strategies effective? What worked? What did not work?
- For next steps in planning, what should be continued? What needs changing?

As a week with children comes to a close, good teachers do not jump immediately into planning for the next week without reflecting about what they observed and identifying what worked and what did not. They use their experiences this week to determine where to go next week. There are two main things to think about when reviewing the week before:

- If something worked well, it does not necessarily need to be changed.
- If something was not successful, it *must* be changed in some way.

The value of this kind of reflective planning is immense when teachers are attempting to integrate standards into a play-based curriculum. They will not have to change the standards they are addressing every week, nor will they have to change the play experiences they offer. Their planning will be meaningful as they honestly evaluate the success of the play experiences, the learning related to standards, the environment, and the teaching strategies.

If teachers determine that certain play experiences were successful, they can plan to continue with them. They do not need to make changes to them because those experiences can be built upon and taken further. Perhaps the children are ready to move to a higher level of complexity in that same play activity. Children can revisit the same materials with new confidence, with developing skills, or with the opportunity to practice and refine what they are learning to do. The old adage "If it ain't broke, don't fix it," applies. If the experience is working well, why not continue and see where the children go with it? Teachers may find provocations and challenges can be more effective when done with play activities where the children are already successful.

In contrast, if a play experience was not successful, it needs to be changed. Perhaps the standard did not match the play. Perhaps the children were not deeply engaged with the materials and did not benefit fully from the experience. Teacher facilitation strategies may not have been successful. Perhaps it was hard for the teacher to gain information about what the children were learning related to the standard. If this is the case, good teachers plan for something different for the next week:

- They change the materials or rearrange the setup of the play area.
- They identify a different goal for the experience (it could be a standard that is less challenging or one that is more so; it could be a standard from a completely different domain).
- They plan for different ways to engage with the children in the play.
- They consider ways to collect information as they observe and interact with children.

Then, the only thing to do is try it out and observe again the next week. Reflective planning is an ongoing process of trial and error and is at the heart of effective teaching. As a plan is formulated, as new play experiences are considered, or as new ways to integrate standards into play are identified, several important questions should also be addressed:

- Is this a familiar experience for the children? What do they already know about it? Where have they been successful in the past? What are they ready for next?
- Is this a new experience for the children? What do I need to introduce and explain to them? Where might they need my assistance? How will I know when I can step back and be nearby, ready to offer guidance or help?

Teacher support will vary depending on whether a play experience is familiar to the children. The less familiar it is, the more direct support is needed. Reflective questions are essential to guide planning for effective integration of standards and play in early childhood classrooms.

Observing for Assessment of Children's Capabilities

In addition to observing and reflecting about the success of play experiences, teachers also observe to assess children's capabilities. They relate their observations to the standards that they set as goals for the play activities and review them to determine where each child is performing related to the standards. Teachers may be using an assessment tool aligned with their standards that guides them in this process. They consider if the child is comfortably demonstrating the expectations of the standard or is not doing so yet. They also recognize when a child is performing beyond the expectations identified. This assessment process also involves reflection and planning. Next steps in planning for child-directed, open-ended play experiences depend on how the child is doing related to the standards involved. Once again, observation and reflection are intertwined.

Teachers observe children all the time. They take in information by watching and listening. With a class of eighteen to twenty-five preschoolers or kindergartners, that can be an overwhelming amount of information to remember and process! Memory is a tricky thing. If teachers do not write down what they are seeing or record it in some way, they may miss important aspects of children's performance. They may forget, they may get distracted by other things happening, or they may not be aware of the details necessary to really determine if the expectations of the standard are being met.

Because of the importance of observation as an assessment process, teachers cannot rely solely on their memory when observing. They must document their observations and write them down. They can write brief notes on sticky pads in the moment with children and fill in the details later, or they can write more extensive observations on notebook paper or special observation forms. They can photograph the children in action to give a visual perspective to the written observation. And they can collect samples of the children's creations (such as drawings, paintings, or writing samples) to add evidence to support their written descriptions of what the child did and said. (Gronlund 2016, 71)

Teachers do not attempt to document *everything* they observe. That would require reams and reams of paper, and they would not have any time to interact with the children.

The most successful teachers pick and choose different documentation strategies and formats and use them at different times of the day. Such teachers are always ready to put down their pen and paper and engage fully with the children. If they have a variety of strategies in mind and use them consistently, they are able to create documentation of their observations that helps them know children better and plan appropriately for them throughout the day. (Gronlund 2016, 72)

Teachers can turn to a variety of books about observation and documentation, including *Focused Observations: How to Observe Young Children for Assessment and Curriculum Planning* (Gronlund and James 2013). Observational assessment tools that have been aligned with the early learning standards of most states are also available.

ASSESSMENT CONSIDERATIONS

To gain the most meaningful information about children's performance in play experiences, teachers need to plan for assessment. As they identify the standard(s) that they will link with the play experience, they also need to determine the best ways to see the standard(s) in action. Here are some questions teachers can ask themselves *before* they begin observing:

- What will I observe children doing that will tell me what they know and can do related to the standard(s)?
- How will I document my observations? In observation notes alone? With additional photographs or video or audio recordings? With work samples of some sort?
- In the play experiences, are there many ways for a child to show what he can do related to the standard?
- Are there questioning techniques or conversations that I can plan with the children to help me learn more about their understanding?
- If I am observing several children playing together, how can I document what they are doing at the same time?

Here again, we can see how closely assessment practices are tied to curriculum planning. It's impossible to separate the two. Teachers think about the standards. They consider effective documentation methods. They plan for child-directed, open-ended play because that will allow more possibilities for children to demonstrate what they can do related to the standards. And they reflect about their own involvement with children as they play. Teaching young children, assessing their performance, and linking play and standards is a complex, thoughtful, and interrelated process.

Observational Assessment in Action

With assessment in mind, let's revisit one of the stories that was shared in a previous chapter and consider how these teachers gathered assessment data as they observed children engaged in this rich, standards-filled play experience.

The Kindergarten Post Office
Remember that Ms. Kenworth and her colleague, Ms. Anders, set up a class post office to encourage children to write in more areas. They provided a variety of writing tools and kinds of paper so that the experience was open ended. Children could choose lined or unlined paper. They could pick the writing tool that worked most successfully for them. In addition, the teachers provided an address book with children's names and addresses (one per page for easy reference). They introduced the post office idea to the children, discussing letter writing and the process of sending and receiving mail.

They were intentional in choosing the materials so that they could observe for a variety of standards related to writing, including the following:

- appropriate grasp and use of writing tools (fine-motor coordination)
- use of emergent writing (making marks, scribbles, letter-like shapes, or recognizable letters and words)
- letter-sound connections as children began to write phonetically

One of the ways these teachers planned to gather assessment information from the post office was by setting up a daily "mail delivery." At the end of each day, at the closing group meeting, a child was designated as the mail carrier and delivered the "letters" to the children to whom they were addressed. This involved being able to read what was written on the envelope and getting the

(cont.)

letter to the right person. Teachers and other children helped the recipients "read" their letters. This daily process gave the teachers the opportunity to review the writing children were doing. They could try to remember what they noticed and write it down after the children left for the day. They could also designate that one of them take brief notes during the mail delivery time. In addition, they could take photographs of the children's writing (with the children's permission, of course) so that they could keep a sample as evidence to support their conclusions about the child's writing skills.

This end-of-day activity was paired with ongoing observations during the playtime earlier in the day. Teachers could pay attention to who was choosing to write in the post office. They could interact with the children there, offering encouragement and assistance as needed.

Because this was a popular choice for children, and they were seeing progress in children's writing over time, Ms. Kenworth and Ms. Anders began to observe for more specific standards. They challenged children to write not only names but addresses as well. They suggested the importance of correct letter formation and spacing between letters and words so that others could easily read what was written. They provided short sentences for copying. Building on the children's interest and motivation, the teachers were now able to observe for the following standards:

- printing many upper- and lowercase letters
- using frequently occurring nouns and verbs
- writing complete sentences
- capitalizing the first word in a sentence
- recognizing and naming end punctuation

As the children wrote their letters to each other, the teachers modeled, demonstrated, and provided scaffolding. They kept a clipboard nearby with a list of children's names so they could jot down brief notes about the various conventions children were using in their writing. And, again, they took photographs of the children's writing to keep as documented evidence to support their assessment conclusions. The key point here is that the teachers took a successful play experience and, with planning and assessment, were able to make it an effective and efficient instructional strategy across many standards.

Child-directed, open-ended play experiences offer many opportunities for teachers to observe children's performance related to standards. It's important that teachers plan for assessment as these two teachers did. Being clear about when to observe, what to look for, and how to document will make the assessment process go smoothly. Teachers will gain a lot of information about how children are learning and growing related to the standards identified (and maybe some others as well).

REPORTING TO FAMILIES

Assessment information is essential for

- identifying children's capabilities;
- planning next curricular steps to build on what children know and can do; and
- introducing new challenges, concepts, and skills.

It's also important for teachers to report assessment information to children's families. Family members are entitled to know how their children are progressing, what their strengths are, where they are challenged, and what strategies teachers are planning to help them continue to grow in skills and capabilities.

Family members may ask directly, "How is my child doing? How does she compare to other children in the class?" Rather than comparing the child to other children, however, teachers need to present assessment results with deeper purposes in mind. It's far more informative to look at what the child is doing compared to standards, to talk about the child's growth and how she is progressing. That gives both teachers and families a clear understanding of how the child is doing related to the expectations for her age. Such a comparison provides an individualized picture that shows what the child's strengths are, where she is showing progress, and what areas are challenging for her.

To come to conclusions about what the child is doing related to the standards, teachers record observations and collect work samples across time. These documents provide evidence so that teachers and family members can compare what the child did previously to what she is doing now. This is criterion-referenced assessment. The criteria are whatever early learning or kindergarten standards are being used. It is also formative assessment, because teachers are using this information over time to determine how the child is progressing and how they will formulate curricular strategies to build on the child's strengths and to address the areas that are challenging.

How do teachers present such assessment information to families? For young children, giving a grade or rating is too simplistic. A grade (such as a B) or a rating (such as "meets expectations") does not reflect the ways in which the child goes about learning various concepts and skills. Grades and ratings do not provide information about times when children benefited from teacher assistance or solved problems on their own. And grades and ratings miss the opportunity to demonstrate the small steps of progress children are making. At a minimum, families should be informed about their children's progress across all the key domains of the state's standards. This is an excellent way to teach families about the standards and how you use them in your practice. You are reminding everyone about the importance of taking a whole-child approach in assessing growth and development.

There are three informative ways to report to families about children's performance related to standards:

1. Portfolio documentation
2. Checklists
3. Narrative summaries

Let's consider each of these in more detail.

Portfolio Documentation

Many teachers have found that they are more successful at keeping track of what they are learning about each child when they use portfolios to organize their documentation. The portfolio documentation may be kept in a file folder or a binder (one for each student) or in an electronic file. It includes observation notes about the child engaged in play and other activities throughout the preschool or kindergarten day. The notes may be accompanied by photos of the child in action, as well as work samples that demonstrate what the child can do. For preschoolers, portfolios include more photos than paper-and-pencil work. However, children's drawings and writing samples can be informative. For kindergartners, photos are also helpful, showing how children make creations with hands-on materials. And, as kindergartners' writing and representational skills grow, teachers can collect more paper-and-pencil samples as children write in journals, engage in meaningful writing tasks, and begin to represent their mathematical and scientific understandings.

Portfolio documentation collected across time offers numerous benefits. Many teachers identify collection periods of ten to twelve weeks so that they can compare the observation notes, photos, and work samples as the school year proceeds.

Portfolios show the cumulative efforts and learning of a particular student over time. They offer valuable data about student improvement and skill mastery. Along with student reflection, that data provides valuable information about how each student learns and what is important to him or her in the learning process. (McDonald 2011)

The key to making portfolio collection a valuable and effective assessment process is to relate the documentation to standards. This can be done by planning ahead of time or by reviewing the documentation after the fact. As teachers have conferences with family members, they can show items from the portfolio that demonstrate the child's level of performance related to the standards.

Portfolios can be powerful communication tools for family/teacher conferencing. Teachers report that children's family members respond very positively to seeing the portfolio documentation. It provides them a window through which to view what the child is doing in the early childhood program. It helps them see the link between child-directed, open-ended play and early learning or kindergarten standards. Families usually love to see photos of their children and examples of their work. When teachers use the portfolio documentation to identify the child's current level of performance related to specific standards, they can also make clear to families what they are planning to help the child move forward in his learning. They can even invite families to support the child in similar ways at home. The whole process teaches families how to observe their child learning in activities at home (meals, bath time, bedtime rituals).

How do teachers integrate standards into portfolios? How do they plan for portfolio collection? What, exactly, do they document? The standards that are best documented in portfolios are much like the ones we have suggested can be easily addressed in child-directed, open-ended play experiences. They are broader and more application oriented, and they involve children showing their understanding or skill development in a number of ways.

> Some skills are easy to record on a simple checklist, such as letter and sound identifi-cation. Other areas specified in the standards may require writing anecdotal records of what you observe children doing and saying. For example, to document science-as-inquiry standards, record observations of children at play in the water table and the science/discovery area. Write down conversations that provide insight into their understanding. . . . These written records provide pieces of concrete evidence that help document children's progress. (Jacobs and Crowley 2010, 32)

In addition, teachers want to be able to easily compare portfolio documentation across time. Therefore, they must plan to collect information that can show children's progress (or lack of it) related to the same broad standards. Let's consider some standards that lend themselves to portfolio documentation in observation notes, photos, and/or work samples. For each one, we identify what documentation teachers can do, what they can observe for related to the standard, and how they can compare observations to determine the child's progress.

Reading Comprehension

- Teachers can observe and document what children say as they respond to stories read aloud.
- They can focus their observations by asking the following questions:
  - —Are students' comments showing they understand what is happening in the story?
  - —Do they make reasonable predictions about what might happen next?
  - —Do they relate the story content or the characters' actions to their own life experiences?
  - —Do children retell the stories in their own words?
  - —Do teachers see children incorporating the stories into their dramatic or construction play?
  - —Do children draw, paint, make creations, or write related to the themes of the stories?
- Teachers can look for progress over time by noting the number of accurate details children are able to recall and incorporate into their conversations, play, and creations based on stories read.

Engaging in Emerging Writing

- Teachers can observe children writing in a variety of play experiences in the classroom (which means providing writing materials in play areas) and collect writing samples (collecting either the papers themselves or taking photographs of them).
- Teachers can engage children in conversations about their writing and learn more about each child's understanding of concepts of print (such as letter formation, spacing, punctuation) and letter-sound correspondence (as they begin to spell phonetically).
- Teachers can look for progress by comparing children's writing samples over time and looking for the ways their use of emergent writing strategies changes and grows.

Mathematical Problem Solving with Objects

- Teachers can observe how children solve mathematical problems (showing their understanding of quantities, geometry, spatial relationships, nonstandard measurement, and comparative language) as they construct with wooden and connecting blocks, as they sort and classify with various manipulatives, and as they engage in play activities throughout the classroom. (How many chairs will fit around a table? How will we divide the playdough among several children?)

- Teachers can write descriptions of what they see the children doing and hear them saying, as well as take photographs of their constructions, creations, and groupings of objects.
- Teachers can look for progress over time by watching for an increase in quantification (counting to higher numbers with understanding), in complexity of constructions and creations with evidence of symmetry and deeper geometrical and spatial understanding, in more use of measurement terminology and tools, and in more-complex classification strategies (including patterning).

Scientific Investigations

- Teachers can observe as children engage in child-initiated scientific explorations with stability, force, and motion in the block area, with natural phenomena and living things outdoors, and with properties of water and other materials at the sensory table or in the art area. They can also observe in teacher-initiated scientific investigations, such as growing plants from seeds, experimenting with freezing and heating water, or mixing different substances (vinegar and baking soda).
- Teachers can write descriptions of what they see the children doing and hear them saying with specific attention to scientific understanding and inquiry. They can encourage children to write and/or draw about their investigations and collect the papers or take photographs of them.
- Teachers can look for progress over time by noting children's levels of curiosity, investigative strategies, and use of scientific terminology.

Self-Reflections

One way for teachers to collect portfolio documentation that addresses standards in the domains of Approaches to Learning and Social-Emotional Development is by inviting children to engage in self-reflection.

- Teachers can engage in conversations with children as they play, and they can encourage children to draw and write as well. Here are some suggested questions to initiate self-reflection with preschoolers and kindergartners:
    —What is your favorite thing to do at school?
    —What is your favorite play area or activity?
    —What is something you are really good at?
    —What is something you want to get better at?
    —What is something you want to learn more about?
    —Is there anything else you want to tell?

- Teachers can encourage children to tell, draw, write, and/or show their answers. Or teachers can write for the children, can record them through audio- or videotaping, or can take photographs of the children demonstrating their answers.
- Teachers can look for progress by comparing children's answers over time. And they can invite children to do the same. They may be surprised by the children's analysis of their own self-reflections and can include a description of their response in the portfolio.

Checklists

A portfolio cannot provide documentation of all the standards teachers are addressing in preschool and kindergarten classrooms. The more specific, skill-discrete benchmarks do not warrant full documentation in a portfolio. Instead, they are much more efficiently recorded in a checklist format. Teachers can create checklists that are related to specific domains or they can create formats with all of the children's names and places to note specific benchmarks they observed children demonstrate. But the format only needs a small space for a check mark or a brief note.

Even with checklist documentation, teachers can still observe children engaged in child-directed, open-ended play. By identifying what they are looking for and having the checklist format prepared and close at hand (on a clipboard or in a notebook), teachers can be ready to quickly document what they see children do as they engage with materials and other children. Here is a suggested strategy for checklist documentation related to mathematics:

Make a checklist of mathematical knowledge, skills, and concepts you want to help children acquire. Ask children to demonstrate individually their understandings of items on the list during day-to-day experiences with hands-on materials, such as counting out cups needed for snack or measuring the bean seedling they planted. Observe children counting items to assess their counting skills. Do they have a strategy for counting accurately, such as moving an item aside after it has been counted? Ask children to demonstrate their thinking about how to solve problems using manipulatives and drawings. . . . Watch as children make patterns in the art area or sort objects in the math area and ask them to describe their process. (Jacobs and Crowley 2010, 87)

Many specific benchmarks lend themselves to checklist documentation across several domains. Here are a few examples:

- Language and Literacy
  - —letter identification
  - —letter-sound correspondence
  - —listening and following multiple-step directions
  - —syllabification
- Mathematics
  - —counting with one-to-one correspondence
  - —identification of shapes
- Physical Development
  - —gross-motor skills, such as hopping, jumping, skipping
  - —fine-motor skills, such as correct pencil grasp and eye-hand coordination

Some teachers are using assessment tools that have checklists designed and correlated with their state's early learning standards or kindergarten standards. It is perfectly appropriate to make use of such tools when the alignment has been recognized by your state and/or your district. Combining portfolio and checklist documentation provides a wealth of information about how children are learning and growing.

Narrative Summaries

Narrative summaries are the way to pull together the information in portfolios and checklists. They help both teachers and family members see the big picture of the child's development, progress, strengths, and challenges. They involve both parties in reflecting on the child's performance related to standards thus far, and in looking ahead at ways to support the child's continued success. When teachers share only checklist information with families, the information can be overwhelming and too detailed. In contrast, when teachers write narrative summaries and show items from the child's portfolio as evidence to support the conclusions in the narrative, family members get a more reasonable amount of information and a truer picture of how their child is doing.

Teachers can design their own narrative summaries or consider organizing the report in such a way that for each domain they are providing the following information about the child:

- Growth and accomplishments: In this domain, the child can . . .
- Progress shown: In this domain, the child has shown progress in . . .
- Plans for next steps: In this domain, here are the ways that teachers are going to address the child's challenges and plan for next steps . . .
- Some teachers also include plans for next steps at home: In this domain, you could help at home by . . .

CONCLUSION

Again, narrative summaries show the integration of reflection and observation. The process of integrating standards in play and being true to what is right for young children is evident in these assessment practices. Standards do not require standardized testing for young children. Rather, teachers can use authentic assessment measures, based on observation and reflection, to show family members and others what each child can do, to plan next steps in curricular strategies, and to continue to link standards and child-directed, open-ended play.

In the final chapter of this book, we investigate advocating for the importance of play-based approaches and give many supportive suggestions to keep play at the forefront of preschool and kindergarten education.

Implementation Ideas for Teachers:
ASSESSMENT IN PLAY

Something you can do right now is consider your reflection and assessment practices:

- How do you reflect about the success of your efforts to integrate learning and play?
- What adjustments and changes do you make related to that reflection?
- How do you observe for standards in children's play?
- What kind of evidence do you collect for portfolio documentation?
- For what standards have you found checklist documentation to be most effective?
- How do you summarize a child's performance, progress, and next steps for families?
- What ideas from this chapter will you try in your program?

ASSESSMENT IN PLAY

Administrators can also consider reflection and assessment practices:

- What assessments are required to be done?
- How would you rate the quality of the assessments? How authentic are they? (Bagnato, Neisworth, and Pretti-Frontczak [2010] demonstrate eighty-one assessments across eight dimensions: accountability, authenticity, collaboration, evidence, multifactors, sensitivity, universality, and utility.)
- Do you and your staff know the purpose of each assessment: screening, eligibility for special services (special education, English-Language Learner), program planning, progress monitoring, program outcomes evaluation and accountability? Transparency about the purpose of all assessments is paramount.
- In what ways can you help your teachers use authentic assessment procedures to better capture the true abilities of children as they play?
- What opportunities can you provide for your teachers to collaborate regarding observation and reflection?
- What additional training do teachers need to use authentic assessment to its fullest?

CHAPTER 14

Saving Play in Preschool and Kindergarten Classrooms: Strategies for Effective Advocacy

PROVOCATIVE QUESTION: Can play be saved?

Tom: The Administrator's Perspective

If we are going to save play, doing so will require building a coalition of like-minded individuals that includes both administrators and teachers. Unfortunately, some administrators are put off or intimidated by outspoken staff members. Yet encouraging teachers and parents to speak their mind, providing safe spaces for open and frank conversations, moving people from reactive to thoughtful action, and channeling high emotions into strategic steps toward desired change are the hallmarks of real leadership. Teachers, especially those who are least likely to speak out, need support and encouragement to be more active. They will appreciate a leader who listens and provides guidance for the best way to promote change at a district or program, state or national level. Advocacy should always begin and end with building people up and empowering them to be leaders.

Gaye: The Practitioner's Perspective

Preschool and kindergarten teachers sometimes feel like they are lone voices shouting in the wilderness. They feel like they are trying to remind a world gone mad that little children need different educational approaches than older ones. Sometimes the forces of educational reforms and higher expectations come sweeping down without regard for recommended practices in early childhood programs. Teachers can get caught in the middle trying to protect children, to continue to do what they know is best for them, and to meet the demands of education departments, school boards, and administrators. We hope that this book has given both teachers and administrators information and strategies to continue to do what's right for preschool and kindergarten children. We want teachers and administrators to join together as advocates for saving play and to be ready to explain to others why that effort is so important.

The Importance of Advocacy

Teachers and administrators need to be strong and effective advocates. They need to stand up to pressures that seek to denigrate play or marginalize its use. They need to continue to push hard for appropriate practices that include play, and they need to be able to make a credible and articulate case for why play is an effective curricular approach. This book is about making that case. As we conclude, we want to address the responsibilities of teachers and administrators to protect and promote play.

Just implementing effective practices is not enough if play is to remain an essential part of preschool and kindergarten classrooms. Larger pressures are present in our educational system that work against the links between play and standards that we have discussed. In this chapter, we present a number of approaches for saving play.

First, we discuss what we see as the responsibilities of teachers and administrators to advocate on behalf of children and their ability to play. We show the benefits of taking an active role in making necessary changes and suggest the skills needed to be an effective advocate and change agent.

Second, we identify some of the pressures facing teachers and administrators that undermine efforts to link play and standards and to allow children the opportunity to play on a daily basis. We discuss the dynamics inherent in that pressure and provide explicit suggestions for how to explain why play still makes sense despite or even because of that pressure.

Third, we look at a number of policy initiatives that could influence play in early childhood classrooms and discuss how play can fit into those initiatives.

Finally, we examine the role of everyday people in helping shape policy as it appears in regulation and legislation. Good advocates know how policy is developed and established, so they can be effective at shaping policy that will value and safeguard play within our educational system.

The "What" of Advocacy

Merriam-Webster defines *advocate* as a person who publicly supports or recommends a particular cause or policy (www.merriam-webster.com). The key word here is *publicly*. Advocacy is not a private matter, but one that moves what may be private concerns into the public sphere. Robinson and Stark (2002) talk about three kinds of advocacy: personal advocacy, public policy advocacy, and private-sector advocacy. Let's look at how each of these is defined.

- **Personal advocacy** is generally targeted at other individuals or groups, explaining a particular point of view on a topic that needs attention.
- **Public policy advocacy** addresses policies that may be part of regulation or legislation. It means inserting oneself, and organizing others to do the same, into the process of policy development. Policy usually results in regulation or guidance in the case of government agencies at an organizational, municipal, state, or national level. It is public policy because the institutions creating the policy are public.
- In contrast to public, in **private sector advocacy** one is interested in changing or addressing policies of private institutions.

It is important to understand what needs to change and where that change can occur so that it makes the biggest difference. Let's consider a hypothetical example.

A principal asks a teacher to shut down her play areas. The teacher, concerned about this action, talks with parents or colleagues about the principal's request. That would be private advocacy. Just that private conversation might be enough. It might lead to other teachers or parents talking with the principal and the principal reversing his action. But suppose the principal established a policy to ban play areas with the support of a school board or a program's board of directors. The next step might be public or private sector advocacy, depending on whether the institution was public or private. That policy could be at the institutional level (the school board) or at the state level (part of educational legislation or regulation), or even at the federal level. These would all require a public policy advocacy response because the need to change is a policy requirement.

We say it is a responsibility of teachers and administrators to be advocates because we believe that ensuring play for children is the right thing to do. According to NAEYC's Code of Ethics, early childhood professionals are to

> acknowledge our responsibility to provide the best possible programs of care and education for children and to conduct ourselves with honesty and integrity . . . [and to] acknowledge a collective obligation to advocate for the best interests of children within early childhood programs and in the larger community and to serve as a voice for young children everywhere. (NAEYC 2005a, 6)

The code also states that professionals are to "support the right of each child to play and learn in an inclusive environment that meets the needs of children with and without disabilities" (2). Advocacy is a duty of early childhood professionals. It is just the right thing to do.

Why Advocate?

While it is an ethical duty to advocate on behalf of play, it is also an activity that has its own rewards and benefits. Benefits of advocacy may include

- sharpening thinking about the issue and feeling driven to learn more,
- developing a community of supporters, and
- increasing communication and organizational skills.

Sharpening Thinking

Articulating clearly why play is important, how it benefits children, and how it can and must be a part of young children's educational experiences requires us to increase our knowledge of the science of play and learning. When we have to explain why certain practices make sense, we invariably refine those practices, make them sharper, and make them more effective across a variety of circumstances. Advocating makes us smarter about what we are promoting.

Here's how it works: we speak out on behalf of play and sooner or later (if we do it enough), opposition comes. People push back, argue against us, and criticize us or our ideas. As hard as it is to hear opposition to something we believe in strongly, it is necessary information that can strengthen our thinking and make our reasoning clearer and our claims more accurate. Disagreements can also teach us how to have conversations that shed more light than heat. Such learning is important to be a good advocate, but it only comes through active advocacy itself.

Developing a Community of Supporters

Not everyone who hears us speaking out will oppose us. Many will applaud and welcome what we say. Smart advocates form alliances with people who have a common cause. Advocacy helps us build wider networks of relationships that can support our work. The wider that network and the more people involved, the stronger our power to make the changes we need to make.

Increasing Communication and Organizational Skills

As we speak out and create networks of supporters, we are exercising our communication and organizational skills. As lifelong learners, we can always be open to the challenge of learning more and becoming better informed. Everyone can and should become a better communicator. Finding your voice and sharing it is one of the most powerful ways to claim your identity and present it to the world around you. By doing so, we become more truly who we are (Covey 2004). Advocacy opens many such opportunities. As we practice being skilled communicators, we are learning how to do the following:

- identify our audience
- craft simple, succinct, and compelling messages
- effectively use various communication channels (public speaking, social media, one-on-one meetings, newsletters, mailings)
- construct coherent, rational, and understandable arguments
- dramatize and visualize our messages through images, storytelling, or art

Coupled with communication skills are organizational skills. Organizing is a learned skill. It is a set of practices that helps us know how to push for change as a united group of folks rather than lone voices in the wilderness. These skills include being able to do these things:

- mobilize stakeholders who share common concerns, values, and goals
- create transparent organizations with good mechanisms for internal communication
- distinguish between problems and issues so they can be properly framed (everyone involved needs to understand what is at stake and what change is needed)
- identify power structures and leverage points
- develop strategies and tactics for joint action (simple ones are better)
- begin to take a long-range view and learn from mistakes

Our best recommendation for inspiring examples of how to be an advocate and change agent is to read *Learning as a Way of Leading: Lessons from the Struggle for Social Justice* (Preskill and Brookfield 2009).

ADDRESSING THE CHALLENGES TO PLAY

Many teachers and administrators face challenges in their attempts to make play a central part of preschool and kindergarten classrooms. In the following table, we name various challenges and cite key messages educators can use to describe how child-directed, open-ended play can support children's learning.

CHALLENGES TO PLAY	KEY MESSAGES TO EXPLAIN AND DESCRIBE HOW PLAY SUPPORTS LEARNING
The attitude that it is "just play" and not true learning.	• Play is a natural way for humans to learn. It involves investigation, problem solving, innovation, teamwork, and cooperation, all important life skills. • Teachers engage in careful planning for play. • The goal is for children to engage in high-level play experiences (not chaotic or simplistic). • Teachers engage with children as they play, observing and interacting to support and enhance children's learning.
There is no time for play in the school day.	• If play is a key strategy for learning, how can schools not allow time for learning? If schools allow time for learning, why can't some of that time be used for play-based learning?
Play requires a lot of planning, and there is no time for that.	• It does take a lot of time. But investments in careful and thorough planning time in the beginning mean less time is necessary later on.
Our early childhood teachers do not have strong early childhood backgrounds.	• The important characteristic that many early childhood teachers have, which really all teachers should have, is responsiveness to individual students. • Many teachers are more responsive to materials, curricula, standards, school culture, and external expectations. • Create professional development opportunities that emphasize child-focused and responsive practices. In other words, if your teachers do not have the skills to teach young children, teach them.
Play is part of early childhood, and that is not where real academic learning takes place.	• Early childhood education is not just watered-down curriculum from later grades. Preschool and kindergarten education is building the foundation for all future learning. • Young children are acquiring a vast amount of knowledge and developing great varieties of skills, and their thinking is deep and complex. Some of the barriers to seeing that complexity lie in their undeveloped communication skills. Real academic learning is indeed taking place as children play.

Policies That Interfere with Play

Many educational systems have implemented a variety of policies and approaches that have the potential of interfering with play. We do not believe teachers and administrators have to accept policies that go against the interests of young children. Instead, we think there are ways to respond to or work within policy initiatives and still provide rich, child-directed, open-ended play experiences in preschools and kindergartens. In the appendix, we look at a few of these policies and provide some ways to respond regarding play by addressing the following:

- district-mandated, scripted curricula
- research-based instructional practices
- Multi-tiered Systems of Support (MTSS) or Response to Intervention (RTI)
- Quality Rating and Improvement Systems (QRIS)
- workforce reforms (such as teacher certification requirements)
- program standards

The Lever of Policy

The secret to broad social change is to focus on policies. Policies are social levers that change organizations, systems, and societies from the inside out. Archimedes is reputed to have said, "Give me a lever long enough and . . . single-handed I can move the world." Policies are just as central to real movement, and if they are "long enough," they can bring about permanent change.

This is a plea to focus advocacy efforts on policy. The universe of public policy is enormous, so where do you start? We recommend three areas: early learning standards, professional standards, and program standards. Advocacy agendas should include efforts to change these standards so that play is more central, more important, and seen as more necessary in early learning programs.

Policy occurs on many levels: program, district, municipality, county, state, and nation. At every level, policies exist that govern how programs should operate. Professionals should look first at the program level for opportunities to adopt or fully implement standards into the school district or program. What might be done to ensure that NAEYC Accreditation standards, along with all of its emphasis on play, become the quality standard for your school? When Boston Public Schools underwent the ambitious goal to accredit all their early childhood classrooms, including kindergarten, the results were dramatic (Sachs and Weiland 2010).

Early learning standards or professional standards are usually best addressed at the state level. But in the development of these policies, government agencies often look to professionals to serve on committees that help draft policy. Make sure you are on those mailing lists and volunteer. The best way to get policies you like is to be part of the team that is writing them.

More and more, early childhood program experiences are being shaped by federal policy. Federal policy advocacy begins with letter-writing campaigns and contacting your state's congressional delegation (your two senators and one representative). Strong advocates should be regular correspondents with legislators, keeping them informed about how policies currently affect you as a constituent and should be changed. Believe it or not, our congressional representatives do care about how federal policy is impacting our lives. If possible, supplement your correspondence with a trip to Washington, DC. NAEYC annually sponsors an advocacy forum. Work with your state affiliate to see if you can attend. Pay attention to legislative recesses when members of Congress return to their home states. Invite them to visit your early childhood program. Show them how play works with children, how you link play and standards, and how you enhance children's learning.

At the state and federal level, teachers and administrators can join professional organizations such as NAEYC or DEC. These organizations provide a united and collective voice to promote stronger policies on behalf of play. In addition, there are other organizations specifically dedicated to promoting play, including these:

- The International Play Association (www.ipaworld.org)
- NAEYC Play, Policy, and Practice Interest Forum (www.naeyc.org/community /interest-forums)
- The Ultimate Block Party: The Arts and Sciences of Play (www.ultimateblockparty.com)
- The Alliance for Childhood (www.allianceforchildhood.org)
- Defending the Early Years (www.deyproject.org)

CONCLUSION

Margaret Meade famously said, "Never doubt that a small group of thoughtful, committed citizens can change the world. Indeed, it is the only thing that ever has" (Lutkehaus 2008, 261). You are that thoughtful, committed citizen and you *can* change the world. You can make sure that young children's right to play is protected, enhanced, and elevated to the important position it deserves in preschool and kindergarten classrooms. Your advocacy efforts must begin with three clear commitments on your part:

- a deep belief and knowledge that this is the right thing to do
- understanding the subject matter of play, why it's important, and how play and learning are connected
- a willingness to speak out and do more research to best understand where and how you can make the biggest difference

We hope the resources we have provided in this book will encourage you to join us and work to save play in preschools and kindergartens. We know the challenges to play are formidable. But we believe wholeheartedly that it is our obligation as advocates for young children to work hard to overcome those challenges. Early educators like you can make a difference by advocating for what is right for children—and what is right is providing learning environments that encourage child-directed, open-ended play.

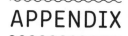

APPENDIX

Policies That Seem to Interfere with Play

POLICY	WHAT IT IS	SUGGESTED RESPONSES TO INTEGRATE POLICIES WITH PLAY
Program-mandated, scripted curricula	Curricula that include written scripts for what teachers should say and do. Some programs require teachers to follow these verbatim. Such rigid control over how teachers teach can interfere with efforts to promote child-directed, open-ended play.	• Scripted curricula do not allow for teachers to be truly responsive to children's engagement in play. • Teachers need to be ready and able to address the teachable moments that arise as children play and not be locked into a scripted response. • Scripted curricula should be studied carefully so recommended verbiage is well understood. They are not necessarily designed to be used verbatim but can be a resource for suggestions when interacting with children in play. • Modifications are appropriate and often necessary to address the needs of each child.

POLICY	WHAT IT IS	SUGGESTED RESPONSES TO INTEGRATE POLICIES WITH PLAY
Required research-based instructional practices	Instructional practices that are considered "research based" are sometimes required by programs. They can include the following: • instructional protocols • specified sequences for introducing skills, concepts, and information • required allotments of time to spend on different topics and skills development	• The research support for children's play must be revisited and communicated to decision makers so that all are clear that many studies support the value and benefits of play for young children. • Research should be scrutinized for long-term versus short-term gains. Some short-term gains are clear and measurable, but they fade away or make a superficial impression. • Research should be scrutinized for whether the generalization of skills was addressed. In other words, can children perform the skill in a variety of settings and not just the one tested for? That suggests deeper and more permanent learning. • If the instructional protocols include opportunities for skill development and practice, see if there are ways in which the skills can be practiced through play. If not, then add play to do just that.

POLICY	WHAT IT IS	SUGGESTED RESPONSES TO INTEGRATE POLICIES WITH PLAY
MTSS (Multi-tiered Systems of Support) or RTI (Response to Intervention)	MTSS or RTI are strategies for providing high-quality teaching using different levels of support for children so that those who need additional support receive it through more intensive and more individualized instruction with a goal that all children learn (DEC, NAEYC, and NHSA 2013).	• Nothing is explicitly stated in MTSS or RTI documents that prohibits the use of play. In fact, the DEC, NAEYC, and NHSA (2013) position paper states: "Regardless of tier, all teaching and caregiving efforts should be planned and delivered in developmentally appropriate ways that build on children's strengths, interests, and preferences. Further, teams enhance learning and development across tiers by incorporating a variety of materials and toys within playful activities, games, and regular daily routines, and by creating interesting and engaging learning environments" (7). • It is hard to imagine this statement not encouraging teachers to provide more opportunities for play. The more teachers connect play with standards the more legitimate their approach will seem like "high-quality teaching." • In practice, sometimes RTI is implemented "incorrectly" by making the higher-tier interventions (what is done when children are not learning as expected with the regular instruction) merely louder and longer (VanDerHeyden et al., 2016). We suggest that Tier 2 or 3 interventions could include play as an alternative approach to teaching students who are not succeeding with the universal instruction provided.

POLICY	WHAT IT IS	SUGGESTED RESPONSES TO INTEGRATE POLICIES WITH PLAY
Quality Rating and Improvement Systems (QRIS)	QRIS is a "systemic approach to assess, improve, and communicate the level of quality in early and school-age care and education programs" (ACF 2013, 1)	• Because most QRIS systems are based on program standards, find out whether any consideration is given for play in your state's QRIS system. If not, that might be an avenue for advocacy. (For a list of state QRIS systems, go to https://qrisguide.acf.hhs.gov/files/QRIS_Definition.pdf.) • Review the program standards that are the basis of your state's QRIS and explore where play is addressed. Many states use the Environmental Rating Scale (Clifford, Harms, and Cryer 2015). ECERS does include an assessment of play areas such as blocks, sand/water, arts, and dramatic play. It also assesses communication and engagement of children during "free play." See also a discussion of program standards below. • Because of play's importance and effectiveness, it should be considered a mark of quality. • A key challenge will be determining how to measure a program's adherence to a play-oriented approach. • If the emphasis in your state's QRIS is on quality efforts that deemphasize play, consider ways to redefine those efforts so they include and even promote play.

POLICY	WHAT IT IS	SUGGESTED RESPONSES TO INTEGRATE POLICIES WITH PLAY
Workforce reforms	Efforts are occurring across the country to strengthen educational requirements for teachers and the competencies required to become licensed (IOM and NRC 2015).	• The basis for all education is the teaching workforce. This should be the starting place if we want to make lasting change in the trend to exclude play from education. • How can we make sure every early childhood educator can effectively link play and standards? Start first with teacher licensure. Advocates may want to investigate state requirements for licensed teachers to see if play is mentioned and what expectations your state has for teacher competence. • Second, ask about the accreditation process for teacher preparation programs. How does that process reassure the state that a particular program of study prepares teachers well for an early childhood classroom where play is present? Where does using play as pedagogy appear in the syllabi of required coursework that addresses curriculum and instruction? • Third, ask whether teaching educators using play as an effective learning strategy would open the doors to ensuring that teachers are exposed to techniques such as those we discuss in this book.

POLICY	WHAT IT IS	SUGGESTED RESPONSES TO INTEGRATE POLICIES WITH PLAY
Program standards	Program standards are those things programs have to do to achieve some level of quality. The most common sets of program standards for preschool or centers are NAEYC Accreditation Criteria (NAEYC 2005b) and the Head Start Program Performance Standards. States also have requirements for their early childhood programs. The National Institute for Early Education Research publishes a yearbook on the status of state-funded preschool state by state. They grade each state based on ten standards and provide one way to assess the quality and rigor of the standards required by your state (http://nieer .org/yearbook).	Both NAEYC accreditation criteria and Head Start Program Performance Standards (HSPPS) include mentions of play and require play to be part of children's experiences. NAEYC's criteria contains many specific recommendations reflecting the practices we encourage in this book. Without the specificity of NAEYC's criteria, the HSPPS also recognize and encourage play as an essential part of children's daily experiences. Advocates may find it helpful to see a list of specifically where play is mentioned and encourages NAEYC and HSPPS (and other Head Start resources): • 1.C.02 and CFR 45 1302.31(b)(1)(i) HSELOF, Goal P-SE 3, p. 30 • 2.A.11 and CFR 45 1302.31(c) 2.A.12, 1302.31(a)(1)(ii); see also HSELOF, p. 2 • 2.L.04 and HSELOF, Goal P-ATL 10, p. 20; Goal P-SE 4, p. 30 • 3.D.10 and CFR 45 1302.31(c) & (d) • 3.F.02 and CFR 45 1302.31(c) • 4.D.08 and CFR 45 1302.33(b). Also assessment of HSELOF Goals: P-ATL 6 (p. 18); P-ATL 10 (p. 20); P-ATL 13 (p. 21); P-SE 4 (p. 30); P-LC 6 (p.44); & P-PMP 1 (p. 72) • 5.A.06 and CFR 45 1302.21(d)(2) & 1302.31(c), (d) & (e)(4) • 9.A.04 and CFR 45 1302.21(d), 1302.31(d), 1302.47(b)(2), & 1302.31(e)(4) • 9.A.08 and CFR 45 1303.31(c)(2) & 1303.31(d) • 9.A.12 and CFR 45 1302.21(d) & 1302.31(d) • 9.B.01 and 1302.31(e)(4) HSELOF = Head Start Early Learning Outcomes Framework, available at https://eclkc.ohs.acf.hhs.gov/policy /45-cfr-chap-xiii

REFERENCES

ACF (Administration for Children and Families). 2013. *QRIS Definition and Web Sites.* https://qrisguide.acf.hhs.gov/files/QRIS_Definition.pdf.

Adams, Gary, and S. Engelmann. 1996. *Research on Direct Instruction: 20 Years beyond DISTAR.* Seattle: Educational Achievement Systems.

AECF (Annie E. Casey Foundation). 2010. *Early Warning! Why Reading at the End of Grade 3 Matters.* www.aecf.org/m/resourcedoc/AECF-Early_Warning_Full_Report-2010.pdf.

Baenninger, M., and N. Newcombe. 1995. "Environmental Input to the Development of Sex-Related Differences in Spatial and Mathematical Ability." *Learning and Individual Differences* 7 (4): 363–79.

Bagnato, S. J., J. T. Neisworth, and K. Pretti-Frontczak. 2010. *LINKing Authentic Assessment and Early Childhood Intervention: Best Measures for Best Practices.* Baltimore: Brookes.

Baroody, A. J., M. Lai, and K. S. Mix. 2006. "The Development of Young Children's Early Number and Operation Sense and Its Implications for Early Childhood Education." In *Handbook of Research on the Education of Young Children*, 2nd ed., edited by B. Spodek and O. N. Saracho, 187–221. Mahwah, NJ: Lawrence Erlbaum.

Bergen, D., and D. Mauer. 2000. "Symbolic Play, Phonological Awareness, and Literacy Skills at Three Age Levels." In *Play and Literacy in Early Childhood: Research from Multiple Perspectives*, edited by K. A. Roskos and J. F. Christie, 45–62. Mahwah, NJ: Lawrence Erlbaum.

Berke, K., C. Heroman, P. O. Tabors, T. Bickart, and D. C. Burts. 2011. *Teaching Strategies GOLD.* Bethesda, MD: Teaching Strategies.

Bodrova, E., and D. Leong. 2003. "The Importance of Being Playful." *Educational Leadership* 60 (7): 50–53.

Bornfreund, L., S. Cook, A. Lieberman, and A. Loewenberg. 2015. *From Crawling to Walking: Ranking States on Birth–3rd Grade Policies That Support Strong Readers.* Washington, DC: New America Foundation. https://www.newamerica.org/education-policy/policy-papers/from-crawling-to-walking/.

Brown, Stuart. 2009. *Play: How It Shapes the Brain, Opens the Imagination, and Invigorates the Soul.* New York: Penguin.

Brown, W. H., K. A. Pfeiffer, K. L. McIver, M. Dowda, C. L. Addy, and R. R. Pate. 2009. "Social and Environmental Factors Associated with Preschoolers' Non-Sedentary Physical Activity." *Child Development* 80 (1): 45–58. doi.org/10.1111/j.1467-8624.2008.01245.x.

Brynie, F. 2010. "Infant Brains Are Hardwired for Language." *Brain Sense. Psychology Today.* www.psychologytoday.com/blog/brain-sense/201002/infant-brains-are-hardwired-language.

Burns, Anne, and Helen de Silva Joyce, eds. 2005. *Teachers' Voices 8: Explicitly Supporting Reading and Writing in the Classroom.* Sydney: National Centre for English Language Teaching and Research, Macquarie University.

CASEL (Collaborative for Academic, Social, and Emotional Learning). 2015. "State Scan Scorecard Project." www.casel.org/state-scan-scorecard-project.

CCSS (Common Core State Standards) 2015a. "Why Are the Common Core State Standards Important?" www.corestandards.org/about-the-standards/frequently-asked-questions/.

———. 2015b. "English Language Arts Standards » Introduction » How to Read the Standards." www.corestandards.org/ELA-Literacy/introduction/how-to-read-the-standards/.

———. 2015c. "Mathematics Standards: Understanding Mathematics." www.corestandards.org /Math/.

Center for Parent Information and Resources. 2015. The Short-and-Sweet IEP Overview. www .parentcenterhub.org/repository/iep-overview/.

Chard, S. 1994. *The Project Approach: Making Curriculum Come Alive.* New York: Scholastic.

Christie, J., and K. Roskos. 2006. "Standards, Science and the Role of Play in Early Literacy Education." In *Play = Learning: How Play Motivates and Enhances Children's Cognitive and Social-Emotional Growth*, edited by D. Singer, R. M. Golinkoff, and K. Hirsh-Pasek, 57–73. New York: Oxford University Press.

Clements, D., S. Swaminathan, M. Hannibal, and J. Sarama. 1999. "Young Children's Concepts of Shape." *Journal for Research in Mathematics Education* 30 (2): 192–212.

Clifford, R., T. Harms, and D. Cryer. 2015. *Early Childhood Environmental Rating Scale.* 3rd ed. New York: Teacher's College Press.

Colby, S. L., and J. M. Ortman. 2015. *Projections of the Size and Composition of the U.S. Population: 2014 to 2060 Population Estimates and Projections Current Population Reports.* Washington, DC: U.S. Census Bureau. www.census.gov/content/dam/Census/library/publications/2015/demo /p25-1143.pdf.

Conley, D. T. 2014. *The Common Core State Standards: Insight into Their Development and Purpose.* Washington, DC: Council of Chief State School Officers. www.ccsso.org/Resources/Publications /The_Common_Core_State_Standards_Insight_into_Their_Development_and_Purpose.html.

Conn-Powers, Michael. 2006. *All Children Ready for School: Approaches to Learning.* Early Childhood Briefing Paper Series. Bloomington: Indiana Institute on Disability and Community.

Cook, Shayna. 2015. "Why We Don't Need to Get Rid of Common Core to Have Play in Kindergarten." *New America EdCentral*, April 1. Washington, D.C.: New America Foundation. www.edcentral .org/kinder-commoncore.

Copple, C., and S. Bredekamp, eds. 2009. *Developmentally Appropriate Practice in Early Childhood Programs Serving Children from Birth through Age 8.* 3rd ed. Washington, DC: National Association for the Education of Young Children.

Covey, S. 2004. *The 8th Habit: From Effectiveness to Greatness.* New York: Free Press.

Cross, Terry, B. Bazron, K. Dennis, and M. Isaacs. 1989. Towards a Culturally Competent System of Care, vol. 1. Washington, DC: Georgetown University Child Development Center, CASSP Technical Assistance Center.

CSEFEL (Center on the Social and Emotional Foundations for Early Learning). n.d. "Building Positive Teacher-Child Relationships." Handout 12. Accessed January 16, 2017. http://csefel.vanderbilt.edu /briefs/handout12.pdf.

DEC (Division for Early Childhood, Council for Exceptional Children). 2014. *DEC Recommended Practices in Early Intervention/Early Childhood Special Education* 2014. www.dec-sped.org /recommendedpractices.

DEC/NAEYC (Division for Early Childhood, Council for Exceptional Children, and National Association for the Education of Young Children). 2009. *Early Childhood Inclusion: A Joint Position Statement of the Division for Early Childhood (DEC) and the National Association for the Education of Young Children.* Chapel Hill: University of North Carolina, FPG Child Development Institute. www.naeyc.org/files/naeyc/file/positions/DEC_NAEYC_EC_updatedKS.pdf.

DEC, NAEYC, and NHSA (Division for Early Childhood, Council for Exceptional Children, National Association for the Education of Young Children, and National Head Start Association). 2013. *Frameworks for Response to Intervention in Early Childhood: Description and Implications.* www .naeyc.org/files/naeyc/RTI%20in%20Early%20Childhood.pdf.

Defending the Early Years. 2012. *Position Statement on Standards and Testing for Young Children.* https://deyproject.files.wordpress.com/2012/11/position-paper-standards-and-testing-for -young-children.pdf.

Diamond, A., W. S. Barnett, J. Thomas, and S. Munro. 2007. "Preschool Program Improves Cognitive Control." *Science* 318 (5855): 1387–88. doi:10.1126/science.1151148.

Dickinson, D. K., and J. Moreton. 1991. "Predicting Specific Kindergarten Literacy Skills from Three-Year-Olds' Preschool Experiences." Paper presented at the Biennial Meeting of the Society for Research in Child Development, April 18–20, 1991. Seattle, WA.

Dweck, Carol. 2006. *Mindset: The New Psychology of Success.* New York: Ballantine Books.

Eberle, Scott G., 2014. The Elements of Play: Toward a Philosophy and a Definition of Play. *American Journal of Play* 6 (2): 214–33.

ECI (Early Childhood Iowa). 2012. *Iowa Early Learning Standards.* Rev. ed. www.state.ia.us /earlychildhood/files/early_learning_standarda/IELS_2013.pdf.

Elias, C. L., and L. E. Berk. 2002. "Self-Regulation in Young Children: Is There a Role for Sociodramatic Play?" *Early Childhood Research Quarterly* 17 (2): 216–38. doi:10.1016/S0885-2006 (02)00146-1.

Emerson, Ralph Waldo. 2007. *The Collected Works of Ralph Waldo Emerson.* Vol. 7, *Society and Solitude.* Cambridge, MA: Belknap Press.

Epstein, Ann. 2014. *The Intentional Teacher: Choosing the Best Strategies for Young Children's Learning.* Washington, DC: NAEYC; Ypsilanti, MI: HighScope Press.

Erikson, Erik. 1950. *Childhood and Society.* New York: W. W. Norton.

Family Communications. 1995. *Mister Rogers' Plan and Play Book: Activities from Mister Rogers' Neighborhood for Parents and Care Providers.* 4th ed. Milwaukee, WI: Hal Leonard.

Fantuzzo, J., and C. McWayne. 2002. "The Relationship between Peer-Play Interactions in the Family Context and Dimensions of School Readiness for Low-Income Preschool Children." *Journal of Educational Psychology* 94 (1): 79–87.

Fernandez-Fein, S., and L. Baker. 1997. "Rhyme and Alliteration Sensitivity and Relevant Experiences among Preschoolers from Diverse Backgrounds." *Journal of Literacy Research* 29 (3): 433–59.

Fink, L. Dee. 2003. *Creating Significant Learning Experiences.* San Francisco: John Wiley & Sons.

Fisher, E. P. 1992. "The Impact of Play on Development: A Meta-Analysis." *Play & Culture* 5 (2): 159–81.

Foley, Jordan, and Jarrod Green. 2015. "Supporting Children's Reflection with Phones and Tablets." *Teaching Young Children* 8 (5): 21–23.

Fox, L., and M. A. Duda. 2017. *Positive Behavior Support.* Tampa: University of South Florida, Technical Assistance Center on Social Emotional Intervention for Young Children. Accessed February 22. http://challengingbehavior.fmhi.usf.edu/explore/pbs_docs/pbs_complete.doc.

Freeman, Don. 1968. *A Pocket for Corduroy.* New York: Viking Press.

Gelman, R. 2006. "Young, Natural-Number Arithmeticians." *Current Directions in Psychological Science* 15 (4): 193–97. doi:10.1111/j.1467-8721.2006.00434.x.

Gestwicki, C. 2016. *Developmentally Appropriate Practice: Curriculum and Development in Early Education.* Belmont, CA: Wadsworth Publishing.

Ginsburg, Kenneth R. 2007. "The Importance of Play in Promoting Healthy Child Development and Maintaining Strong Parent-Child Bonds." *Pediatrics* 119 (1): 182–91. doi:10.1542/peds.2006-2697.

Goleman, Daniel, Richard Boyatzis, and Annie McKee. 2013. *Primal Leadership: Learning to Lead with Emotional Intelligence.* Boston: Harvard Business Review Press.

Gronlund, Gaye. 2013. *Planning for Play, Observation, and Learning in Preschool and Kindergarten.* St. Paul, MN: Redleaf Press.

———. 2014. *Make Early Learning Standards Come Alive: Connecting Your Practice and Curriculum to State Guidelines.* 2nd ed. St. Paul, MN: Redleaf Press.

———. 2016. *Individualized, Child-Focused Curriculum: A Differentiated Approach.* St. Paul, MN: Redleaf Press.

Gronlund, Gaye, and Marlyn James. 2008. *Early Learning Standards and Staff Development: Best Practices in the Face of Change.* St. Paul, MN: Redleaf Press.

———. 2013. *Focused Observations: How to Observe Young Children for Assessment and Curriculum Planning.* 2nd ed. St. Paul, MN: Redleaf Press.

Harvard T. H. Chan School of Public Health. 2016. "Early Child Care Obesity Prevention Recommendations: Complete List." Obesity Prevention Source. www.hsph.harvard.edu/obesity-prevention-source/obesity-prevention/early-child-care/early-child-care-obesity-prevention-recommendation-complete-list.

Hattie, John. 2009. *Visible Learning: A Synthesis of Over 800 Meta-Analyses Relating to Achievement.* New York: Routledge.

Heitin, L. 2015. "Debate Persists around Early-Reading Standards." *Education Week*, May 5. www.edweek.org/ew/articles/2015/06/05/debate-persists-around-early-reading-standards.html.

Hernandez, D. J. 2011. *Double Jeopardy: How Third-Grade Reading Skills and Poverty Influence High School Graduation.* Baltimore, MD: Annie E. Casey Foundation. www.aecf.org/m/resourcedoc/AECF-DoubleJeopardy-2012-Full.pdf.

Hest, Amy. 2007. *Off to School, Baby Duck!* Somerville, MA: Candlewick.

HighScope. 2014. *COR Advantage User Guide.* Ypsilanti, MI: HighScope Press. http://secure.highscope.org/productcart/pc/catalog/pdf/cor_userguideall_web.pdf.

Hirsh-Pasek, Kathy, and Roberta Michnick Golinkoff. 2014. "Playful Learning: Where a Rich Curriculum Meets a Playful Pedagogy." *Preschool Matters . . . Today!* March 6. http://preschoolmatters.org/2014/03/06/playful-learning-where-a-rich-curriculum-meets-a-playful-pedagogy.

Hirsh-Pasek, Kathy, Roberta Michnick Golinkoff, Laura E. Berk, and Dorothy Singer. 2009. *A Mandate for Playful Learning in Preschool: Presenting the Evidence.* New York: Oxford University Press.

Hutchins, Pat. 1971. *Rosie's Walk.* New York: Simon and Schuster.

IDEA (Individuals with Disabilities Education Improvement Act of 2004). Pub. L. No. 108-446, 118 Stat. 2647 2004.

IOM and NRC (Institute of Medicine and National Research Council). 2015. *Transforming the Workforce for Children Birth through Age 8: A Unifying Foundation.* Washington, DC: National Academies Press. www.nap.edu/catalog/19401/transforming-the-workforce-for-children-birth-through-age-8-a.

Jablon, Judy R., and Michael Wilkinson. 2006. "Using Engagement Strategies to Facilitate Children's Learning and Success." *Beyond the Journal: Young Children on the Web.* www.naeyc.org/files/yc/file/200603/JablonBTJ.pdf.

Jacobs, Gera, and Kathy Crowley. 2010. *Reaching Standards and Beyond in Kindergarten: Nurturing Children's Sense of Wonder and Joy in Learning.* Thousand Oaks, CA: Corwin Press; Washington, DC: NAEYC.

Joseph, G. E., P. Strain, T. Yates, and M. L. Hemmeter. 2010. *Social Emotional Teaching Strategies, Module 2.* Champaign-Urbana, IL: Center for the Social Emotional Foundations for Early Learning. http://csefel.vanderbilt.edu/modules/module2/script.pdf.

Justice, L. M., and P. C. Pullen. 2003. "Promising Interventions for Promoting Emergent Literacy Skills: Three Evidence-Based Approaches." *Topics in Early Childhood Special Education* 23 (3): 99–113.

Kaefer, Tanya, S. B. Neumann, and A. M. Pinkham. 2015. "Pre-Existing Background Knowledge Influences Socioeconomic Differences in Preschoolers' Word Learning and Comprehension." *Reading Psychology,* 362: 203–31. doi:10.1080/02702711.2013.843064.

Kagan, Sharon Lynn, E. Castillo, R. E. Gomez, and S. Gowani. 2013. "Understanding and Using Early Learning Standards for Young Children." *International Journal of Child Care and Education Policy* 72: 53–66.

Kantor, Rebecca, and Kimberlee L. Whaley. 1998. "Existing Frameworks and New Ideas from Our Reggio Emilia Experience: Learning at a Lab School with 2- to 4-Year-Old Children." In *The Hundred Languages of Children: The Reggio Emilia Approach: Advanced Reflections,* 2nd ed., edited by Carolyn Edwards, Lella Gandini, and George Forman, 313–34. Greenwich, CT: Ablex Publishing.

Kentucky Governor's Office of Early Childhood. 2013. *Building a Strong Foundation for School Success: Kentucky's Early Childhood Standards.* http://kidsnow.ky.gov/School%20Readiness/Documents/Kentucky%20Early%20Childhood%20Standards.pdf.

Linder, T. 2008. *Transdisciplinary Play-Based Assessment.* 2nd ed. Baltimore: Brookes.

Lutkehaus, Nancy C. *Margaret Mead: The Making of an American Icon.* Princeton, NJ: Princeton University Press, 2008.

Marzano, R. J. 2004. *Building Background Knowledge for Academic Achievement.* Alexandria, VA: ASCD. www.ascd.org/publications/books/104017/chapters/The-Importance-of-Background -Knowledge.aspx.

Massachusetts Department of Early Education and Care, Massachusetts Department of Elementary and Secondary Education, and Staff at the Institute for Community Inclusion, University of Massachusetts, Boston. 2015. Massachusetts Standards for Preschool and Kindergarten: Social and Emotional Learning, and Approaches to Play and Learning. www.doe.mass.edu/kindergarten /SEL-APL-Standards.pdf.

McDonald, Emma. 2011. *Student Portfolios as an Assessment Tool.* Colchester, CT: Education World. www.educationworld.com/a_curr/columnists/mcdonald/mcdonald025.shtml.

Meisels, S. J., D. B. Marsden, J. R. Jablon, and M. Dichtelmiller. 2015. *Work Sampling System.* 5th ed. New York: Pearson Education.

Miller, Edward, and Joan Almon. 2009. *Crisis in the Kindergarten: Why Children Need to Play in School.* College Park, MD: Alliance for Childhood.

Mindes, G. 2005. "Social Studies in Today's Early Childhood Curricula." *Beyond the Journal: Young Children on the Web.* September. www.naeyc.org/files/yc/file/200509/MindesBTJ905.pdf.

Morris, Ann. 1989. *Hats, Hats, Hats.* New York: Lothrop, Lee & Shepard.

Murphy, P. K., M. L. Rowe, R. Ramani, and R. Silverman. 2014. "Promoting Critical-Analytic Thinking in Children and Adolescents at Home and in School." *Educational Psychology Review* 26 (4): 561–78.

NAE and NRC (National Academy of Engineering and National Research Council). 2014. *STEM Integration in K–12 Education: Status, Prospects, and an Agenda for Research.* Washington, DC: National Academies Press. www.nap.edu/read/18612/chapter/1.

NAEYC (National Association for the Education of Young Children). 2005a. Code of Ethical Conduct. www.naeyc.org/files/naeyc/file/positions/PSETH05.pdf.

———. 2005b. *NAEYC Early Childhood Program Standards and Accreditation Criteria: The Mark of Quality in Early Childhood Education.* Washington, DC: NAEYC.

NAEYC and NAECS/SDE (National Association of Early Childhood Specialists in State Departments of Education). 2002. *Early Learning Standards: Creating the Conditions for Success.* www.naeyc .org/files/naeyc/file/positions/position_statement.pdf.

National Scientific Council on the Developing Child. 2007. *The Science of Early Childhood Development: Closing the Gap between What We Know and What We Do.* www.developingchild .harvard.edu.

Neill, P. 2015. "Going from Me to We: Social Studies in Preschool." *HighScope Extensions* 29 (1): 1–10. www.highscope.org/file/NewsandInformation/Extensions/Extensions_Vol29No1_web-SocialStudies.pdf.

Neisworth, J. T., and S. J. Bagnato, 2004. "The Mismeasure of Young Children: The Authentic Assessment Alternative." *Infants and Young Children* 17 (3): 198–212.

Ness, Daniel, and Stephen J. Farenga. 2007. *Knowledge under Construction: The Importance of Play in Developing Children's Spatial and Geometric Thinking.* Lanham, MD: Rowman and Littlefield.

Neuman, Susan, and Kathleen Roskos. 1992. "Literacy Objects as Cultural Tools: Effects on Children's Literacy Behaviors during Play." *Reading Research Quarterly* 27 (3): 202–26.

Next Generation Science Standards. 2015. www.nextgenscience.org.

NIEER (National Institute of Early Education Research). 2014. *The State of Preschool 2014*. New Brunswick, NJ.

Paley, Vivian. 1981. *Wally's Stories: Conversations in the Kindergarten*. Cambridge, MA: Harvard University Press.

Parr, Todd. 2006. *The Grandma Book*. New York: Little, Brown.

Pennsylvania Office of Child Development and Learning. 2014. Pennsylvania Learning Standards for Early Childhood Prekindergarten. www.education.pa.gov/Documents/Early%20Learning/Early%20Learning%20Standards/Early%20Learning%20Standards%20-%20Prekindergarten%202014.pdf.

Perry, Bruce D. 2001. "Curiosity: The Fuel of Development." http://teacher.scholastic.com/professional/bruceperry/curiosity.htm.

Pepler, Debra J., and Hildy S. Ross. 1981. The Effects of Play on Convergent and Divergent Problem Solving. *Child Development* 52 (4), 1202–1210. doi:10.2307/1129507.

Pessoa, Luiz. 2013. *The Cognitive-Emotional Brain: From Interactions to Integration*. Cambridge, MA: Massachusetts Institute of Technology Press.

Pondiscio, Robert. 2015. "Is Common Core Too Hard for Kindergarten?" *Common Core Watch*, February 11. http://edexcellence.net/articles/is-common-core-too-hard-for-kindergarten.

Preskill, Stephen, and Stephen D. Brookfield. 2009. *Learning as a Way of Leading: Lessons from the Struggle for Social Justice*. San Francisco: Jossey-Bass.

Ramani, G., and R. S. Siegler. 2008. "Promoting Broad and Stable Improvements in Low-Income Children's Numerical Knowledge through Playing Number Board Games." *Child Development* 79 (2): 375–94.

Raver, C., and J. Knitzer, 2002. *What Research Tells Policymakers about Strategies to Promote Social and Emotional School Readiness among Three- and Four-Year-Old Children*. New York: National Center for Children in Poverty. www.nashp.org/sites/default/files/abcd/abcd.readytoenter.pdf.

Rich, Motoko. 2015. "Kindergartens Ringing the Bell for Play inside the Classroom." *New York Times*, June 10. www.nytimes.com/2015/06/10/education/out-of-the-books-in-kindergarten-and-into-the-sandbox.html?_r=0.

Riley-Ayers, S., J. S. Boyd, and E. Frede. 2008. *Early Learning Scale Preschool Assessment*. Carson, CA: Lakeshore Learning.

Rimm-Kaufman, S., and C. S. Hulleman. 2015. "SEL in Elementary School Settings: Identifying Mechanisms That Matter." In *Handbook of Social and Emotional Learning: Research and Practice*, edited by J. A. Durlak, C. E. Domitrovich, R. P. Weissberg, and T. P. Gullotta, 151–66. New York: Guilford.

Robinson, A., and D. Stark. 2002. *Advocates in Action: Making a Difference for Young Children*. Washington, DC: NAEYC.

Roderick, M., and M. Engle. 2001. "The Grasshopper and the Ant: Motivational Responses of Low-Achieving Students to High-Stakes Testing." *Educational Evaluation Policy Analysis* 23 (3): 197–227.

Rogers, C. S., and J. K. Sawyers. 1988. *Play in the Lives of Children.* Washington, DC: NAEYC.

Roskos, Kathleen, and James Christie. 2004. "Examining the Play-Literacy Interface: A Critical Review and Future Directions." In *Children's Play: The Roots of Reading,* edited by Edward F. Zigler, Dorothy G. Singer, and Sandra J. Bishop-Josef, 95–123. Washington, DC: Zero to Three Press.

Sachs, J., and C. Weiland. 2010. "Boston's Rapid Expansion of Public School-Based Preschool: Promoting Quality, Lessons Learned." *Young Children* 65 (5): 74–77.

Senge, Peter M. 1990. *The Fifth Discipline: The Art & Practice of the Learning Organization.* New York: Currency Doubleday.

Seo, K., and H. P. Ginsburg. 2004. "What Is Developmentally Appropriate in Early Childhood Mathematics Education? Lessons from New Research." In *Engaging Young Children in Mathematics: Standards for Early Mathematics Education,* edited by D. Clements and J. Sarama, 91–104. Mahwah, NJ: Lawrence Erlbaum.

SHAPE (Society for Health and Physical Educators). 2009. *Active Start: A Statement of Physical Activity Guidelines for Children from Birth to Age 5.* Reston, VA: National Association for Sport and Physical Education.

Sneiderman, Joshua M. 2013. "Engaging Children in STEM Education Early!" *Natural Start Alliance,* December. http://naturalstart.org/feature-stories/engaging-children-stem-education-early.

Snow, Kyle. 2015. "Research News You Can Use: Debunking the Play vs. Learning Dichotomy." www.naeyc.org/content/research-news-you-can-use-play-vs-learning.

Strain, P. S., and M. Hoyson. 2000. "The Need for Longitudinal, Intensive Social Skill Intervention: LEAP Follow-Up Outcomes for Children with Autism." *Topics in Early Childhood Special Education* 20 (2): 116–22.

Tinzmann, Margaret Banker, Beau Fly Jones, Todd F. Fennimore, Jan Bakker, Carole Fine, and Jean Pierce. 1990. *The Collaborative Classroom: Reconnecting Teachers and Learners.* Elmhurst, IL: North Central Regional Educational Laboratory. http://files.eric.ed.gov/fulltext/ED327931.pdf.

Tremblay, A., P. S. Strain, J. M. Hendrickson, and R. E. Shores. 1981. "Social Interactions of Normal Preschool Children Using Normative Data for Subject and Target Behavior Selection." *Behavior Modification* 5 (2): 237–53.

United Nations Human Rights, Office of the High Commissioner, Committee on the Rights of the Child. 1990. Convention on the Rights of the Child. www.ohchr.org/en/professionalinterest /pages/crc.aspx.

VanDerHeyden, A., M. Burns, R. Brown, M. R., Shinn, S. Kukic, K. Gibbons, G., Batsche, and W. D. Tilly. 2016. "Four Steps to Implement RTI Correctly." *Education Week* 351 (5): 25.

Vermont Agency for Education and Agency for Human Services. 2015. *Vermont Early Learning Standards.* http://education.vermont.gov/documents/edu-early-education-vels.pdf.

Vollmer, Jamie. 2002. "The Blueberry Story: The Teacher Gives the Businessman a Lesson." *Education Week* 21 (25). www.jamievollmer.com/blueberries.html.

Washington State Department of Early Learning. 2012. *Washington State Early Learning and Development Guidelines: Birth through 3rd Grade.* www.del.wa.gov/publications/development/docs/guidelines.pdf.

Weisberg, D. S., K. Hirsh-Pasek, and R. Golinkoff. 2013. "Guided Play: Where Curricular Goals Meet a Playful Pedagogy." *Mind Brain and Education* 7 (2): 104–12. doi:10.1111/mbe.12015.

Wenner, Melinda. 2009. "The Serious Need for Play." *Scientific American Mind*, February/March.

Wyoming Early Childhood State Advisory Council. 2013. *Wyoming Early Learning Foundations for Children Ages 3 to 5.* http://edu.wyoming.gov/downloads/early-childhood/2014/14-align-0009-early-learning-foundations-spreads-1.pdf.

Yair, G. 2000. "Reforming Motivation: How the Structure of Instruction Affects Students' Learning Experiences." *British Educational Journal* 26 (2): 191–210.

Zagarenski, P. 2005. *Where Am I Hiding? / ¿Dónde me escondo?* New York: Houghton Mifflin Harcourt.

Zigler, E. F., D. G. Singer, and S. J. Bishop-Josef, eds. 2004. *Children's Play: The Roots of Reading.* Washington, DC: Zero to Three.

INDEX

motor development standards. *See* physical and motor development standards

motor/movement skills—fine strand, physical and motor development standards, 155–157

motor/movement skills—gross strand, physical and motor development standards, 151, 152–154

Murphy, P. K., 45

narrative summaries, 198

National Association for the Education of Young Children (NAEYC), 67
  advocacy by early childhood professionals, 203
  "Developmentally Appropriate Practice," 9–10
  false dichotomy between play and direct instruction, 52

National Association of Sport and Physical Education, 150, 152

National Physical Education Standards and Minnesota Benchmarks, 160

National Research Council, 122

Nebraska Early Learning Guidelines for Ages 3 to 5, 175

New Jersey Core Curriculum Content Standards for Comprehensive Health and Physical Education, 157

New Mexico Social Studies Standards: Grades K–4, 143

Next Generation Science Standards for kindergarten, 122, 124, 126, 128, 130

North Carolina Essential Standards: Kindergarten Social Studies, 138

North Carolina Foundations for Early Learning and Development, 90, 170

number sense, quantity, and counting strand, mathematics domain, 112–113

Nutrition and Physical Activity Self-Assessment for Child Care instrument, 150

observation
  assessment considerations before beginning, 189–190
  documenting, 188–189
  experience described, 190–192
  importance, 22, 34
  role in assessments, 183, 185–186

Ohio Early Learning and Development Standards: Birth to Kindergarten Entry, 152

Ohio New Learning Standards: Kindergarten through Grade 3, 92

Oklahoma Kindergarten Standards, 155

on-demand tasks, as inauthentic assessments, 184

open-endedness
  in play
    described, 12
    implementation ideas, 17
  in questioning, 34

operations and algebraic thinking strand, mathematics domain, 114–115

Oregon Social Sciences Academic Content Standards (Kindergarten), 146

Paley, Vivian, 34

passivity versus activity, 54

Pennsylvania Learning Standards for Early Childhood
  Infant/Toddler through Kindergarten, 90
  Kindergarten, 167
  Pre-Kindergarten, 100

persistence strand, approaches to learning domain, 88, 95

personal advocacy, 203

phonological awareness strand, language and literacy domain, 99, 104–105

physical and motor development standards
  active physical play strand, 151, 160–161
  health and well-being strand, 157–159
  motor/movement skills—fine strand, 155–157

scaffolding

  for approaches to learning domain

    attention and engagement strand, 90, 91

    curiosity/initiative strand, 86, 87

    persistence strand, 88, 89

    problem solving and creative thinking strand, 92, 93

  developing, 30–31, 62

  for language and literacy domain

    phonological awareness strand, 104, 105, 106

    reading and writing strand, 102, 103, 106, 107

    speaking and listening strand, 100, 101

  for mathematics domain

    geometry and spatial relationships, 118, 119

    measurement strand, 116–117

    number sense, quantity, and counting strand, 113

    operations and algebraic thinking strand, 114–115

  for physical and motor development standards

    active physical play strand, 160, 161

    health and well-being strand, 158, 159

    motor/movement skills—fine strand, 155, 156–157

    motor/movement skills—gross strand, 153, 154

  for science domain

    analyzing and interpreting data strand, 126, 127

    constructing explanations and designing solutions, 128, 129

    developing and using models, obtaining, evaluating, and communicating information, 130, 131

    practice asking questions, defining problems and planning and carrying out investigations, 125

  for social-emotional domain

    emotions strand, 171, 172

    participates cooperatively in play strand, 176, 177

    relationships with adults strand, 168, 169

    self-image strand, 173, 174

  for social studies domain

    community strand, 144, 145

    economics strand, 147

    geography strand, 139

    history strand, 141, 142

  when offering provocations, 32

science domain

  analyzing and interpreting data strand, 126–127

  constructing explanations and designing solutions, 128–129

  developing and using models, obtaining, evaluating, and communicating information, 130–131

  practice asking questions, defining problems and planning and carrying out investigations, 124–125

science standards, addressing in play, 122–124

self-control and self-regulation, developing, 23–24

self-image strand, social-emotional domain, 173–174

Silverman, R., 45

Snow, Kyle, 52, 53

social-emotional domain

  emotions strand, 170–172

  overview of, 165–167

  participates cooperatively in play strand, 175–177

  relationships with adults strand, 167–169

  self-image strand, 173–174

social studies domain

  community, civics, and government strand, 137, 143–145

Play, academics, and standards *can* work together

The increase in standards-based education should be a reason to embed more, not less, play-based learning in early childhood classrooms. Become a strong advocate for saving play in preschool and kindergarten by integrating play and standards, and learn how child-led, open-ended play addresses the domains of child development and Common Core State Standards.

Saving Play is full of research, resources, and practical knowledge that link academic learning and play experiences—giving you the right strategies to take an active role and help restore play as a fun and educational part of early childhood classrooms.

"A timely survival guide. This wonderfully challenging, readable book invites us to sharpen our perceptions of a whole range of state and national standards and to share responsibility for explaining them to teachers and parents and the public. As a standards-resister myself, I've just been won over. Read this book!"

—**Elizabeth Jones**, faculty emerita, Pacific Oaks College, author of *The Play's the Thing* and *Playing to Get Smart*

"A brilliant piece of work! Rendon and Gronlund have set the foundation for putting play right at the heart of the curriculum and high-quality professional development like no other book I have read!"

—**Walter F. Drew**, EdD, founder and executive director of the Institute for Self Active Education, board member for the Association for the Study of Play

"*Saving Play* is a delightful book written by an administrator and a practitioner—a great combination. Playful learning is essential to helping children think, learn, and remember. Bravo for bringing these important ideas to life!"

—**Roberta Michnick Golinkoff**, PhD, University of Delaware, and author of *Becoming Brilliant: What Science Tells Us about Raising Successful Children*

Gaye Gronlund, MA, is a nationally recognized consultant and author who works with early childhood programs across the country. Gaye is the author of *Individualized Child-Focused Curriculum, Focused Observations,* second edition, and *Making Early Learning Standards Come Alive,* second edition.

Thomas Rendon is the coordinator of the Iowa Head Start State Collaboration Office and an active supporter of policy to promote play at a state level.

ISBN 978-1-60554-530-1 $34.95

Redleaf Press®
www.redleafpress.org
800-423-8309

53495

9 781605 545301